COVENTRY'S FORGOTTEN THEATRE

By
Ted Bottle

The Badger Press, Westbury, Wiltshire
2004

Sir Skears Rew
The Founder of the Theatre Royal, Coventry

Coventry Local Studies, Central Library

COVENTRY'S FORGOTTEN THEATRE

The Theatre Royal, Smithford Street, which became the Empire Theatre of Varieties

Including glimpses of other Coventry venues of entertainment and the workings of the English Provincial Theatre during the nineteenth century

By

Ted Bottle

THE BADGER PRESS, WESTBURY, WILTSHIRE

2004

To the memory of

Richard and Helen Leacroft

Published in Westbury, Wiltshire by
The Badger Press

Cover photograph courtesy of Coventry Evening Telegraph

Typesetting by Marlinzo Services

ISBN 0 9526076 7 0

Printed and bound in Great Britain by Antony Rowe Ltd., Chippenham, Wiltshire

Acknowledgements

Babs Adams

John Ashby

Derek Forbes

Ray Fowkes

Gil Robottom

Staff at Coventry City Library and City
    Record office especially Andrew Mealey

Dr David Wilmore

Suz Winspear

Contents

List of Illustrations

Acknowledgements appear on each illustrated page.

Preface

Apart from its associations with the medical world and the field of military battle, the meaning of the word 'theatre' covers both the product and the place where it is performed. Over the years writers have given a lot of attention to the many aspects of theatre so that library shelves groan under the weight of a myriad of books on the subject, but when biographies, tomes on critical analysis, papers dealing with scenic design, lighting and costumes or anything relating to London and Shakespeare have been removed, little is left. London theatres, especially the early ones, have been well documented, but readers seeking information on individual buildings outside the capital, or data about the owners and managers who ran them and artists who performed in them, are poorly served in relative terms. Unlike Mother Hubbard's cupboard, the provincial shelves are not completely bare, but are meagrely stocked at best. Many of the more important city centre playhouses have been documented to some degree, but the smaller theatres, which frequently inhabited the unfashionable suburbs, have always been beyond the pale and relegated way down the pecking order of importance, which meant they received less attention from the press of the day, and official research organisations now. This is a pity since their stories would appear to be just as interesting, if not more so, than those of the number one theatres in town. They may not have had an endless supply of top line performers, but they reflected ordinary working theatrical life and played to the man in the street.

It has to be acknowledged that some excellent research has been carried out by a handful of people. Leicester's theatres are well recorded, thanks to the meticulous work of Richard and Helen Leacroft and Kathleen Barker did a similar service for Bristol, especially the Royal. Lou Warwick produced several volumes of detailed information for the venues of Northampton, including the town's Marefair Theatre, the predecessor of the present Royal and Opera House, and which mirrored the Coventry Theatre Royal in so many ways. Mike Newman has lavished much print on his beloved Coventry Hippodrome [1937–2002] and Philip Ryan covers the Irish capital in his *"Lost Theatres of Dublin"*. Terry Hallett's *"Bristol's Forgotten Empire"* is a rare example of a work which deals with what ended up as a number two provincial music hall, and its story is a fascinating catalogue of this once popular, but rarely written about form of entertainment. We have some knowledge of nineteenth and early twentieth century theatres of Glasgow and Liverpool, from the works of Baynham and Broadbent respectively. C.M.P. Taylor has mapped the Wakefield

Theatre Royals and Sybil Rosenfeld's record of the York Royal goes into much minute detail. This list is not definitive but the combined efforts still represents a drop in the ocean.

The formation and work of the London based Theatres Trust has undoubtedly brought the position of theatres both in London, and the country, to the attention of more people than before. The publication of *'Curtains!!! or a New Life for Old Theatres'* in 1982 began it all, and the Trust's own *'Guide to British Theatres 1750–1950'* [A & C Black, 2000] has considerably furthered the interest previously generated. Apart from making people aware of those buildings in their locality, and especially those capable of restoration, it keeps a watchful brief to ensure that the limited stock of British theatres remains intact and is not further eroded in the interests of big business or as the result of local authority folly.

Bookshops frequently have a section devoted to local matters, and it is sometimes possible to pick up a monograph of a town's theatre or music hall, although many, it has to be said, are superficially written and intended only for casual browsing by readers. They offer little by way of original research.

This volume treats the Coventry Royal and Empire in greater depth, including all the known information on the history of the building, together with details of working practices and information on the better known productions of the day. To add interest, thumb nail sketches of the more important artists who played the theatre, have been included. Details of the opposition, especially the Britannia Music Hall and Sydenham Palace of Varieties, have been recorded as they had a direct influence on the fortunes of the theatre once it had become the Empire.

Our knowledge of how the nineteenth century circuit theatres worked remains relatively sketchy. Broad views of understanding exist, but many gaps of minutiae remain. Some jig-saw pieces have been put together by Moira Field in her fascinating work on the East Anglian Fisher Circuit, and one supposes other companies worked along similar lines. She was fortunate to obtain information from log books kept by the Fisher Company – details that surprisingly survived. Paul Ranger in his *'Under Two Managers'*, (Society for Theatre Research 2001), has done similar interesting spadework into the circuit of Thornton and Barnett in the south, and his findings tend to tie in with the work of Field. Other areas of the country appear to have little or no documentation which would enable the jig-saw to be completed.

So what is special about Coventry and the Theatre Royal, which later became the Empire Music Hall? My attention was drawn to it by a short article in the *'Stage'* newspaper for 7th September, 1893 when it was reported that those attending a Bristol exhibition had listened to part of an ordinary performance via the telephone. This seemed excitingly novel, until I discovered the idea was not new at all and that others had done the same before and elsewhere. None the less the imagination was stimulated into finding out what this previously unknown Empire Theatre was, the only other on record being the Hertford Street Empire, which did not open until 1906. It transpired that the first Empire was a building which originated as the 'Theatre' in the Regency period, a time of considerable theatre growth, managing to survive the great cull of the 1840s and 1850s, whence it entered into the music hall boom of the 1880s and 1890s with much promise, only to expire in the middle of it. This last unexpected turn of events poses many questions to which few immediate answers seem available.

In *'The Development of the English Playhouse'* (Methuen 1973), Richard Leacroft included his own isometric drawings of London's Drury Lane and Covent Garden theatres, which included much minute detail. He had access to early architectural drawings, but there are no existing plans of the Coventry Theatre. Details concerning the internal and external arrangements are conspicuous by their absence. One imagines something was put on paper at one time, but this may not have been thought sufficiently important to keep. On the other hand, Coventry was decimated during the Second World War bombing raids and among the casualties was the main library, which probably explains why some of the original newspapers, dealing with the first ten years of the theatre's life, are missing. Surprisingly these volumes are absent from the British Newspaper Library at Colindale too. The loss of such important primary material is unfortunate. Alternative information, especially in theatrical publications from the mid century, is sparse which is why reliance has occasionally been made on commentaries published by those who had access to the papers before the war. It is possible to make educated assumptions of the building from other theatres that existed at the same time.

Details of performances seen at the Theatre Royal became more interesting on the discovery that many of the London and provincial stars (an overworked term now but one in use during the Victorian period) visited the theatre from time to time, some being successful while others were sent, in the literal sense, to Coventry.

It is highly unlikely the Coventry Theatre was an architectural work of beauty, either inside or out, although had it survived in anything approaching its original form it would have ranked along with the Bristol Theatre Royal, Georgian Theatre Royal at Richmond, Yorkshire, the Bury St Edmunds Theatre Royal and the Glasgow Britannia Music Hall and given listed status by English Heritage. Its location was probably the most unsatisfactory spot in the city its founder could have chosen, and the design was such that despite many subsequent alterations, the theatre proved a thorn in the flesh to those who latterly used it for the modern productions of the day.

Competition from other theatres during the initial days was nothing much to worry about; Birmingham had its New Street Theatre, the Leamington Spa Theatre functioned in Bath Street, the second Warwick Playhouse existed in Theatre Street and there was Northampton's Marefair Theatre, fascinatingly labelled *'Theatre Un-Royal'* by Lou Warwick. Human traffic from one town to another in pre-railway days must have been limited and so audiences were not seriously tempted by greener grass beyond the city boundary. Stratford did not acquire its first permanent theatre until 1827, some 52 years before the opening of the Memorial Theatre (now the Swan), next to the present Shakespeare theatre on the river bank site. Until mid century, local competition within the city of Coventry for entertainment comprised nothing more serious than the occasional concert, fair or travelling circus.

Admission to the theatre was expensive, 3s. for the boxes, 2s. for the pit and 1s. in the gallery, which may not seem exorbitant in an age when seats can cost from £6 to £60 or more, but 1s. then would have been beyond the reach of some working people. Throughout the following pages only the pre-decimal coinage is given. Those who may be unfamiliar with pounds, shillings and pence may like to bear in mind that 3s. (three shillings) is equivalent to 15p, 2s. is equal to 10p and 1s. to 5p. One pound is exactly the same in both currencies but in the imperial system there were 20 shillings to the pound, 12 pence to the shilling and 240 pence to the pound. In like manner the imperial units of measurement have been retained. One inch is represented by 2.54 centimetres and one foot is 30.48 centimetres or 0.3048 metres. For those wishing to carry out conversions a calculator, either mental or electrical, may be helpful. Theatrical productions were not always on tap, as the law curtailed a company's activity to a few weeks a year in any one town, whence the group of thespians had to travel from one theatre to another within their circuit carrying their properties, personal belongings and scenery with them, in order to earn a living throughout the year.

Coventry Theatre Royal had no serious rivals in the field of drama until greater use was made of the Corn Exchange in 1856 and William Bennett opened his Opera House in 1889, whence the old theatre immediately became the Empire Music Hall and here there was opposition in the form of two other halls, each presenting entertainment of a similar nature. Coventry was a working class city and music halls were acknowledged as the working man's entertainment, so this makes the collapse of all three venues of light entertainment within a short space of time all the more puzzling. Probable reasons for their untimely demise will be touched upon in the following pages; in the meantime let us begin where it all started – with that telephone 'broadcast'.

Chapter 1

Broadcasting by Telephone

"Coventry Calling"

On the evening of Wednesday 30th August, 1893, a novel 'broadcast' took place at the Coventry Empire Theatre of Varieties.[1] This was the last of the three names by which the building was known, opening as the Theatre in 1819, becoming the Theatre Royal in 1848 and ending as the Empire Theatre of Varieties in 1889. Possibly because the gas footlights might damage the equipment, the two transmitters (which had been connected into the national telephone system) were

Figure 1   An example of electrophone microphones placed in the footlights of an unknown London theatre, 1904

BT Archives

1

placed on each side of the proscenium arch from where they picked up the once nightly variety show given by performers representing the artistry of the comedian, acrobat, musician, vocalist and dancer. The appreciative audience had paid 1s. in the stalls or dress circle, 6d. in the upper circle and pit and 3d. in the gallery, although late comers after 9.00 p.m. were charged less in some parts of the house. The first half closed with, 'The Gathering of the Clans', a military spectacle involving a large number of well trained juveniles.

The event was especially organised for visitors attending the 'British Industrial and Fine Art Exhibition', held in Bristol on Monday, August 28, the aim being to promote and encourage local businesses – a kind of Victorian trade fair.

> "One of the most attractive features of the exhibition is the telephone room. Connection is established between theatres in Bristol; the Prince of Wales, Birmingham; the Coventry Music Hall and many other places. . ."[2]

A large gathering of people picked up their receivers at the appointed time and heard the Coventry Empire orchestra render Balfe's 'Bohemian Girl' overture during the interval. The entertainment was also available to telephone subscribers in Birmingham and Coventry and, one assumes, they could have listened to the entire show, although anything other than spoken or vocal offerings would have made scant impact. Just why theatres in these specified towns were chosen must remain a mystery, although it is possible that the nearby Coventry Telephone Exchange, opened only a couple of doors from the Empire in June 1889, may have been an influential factor for that city.

A previous demonstration of this form of communication had been held at a Birmingham Midland Institute Conversazione in January 1892, where people listened to music simultaneously relayed from Dudley, Wolverhampton, Stafford and Hanley. With the use of careful timing and synchronised metronomes, the musicians in all four towns played and sang together as though they were in the same room. The result was spectacularly successful.[3]

The Electrophone

The Coventry 'broadcast' was made possible by using the Electrophone, a device designed to maximise the use of telephonic equipment during 'off peak' periods, rather similar to Economy Seven electricity, and many churches were thus wired to enable a wider audience to hear services and sermons on Sundays. In 1892 a British patent was taken out by H.S.J.Booth whereby people in hotels, and the like, could be connected to theatres via a coin operated mechanism attached to the telephone.[4] The idea was originally devised by German born Philip Reis, whose device enabled concerts to be transmitted via the telephone as early as 1861 although at that time speech did not communicate as well as music.[5] The invention was known to Queen Victoria who, whilst staying at Newham House, was pleased to listen to the complete opera, 'Les Cloches de Corneville', relayed from the Liverpool Royal Court Theatre on 11th May, 1880.[6]

In May 1883, the composer Arthur Sullivan had a private telephone installed between his home and the London Savoy theatre, where most of his collaborations with Gilbert were first performed. The occasion was that of his forty-first birthday party (May 13th) when guests, including the Prince of Wales, were gathered for the celebrations and each took turns to hear items from 'Iolanthe', then playing at the theatre.[7]

Telephonic Advertising

Theatre managers were not slow to take advantage of telephonic publicity. George Gaze, manager of the Hastings Gaiety Theatre, had used it in January 1889.[8] H.W.Rowlands followed Coventry's example, in November 1893, publicising his Pleasure Gardens Theatre wares at Folkestone to subscribers in nearby Deal, Dover and Canterbury.[9] The Hastings, Folkestone and Bristol experiments were all concerned with the legitimate or lyrical theatre; the Coventry Empire occasion represents one of the first known 'broadcasts' from a music hall.

The idea was later widened in 1922 by the formation of the British Broadcasting Company, afterwards known as the British Broadcasting Corporation. A small number of outside broadcasts from theatres took place but were stopped in the following year by a committee of theatre managers, who feared that any additional competition would make further inroads into the profitability of an already declining music hall market. The ban was supported by the Variety Artists' Federation, both groups failing to realise the potential audiences from people who, once having heard an act on air, would want to visit the theatre to see it in the flesh.[10]

In the late twenties, George Black permitted monthly relays from the London Palladium Theatre and Sir Oswald Stoll offered broadcasts from the London Coliseum and Alhambra Theatres.[11] In later years short fifteen minute outside broadcasts from various pantomimes and variety bills were regularly heard on radio. One house which featured more frequently than most was the Coventry Hippodrome, whose prestigious orchestra, first under Charles Shadwell and later Bill Pethers, broadcast a weekly programme of music during the day-time. The orchestras of the Dudley and Aston Hippodromes also made their marks in this way.

Boom for Variety but Bust for the Empire

The Coventry transmission of 1893 was made when the fortunes of the Empire Music Hall were buoyant. These were the 'Naughty Nineties', the golden age of music hall when the great circuits founded by Moss, Stoll, Barrasford, MacNaghten, de Freece and others, had been laid down or were in a period of gestation. Such was the popularity of this mainly working class entertainment, now made respectable by the elimination of food and drink from the auditorium, that within fifteen years many well known dramatic houses, the London Lyceum, Birmingham Grand, the Dover Royal, Eastbourne Royal and many others, were converted into twice nightly variety halls. Yet within eighteen months of the 'broadcast', the Coventry Empire was in terminal decline.

Failure is likely to have been largely connected with the building which, in 1887, was described as still having original defects, although these were not enumerated beyond mentioning restricted exits.[12] The building was, no doubt, inconvenient, uncomfortable, a possible fire hazard and structurally well past its sell by date. The lack of drawings or photographs doesn't help our comprehension of how bad things must have been, although it is possible to detect some idea of the internal arrangements by studying the many alterations carried out after 1857.

[1] The Stage, 7 September, 1893.
[2] Coventry Standard, 1 September, 1893.
[3] Midland Daily Telegraph, 19 January, 1892.
[4] Dr Terence Rees and Dr David Wilmore (ed) "British Theatrical Patents 1800–1900", Society for Theatre Research 1996.
[5] National Telephone Journal, March 1907.
[6] Era Magazine, 15 May, 1880.
[7] Herbert Sullivan and Newman Flower. "Sir Arthur Sullivan", Cassell & Company, 1927.
[8] The Stage, 18 January, 1889.
[9] The Stage, 23 January, 1893.
[10] Asa Briggs, "The Birth of Broadcasting", OUP 1961.
[11] Paddy Scannell & David Cardiff, "A Social History of Broadcasting", Volume 1. 1922–1939. Basil Blackwell 1991.
[12] Coventry Herald, 23 September, 1887.

Chapter 2

The Building – A Mystery

There are three maps of Coventry, 1837, 1851 and 1888, which show outlines of the Theatre, however only the last is of a large enough scale to show important detail. A map published in 1807 illustrates the Cavalry Barracks and the adjacent vacant land upon which the theatre was to be built in 1819. The plan view of the

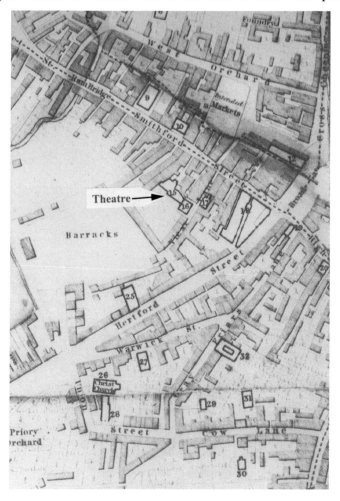

Figure 2   A map of Coventry in 1837 showing Smithford Street and the Theatre (number 15). The accuracy of the tapered stage and the kink in the long wall has to be questioned

Coventry Local Studies, Central Library

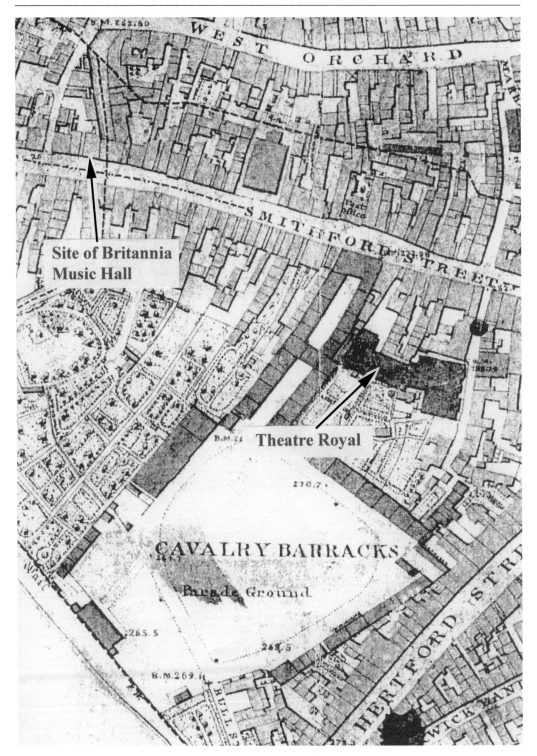

Figure 3 A Board of Health survey map of 1851 showing the Theatre Royal as an oblong figure with the manager's house attached

Coventry Record Office

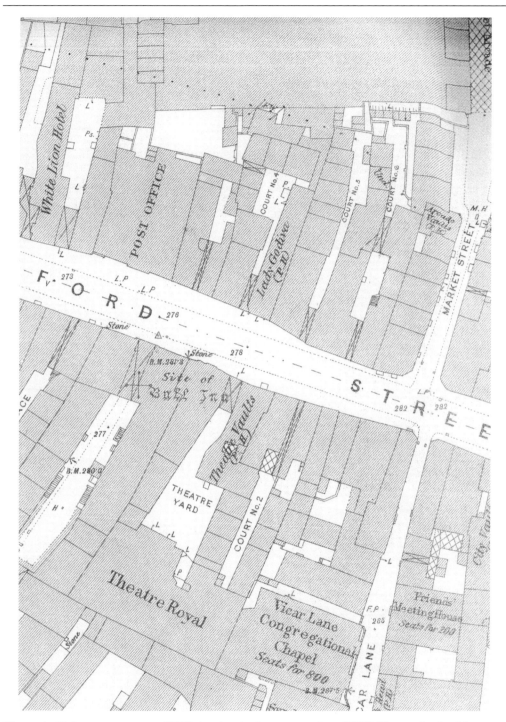

Figure 4 Ordnance survey map of 1888 showing the theatre extensions of 1857. The restricted public access from Smithford Street, beneath a building, can be clearly seen along with the 'dog-leg' passage from Vicar Lane to the scene dock doors. A long narrow passage beneath another building is shown leading to Court No. 2 and is thought to have led to the dressing rooms. Note the position of the Theatre Vaults which feature more prominently when the Theatre became the Empire Music Hall

Coventry Record Office

theatre in 1837 is inconsistent with those of 1851 and 1888 in that it shows certain discrepancies. The southern wall is depicted with a kink not shown in the 1851 or 1888 editions and this is unlikely to have been altered since no major building works were carried out before 1857. Also the tapered stage is not shown elsewhere, however, this was not an ordnance survey map and probably contained certain inaccuracies. They all agree with the position of the manager's house beneath which were the main entrances, public saloons and staircases. When measured with dividers, and appropriately scaled, the dimensions of the building on all maps agree quite well, the width varying by about two to three feet.

Using the large scale map published in 1888, the size of the theatre can be assumed to be ninety six feet in length and thirty four feet in width. Since the Ordnance Survey reckons that the margin of error on large scale maps is no more than one in 500, the dimensions can be taken as more or less correct. The new dressing room block of 1857, together with additional wing and storage spaces, follows the outlines of two dwellings clearly marked on the 1851 map and were conversions of private residences rather than the result of an entirely new construction.

The auditorium and stage were unusually narrow for theatres of this period and this aggravated the problems experienced by managers in later years.

The Exterior

Very few early provincial theatres have been photographed and Coventry Theatre is no exception. Neither has a pen and ink drawing of it surfaced in any publication. Since the theatre was hidden in an alley off the main street, any casual photographer or illustrator was unlikely to stumble upon it by accident. The Coventry City Library has two photographs of the building, one an exterior dating from between 1889 and around 1892, and which shows the main public entrance in the area beneath what had been the manager's house. It is likely the two narrow middle doors formed the entrances, possibly leading to a centrally positioned pay box. The larger doors on either side may have been used for egress. Although the photograph relates to its last few years, the arrangements for going in and out are likely to have been much the same during earlier times. The exception could have been the pit entrance which was probably placed towards the left of the picture and well away from the box clientele. Working from the 1888 ordnance survey map, the frontage measured around twenty three feet six inches in width with a height of nearly thirty feet to the parapet, a figure that can be calculated by proportion. In the early days, it is likely the ground floor of this section was occupied with entrances and staircases, whilst the first and second floors were given over to offices and accommodation for the manager.

To the left of the photograph is a passageway boarded by a wooden door which probably signifies another entrance point, disused by the time the photograph was taken. On the extreme left can be seen the edge of a wall which ran across a narrow entrance and this is clearly shown in the 1888 map. The existence of this

Figure 5 The public entrance to the theatre was beneath the manager's house
situated on the upper two floors. The pecture dates from between 1889
and 1892 when Henry William Thomas re-named it Thomas's Empire

Picture courtesty of Coventry Evening Telegraph

constriction is a mystery and one wonders why, when the extension to the stage house was built in 1857, this area was not then enclosed. It must be assumed this formed an important passageway from the theatre yard, and that it continued to be used, probably for emergency exits, after the alterations had taken place. It may have been the original pit entrance, which would have burrowed beneath the proscenium stage to emerge adjacent to the orchestra on the inside. The photograph shows that a new pit entrance existed in later years which might explain why the former passage was walled across. The only known photograph of the interior does not show a ground floor entrance by the orchestra pit (the usual position in 1819) which probably means it was re-located somewhere along the interior side wall at some time from 1857. It will be seen that the roof over the auditorium comes to an abrupt end indicating that cover for the stage was at a lower height. The photographer was standing in the Theatre Yard with his back to the archway leading directly into Smithford Street. There was little else of the outside to photograph since the theatre, at that time, was hemmed in on three sides by other buildings.

The Stage

This solitary photograph of the interior was taken in its music hall days, a form of entertainment initially linked closely with the idiom of the public house as shown by the beer engines, barrels and bottles, although in the 1890s the format of these halls was changing more to that of a conventional theatre, with neat rows of seats and benches. It became the condition of a music hall's licence that bars should be constructed outside the auditorium as a means of limiting drinking and controlling drunkenness. This marked the point of transition between the informal entertainment in the 'free and easies' and the respectable 'Palaces of Varieties' which, to all intents and purposes, looked just like any other theatre.

The stage appears raked, with wings and a backcloth the top of which is just visible indicating the approximate height of the stage opening. As there was no fly tower, cloths like this would have been rolled up from the bottom using a system of ropes. Wings were held upright by a series of narrow wooden grooves screwed onto the stage floor, and into the roof space, thereby permitting these narrow pieces of scenery to be slid into or out of view. Originally there would have been a front curtain and, later, an act-drop placed immediately behind. Neither is visible here. There are no stage curtains at the sides ruling out those which traversed left and right or those which rose upwards and outwards in tableau fashion, so any curtain is likely to have been rolled or taken up in a series of horizontal swags similar to that at the Richmond Georgian Theatre Royal in Yorkshire. Since the provision of a new act-drop was chronicled in 1892, it is possible that the front curtain had been

Figure 6 The only known interior view of the Empire. The paraphernalia of the public house is clearly visible. Note the narrow orchestra pit and the iron rail to protect artists' costumes from coming into contact with the naked gas footlights

Coventry Local Studies, Central Library

removed, since it was not common practice for small music halls of this period to have both.

The two model figures on either side of the proscenium may have been connected with a Christy Minstrel show; unfortunately the lettering around the base is indecipherable. The tall iron rail at the front of the stage is unusually high and was intended to prevent costumes coming into contact with the naked gas footlights. There is nothing in the photograph to suggest scale but it is known that the proscenium width was narrow – probably no more than sixteen feet. The stage depth was around thirty six feet. Restoration and early Georgian theatres used this depth to display perspective scenery. Under this arrangement a row of painted wooden houses at the back of the stage might only be five feet in height whereas those near the front of the stage would be much taller. As it would be ridiculous for performers to wander amongst two storey houses which were shorter than they were, acting was confined to an oblong platform, the forestage, or 'pro-scenium' (before the scenery), placed in front of the curtain. Access to this acting area was through a proscenium door placed at each side with, possibly, a private box situated directly above. However by the time Coventry had its theatre, action behind the curtain was becoming more common and the fore, or 'pro-scenium' stage, became increasingly redundant. Proscenium doors were also becoming superfluous, although they were often retained as 'call doors' to allow performers to enter at the end of the

Figure 7 The proscenium stage positioned before the curtain and accessed via the proscenium door beneath the private box as seen in the Georgian Theatre Royal, Richmond, Yorkshire in 1998. There is a similar door beneath the photographer. This arrangement is likely to have existed at the Coventry Theatre when it opened in 1819

Photo – Author

play to receive their applause, or disapprobation. It is likely a forestage, with proscenium doors, existed when the theatre opened and in the absence of other information, one might assume they were dismantled, or reduced, in the rebuild of 1857 when a new stage was installed.

After the 1857 extensions to the stage, the scene dock doors, measuring approximately seven feet across, were positioned on stage right of the rear wall opposite an alley way from Vicar Lane. The right-angled bend near the stage wall must have caused difficulties for transporting long pieces of scenery or cloths. The rear stage wall abutted the Vicar Lane Congregational Chapel, but as it would have been unusual for both establishments to function at the same time, it is unlikely there was any interference.

The original dressing rooms were most likely situated beneath the stage and were probably two in number, one for men and the other for women, with an outside access from the Theatre Yard. The rebuild of 1857 changed all that. Two adjacent houses at the end of Court No 2, were acquired and converted into dressing rooms which were accessed from the stage via a wooden staircase and, therefore, technically outside the theatre.

Figure 8 (*Left*) Richard Leacroft was ready to leap onto the stage of the Grand Theatre, Llandudno, by standing of a corner trap (1984). The platform beneath his feet measured approximately twenty seven inches square and was engineered to the same rake as the stage. The hosting ropes and counterweights were missing

Figure 9 (*Right*) An underneath view of a bridge trap as seen from the cellar at the Tyne Theatre, Newcastle-upon-Tyne (1998). The space between the two vertical timbers represents the width of the bridge – usually just over two feet. The circular drum is a mechanical device for raising or lowering the bridge. The vertical distance of the lift at Coventry is not known. One can imagine the perilous journey a group of pantomime nymphs and fairies would have endured being raised on such a narrow platform with no sides, probably in the dark, in a transformation scene

Photos – Author

The Coventry Theatre is likely to have been built with the usual stage traps so familiar to audiences in other theatres at the time. In addition to corner and grave traps it is probable that the stage had at least two bridge lifts. These are openings measuring the width of the proscenium by approximately two feet six inches in breadth and were used in order to raise, or lower, scenery or groups of actors in full view of the audience. These bridge trap openings were covered by two sliders at stage level, each capable of being drawn off into the wings to reveal the gap which would then be filled by the rising bridge. A bridge trap sixteen feet in length would require two sliders each being eight feet long. In order to have sufficient space in which the slider could be removed, each wing would need to be eight feet wide. Therefore, a proscenium opening wider than sixteen or seventeen feet would have made this type of trap difficult to operate since the building was only thirty four feet wide.

The Auditorium

The appearance and design of the auditorium are unknown although it is possible to make educated assumptions using other models and a knowledge of the period. The name of the architect is also a mystery but it is likely he visited other theatres to get ideas. It was not common for one designer to be responsible for swathes of theatres as happened later in the century with Phipps, Matcham, Sprague and others. Samuel Beazley was probably the first architect responsible for more than a couple of theatres, but he worked mainly in London between 1816 and 1851.

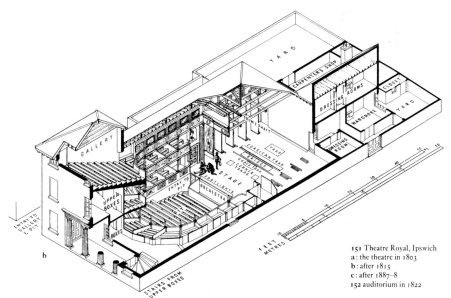

151 Theatre Royal, Ipswich
a: the theatre in 1803
b: after 1815
c: after 1887–8
152 auditorium in 1822

Figure 10 Theatre Royal, Ipswich after alterations in 1815 as shown in '*Theatre and Playhouse*' by Richard Leacroft (1984). There would have been similarities between this and the Coventry Theatre although the latter had a gallery in place of the central upper box tier. The 'U' shaped auditorium at Ipswich would have been similar to that at Coventry after the alterations in 1820/21

Courtesy Methuen Publishing Ltd

There were many buildings which the Coventry designer might have visited, the nearest being: Birmingham, Cambridge, Cheltenham, Derby, Leamington, Leicester, Northampton, Nottingham, Shrewsbury, Tamworth, Warwick and Worcester. Some of these began as small oblong barn like constructions in the eighteenth century and were gradually altered, or rebuilt, from time to time, but exact details concerning the interiors of these theatres have largely passed into oblivion, so direct comparisons are difficult to assess. Slightly further afield, the Bury St Edmunds Theatre Royal also opened in 1819 and four years previously the Ipswich Theatre Royal underwent stage alterations, although the auditorium of 1803 remained relatively untouched. Richard Leacroft, theatre historian, scenic artist and architect, studied these buildings in detail and prepared scale isometric drawings of both.[1] The overall external dimensions of the Ipswich, Bury St Edmunds and Coventry theatres have similarities and are worthy of closer inspection.

The following table compares the approximate dimensions of all three as far as possible.

	Ipswich:	Bury St Edmunds:	Coventry:
Length of auditorium and stage:	99'	96'	96'
Width of the building:	40'	40'	34'
Width of proscenium opening:	20'	22'	(16')?
Width of each wing	10'	9'	(9')?
Stage depth:	27'	36'	36'

All three theatres were of similar length and the extreme narrowness of the Coventry auditorium suggests that the proscenium width was likely to have been around sixteen feet at most. The Northampton Marefair Theatre (opened 1806) had a proscenium opening of seventeen feet by a height of twelve feet six inches. The replacement Coventry Opera House had a stage opening of twenty four feet (still quite narrow) and was considered an improvement upon its predecessor – the Smithford Street Theatre Royal. By comparison, the 1937 Coventry Hippodrome had a stage opening of over forty four feet. Simple arithmetic leads us to calculate that the wing space at the Theatre would have been around eight or nine feet each side. That on stage right was considerably increased after the rebuilding programme in 1857 but the 1887 survey suggested that there was 'plenty of room at the sides of the stage', which is difficult to appreciate especially regarding stage left where no improvements were made.

The orchestra, placed between the pit and 'pro-scenium' stage, held nine players in later days which was modest considering the number of operas staged. Entry to the pit benches is likely to have been via a 'tunnel' on the north side of the orchestra and probably led to the outside through a door directly into the Theatre Yard.

The layout of the house would have taken the usual form of Georgian and Regency theatres, namely seating on the ground floor (called the pit), sloping upwards and backwards to meet the first tier of boxes. Unlike theatres of today, the

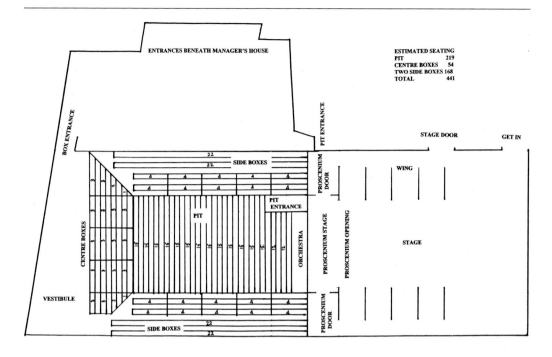

Figure 11 An impression of what the Coventry Theatre pit and first tier of boxes might have looked like in 1819

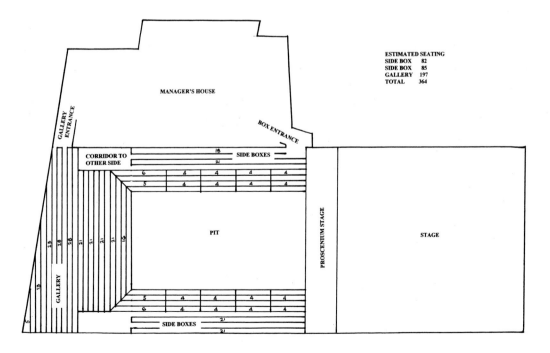

Figure 12 An impression of what the Coventry Theatre second tier of boxes and gallery might have looked like in 1819

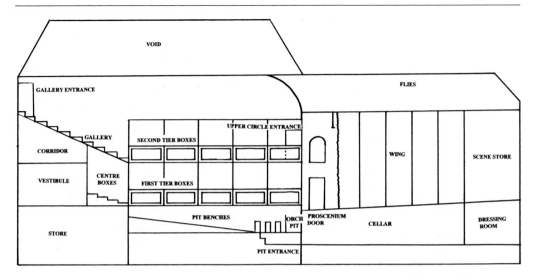

Figure 13 An impression of what the Coventry Theatre auditorium and stage might have looked like in 1819

pit would have been enclosed by a three sided configuration of boxes, the benches of which would be occupied by members of the middle or upper class societies. This arrangement of pit and boxes can be seen at Bury St Edmunds Theatre Royal, the Richmond Georgian Theatre Royal, Yorkshire, and in a modified manner at the Bristol Theatre Royal. In light of alterations recorded a year or so after the opening, we can assume that the Coventry auditorium was originally oblong in shape, like the Georgian Theatre Royal, Richmond in Yorkshire, as opposed to a semi circular arrangement as at the Bury St Edmunds and Bristol theatres. The Ipswich Theatre Royal was more 'U' shaped as Coventry was later to become. Coventry was also much longer, probably having around fifteen rows of benches in the pit as opposed to approximately ten or twelve elsewhere, due to all the entrances being at one side beneath the manager's quarters and not at the end opposite the stage. Public access to the auditorium was at the side for the simple reason that the existence of other buildings prevented doors being placed in the end wall. Unlike Ipswich Theatre Royal, the second tier at Coventry had side boxes with a sloping gallery running in-between. Bristol Theatre Royal opened with this arrangement in 1766, but the side boxes were joined by a middle section of boxes by 1800. The London St James's Theatre had a similar arrangement to Coventry when it opened in 1835. As will be seen later, the upper part of the Coventry Theatre auditorium was subjected to several alterations in that the circle of boxes was completed, removed and further reinstated during its life time.

The word box conjures up a vision of a privately enclosed space seen in our remaining Victorian and Edwardian buildings. Boxes in the Regency period consisted of larger areas into which perhaps a dozen or more people sat and they were separated from the box next door by waist high partitions, examples of which have been retained in the upper circle area of the Bury St Edmunds Theatre Royal. The relatively new Northampton Derngate Theatre, opened in 1983, has a similar arrangement when the interior is modelled into the lyric mode. As will be seen from the simulated plan, there were no gangways to reach many of the benches, the practice of clambering over them being the accepted method of reaching the front, although in some pits the end twelve inches of each bench was made to hinge upwards to facilitate easier access from one row to the other. It is not known whether these were installed in the Coventry Theatre.

Figure 14   The upper circle boxes at the Theatre Royal, Bury St. Edmunds (1984) showing the typical waist high divisions. These boxes held four chairs but those in other theatres could be much larger

Photo – Author

The rear wall of the auditorium was not at right angles to the side walls, this being caused by the lay out of adjacent property.

Calculating the capacity of an auditorium furnished with benches can never be an exact science since the number occupying a bench has to be a variable quantity. Henry Holland, of London's Drury Lane in the early nineteenth century, allowed eighteen inches per person in the boxes and fourteen inches elsewhere. In 1835, the proprietor of the London St James's Theatre unleashed his generosity in permitting pit persons to have fifteen inches of bench to themselves. For the purpose of estimating the capacity of Coventry's Theatre, Holland's figures have been adhered to. The entire theatre would have consisted of benches; chairs were not introduced for the higher priced seats until 1857. The only known fact of the interior is that, before the alterations of 1857, the pit held 200 people. This number could have been accommodated on fifteen benches, each being approximately seventeen feet long, and two around fifteen feet in length. (see Figure 11, page 15) A space of two feet was allowed for each bench and legs before the next row, therefore the pit would have extended back around thirty two feet before meeting the first tier of boxes. When alterations took place to slightly curve the box fronts from an oblong format to that of a long letter 'U' in the first or second year of opening, a few pit benches would have been sacrificed at the corners, but this has been allowed for. A single entrance to the pit was common practice and this is likely to have tunnelled beneath the 'pro-scenium' stage and into the Theatre Yard to the north.

The depth of the centre box level would have been approximately seventeen feet, and as the second tier (the gallery) is unlikely to have overhung the lower boxes this would have had a similar measurement. Exactly how much of the first tier was occupied with benches and how much was given to vestibule space is not known. As the alterations of 1857 enabled this area to be deepened, there must have been space into which the additional accommodation encroached. Whether the generous vestibule was merely an area for gathering, or whether refreshments were available there, as in the some London houses, is not known either. It is unlikely there was sufficient room for assembly outside the auditorium as space in the lower regions of the manager's house would have been taken up with corridors and staircases. As the house seemed not to be used for residence purposes in later years, some additional space might have been devoted to cloak room and refreshment facilities after 1857, but this is mere speculation.

Initially the side gallery width of approximately eight feet is unlikely to have included a separate access corridor as this appears to have been added during the alterations of 1820/21. As elsewhere, benches in the side boxes were no doubt reached by passing through other adjacent boxes, as happens at the Richmond Georgian Theatre Royal now. Each side gallery would have been divided into a number of smaller boxes, perhaps up to five on each side.

The seating capacity at the 1819 opening is not recorded but the following estimates are suggested:

pit: 219; first tier boxes (central portion) 54; first tier boxes (both side sections) 168; second tier boxes (both side sections) 167; gallery; 197. This makes a grand total of 805 which, on the face of it seems large, but may, in part, be accounted for by the fact that the long auditorium was the result of the entrances being at the side and not at the end of the building. Prices of entry were fairly standard over the country and ranged from 3s. in the boxes, 2s. for the pit and 1s. in the gallery. A full house would therefore yield circa £58 6s. for the boxes, £21 18s. for the pit and £9 17s. in the gallery or a total of around £90 1s.

Paul Ranger[2] informs us that the Guildford Theatre, opened around 1789, measured sixty three feet by thirty eight feet and held around 400 people, which provides a useful comparison.

Having surmised on the appearance of the Coventry Theatre Royal, we can look at its relatively long and fascinating history which has escaped the attention of previous theatre historians. It epitomised a typical nineteenth century provincial theatre, managing to survive the down turn of the 1840s and 1850s, but surprisingly died during the greatest expansion of theatres and music halls this country has ever seen. It ranks as one of the few long serving theatres which never suffered a serious fire, a fate which befell so many others in the middle and late Victorian years.

---

[1] Richard Leacroft, "Theatre and Playhouse", Methuen 1984.
[2] Paul Ranger, "Under Two Managers", Society for Theatre Research 2001.

Chapter 3

Opening of the Theatre

Samson Penley. The First Manager. [d. 1838]

In 1752, a new Coventry theatre opened in what had been a Riding School, situated down a large open yard close by St. John's Bridge and where Kemble acted in *'Measure for Measure'*.[1] The building, which would have been used on infrequent occasions was, no doubt, large enough to be financially viable, as dramatic companies were commercial concerns and the word 'subsidy' was an un-dreamt of concept. Another venue brought into intermittent use was a capacious barn on the north side of Spon End, but this closed when the new theatre opened off Smithford Street on Easter Monday, 12th April, 1819. The whole area was heavily redeveloped after the last war, but the Theatre can be calculated to have been somewhere near the present City Library. It was not to be called 'Royal' until much later. Patrons made their way along a narrow passageway between Smithford Street and the Theatre, which had been built on land adjacent to the Cavalry Barracks. This one and only access to the playhouse restricted the movement of a large crowd of people and must have been a contributory factor to the theatre's lack of success in later years. According to Paul Ranger, a similar situation existed at Chelmsford where the 1792 theatre was constructed along a long blind alley leading from Conduit Street.[2]

The Coventry Theatre was built by Sir Skears Rew [1758–1828], a respected local magistrate, alderman and mayor of Coventry between 1815 to 1817. A plumber and glazier by trade, and knighted during his mayoralty for presenting a loyal address to the Prince Regent at Coombe Abbey in 1817, he had offices on Smithford Street, which must have been the most likely reason the theatre was built there. He moved his office into the front part of the theatre and an undated newspaper cutting in the local city library indicates that Rew's house was situated in what became known as the Theatre Yard. It seems likely that his office occupied the storeys above the public entrances on the north side of the building. After Rew's time the upper floors became the manager's house. Just why Rew built a playhouse at all is not clear, for he was a tradesman and a politician, not a theatrical entrepreneur. Theatre buildings were usually built by managers of existing companies, who had an eye on expanding their businesses, or by public subscription. Coventry fits into neither of these categories. Who did Rew think would run it? Was Penley in his mind all along and, if so, how were the two acquainted, given the distance between Coventry and

Windsor? If a speculating manager was interested on expanding his empire in a new town, it was customary for him to test the water by using a barn, or some such building, for a couple of seasons to size up the demand. Plays had been performed in Coventry barns for some time, so possibly the inhabitants had passed that hurdle. The beginning of the nineteenth century was a period of considerable theatre expansion and perhaps it was deemed an act of public spiritedness for a well respected local figure to provide such an amenity for the town, although one has to bear in mind there was a strata of society which viewed play acting with disfavour. Perhaps Rew enjoyed the drama and had the wherewithal to provide it with a permanent home. Coventry's theatre did not replace an older building, but merely added to the numbers already existing in the country.

There is a story that on the occasion of an election, Rew sent his apprentices out to assist in harrying the opposition. On their return he wanted to know the extent of their exploits and, when they told him they had smashed all the windows in such and such a building, he was aghast for he was under contract at a fixed price to keep those windows in good repair.

Figure 15   Sir Skears Rew who built the theatre in 1819.
This painting is a miniature of a larger work donated by the
Shepheard Family to the Coventry Art Gallery in 1926
Coventry Local Studies, Central Library

In 1819, Coventry numbered 21,000 inhabitants, over half of whom were employed in the silk trade, an occupation frequently in recession. In that year Peter Moore attempted to get a bill through Parliament which would enable local magistrates to regulate weavers' wages to a farthing a yard, as happened in Spitalfield and Dublin, but the bill was thrown out. (A farthing was a quarter of one old penny). Another bill attempted to limit the age and hours that could be worked by young chimney-sweep apprentices. At the other end of the social spectrum, the year was marked by the visit to Coventry of King Leopold of the Belgians, married to our Princess Charlotte. In addition to being given the freedom of the city, the Prince was on a nation-wide tour of the country.[3]

The honour of opening the new theatre went to Mr Samson Penley, whose theatrical company was based at Windsor's Theatre Royal in Thames Street. He was of a theatrical family having two brothers in the business, Belville and Montague, the latter being the first manager of the Grey Street Theatre Royal, Newcastle-upon-Tyne in 1837. The inaugural performance was Philip Massinger's '*A New Way to Pay Old Debts*' (advice which ought to have proved a source of useful instruction to later managements), and '*The Irishman in London*'.[4] The former was one of many plays with a moral message. Songs were rendered during the interval by Mr R. L. Jones. Among those in the company were: Messrs Salter, Bennett, Burton, Willmott, Prior, R.L.Jones and Misses Penley and Fisher. Penley, and his business partner John Jonas, were established joint managers at Lewes and Eastbourne with fingers in theatrical pies at Folkestone, Rye, Tenterden and Henley at the beginning of the nineteenth century. In 1805 they built a new playhouse in Henley, now the Kenton Theatre although with a different interior. It would seem strange that Penley should venture outside his southern territory and take a solitary venue in the Midlands, especially in pre-railways days when transporting scenery and properties over long distances had its problems and was not without cost. Nye Chart was to do the same in the late 1850s. The most likely explanation was the need to keep their companies intact after the main season at their respective base theatres had closed. Dispersal of the company would mean searching for fresh actors and actresses at the start of the new season as the better ones, especially, would have secured employment elsewhere. Maybe Penley was influenced by great improvements to the southern section of Watling Street, engineered by Thomas Telford in 1815, and which passed close to Coventry. Unless he used the older route through Oxford, it is likely that the actor-manager made his way along the improved road as far as Weedon and branched along the Birmingham Road through Dunchurch. The road to Birmingham, in fact, went along Coventry's Smithford Street so it was a fairly direct route from Windsor.

Although inhabitants of a town mainly remained in one place for most of their lives, extensive travel along turnpike roads was not unrealistic before railways but certainly more expensive. In 1824, it was possible to board a daily stage coach at Leamington at 4.00 p.m. and be in Liverpool the following morning. Likewise night journeys to London from Warwick were regularly advertised in the local press.

Turnpike roads were divided into several lengths each being entered through a gate after a toll had been paid. The toll was intended to keep the road, or track, in proper repair and to provide an income for those who leased that section of road. In 1822 various gates on the Studley to Birmingham road were auctioned. Those at Withwood and Bordesley were advertised as accruing £701 during the previous year, therefore travelling could be costly and certainly brought additional financial burdens to theatre companies transporting their equipment from one town to another.[5]

Coventry was situated on several turnpike roads and became a centre for both cart and coach services to London, Birmingham, Great Yarmouth to the East via Stamford, and north to Liverpool and Chester, not forgetting the local areas of Rugby, Leamington and Northampton. The opportunity for companies and 'stars' to travel was better here than in some other parts of the country.

Penley, who also had associations with Drury Lane[6], inaugurated a plan of non-transferable discount subscription tickets (whereby one booked for several performances at a reduction) which was probably similar to schemes favoured by present day managements. Penley's arrangement cost two guineas for the season. He actively discouraged the visitation of anyone behind the scenes.[7] The days when highly-priced seats for the nobility were placed at the sides of the acting stage had disappeared, therefore reasons for going backstage would have been more for personal than dramatic purposes.

The size of the auditorium governed what could be taken at the box office which, in turn, determined the viability of the company. Theatres were commercial ventures and the only subsidies came from the pocket of which ever manager was in charge at the time, an occurrence which did not repeat itself too often, at least not with the same lessee. The same problem of size exists today, which is why the small subsidised theatres built in the 1960s and 1970s are less able to profitably attract a wide range of professional companies after the cutting, or withdrawal, of Local Government or Arts Council subsidies in recent times.

Circuits

Individual theatres, within a limited geographical area, were often combined into what was called a circuit. This group of theatres was under the control of an actor-manager who was responsible for the company of players and the productions in which they appeared. The number of venues in any particular circuit varied. If there were two or more companies operating under one manager, the number of outlets naturally increased. Tracing which theatres belonged to which circuit is not always easy as from time to time, and often for financial reasons, managers shed or acquired buildings. For quite a long period of time Coventry was linked with the Worcester, Shrewsbury and Wolverhampton circuit. The distance between any two of these theatres was upwards of fifty miles, which was a long way to walk and trail wagons of scenery along ill made and poorly maintained roads. This type of circuit system survived until the mid nineteenth century when swathes of provincial theatres, especially those in rural areas, disappeared. A similar situation occurred in the 1950s when the wholesale closure of theatres and music halls, resulting from the introduction of television, decimated the touring circuits. In many ways the nineteenth century circuit system was mirrored by those of the music hall magnates in the twentieth century where organisations such as: Moss Empires, Stoll's, Howard and Wyndham's, F.J.Butterworth and others, operated many buildings the length and breadth of the country. At one time an artist booked on the Moss tour would secure half a year's work at a stroke.

Penley returned to Coventry on June 2nd, 1820 for a new season after having the new theatre redecorated. The advertised redecoration may have added to the theatre's attractions, although it is not certain just how much re-embellishment was done, but there is little doubt the use of candles for lighting purposes deposited soot over the interior surfaces and this needed removing quite frequently. The situation did not improve after the introduction of gas. Penley's two daughters, Miss Penley and Miss R. Penley, returned with the company although their acting ability is difficult to assess since the *Coventry Herald* printed no criticisms of any play. There was another daughter, a Miss E Penley, and all three sisters appeared together during Elliston's regime at Coventry. Records suggest that Samson Penley did not personally take to the boards except for his benefit when he, and John Jonas, acted in the comedies, '*Speed the Plough*' and '*The Midnight Hour*'. It was advertised that '*God Save the King*' would be played prior to the performances. The remainder of the season included a mixture of comedies and dramas that mean little today apart from the classics, '*The Rivals*' and '*School for Scandal*'. The theatre was open for business on Monday, Tuesday, Thursday and Friday evenings, the doors were unlocked at 6.30 p.m. and the entertainment commenced at 7.00 p.m. prompt, with half price admission allowed from 8.45 p.m. A different production was usually staged each night.

Information on forthcoming performances appeared in the weekly press and covered the following seven days from the date of publication. Bigger productions, especially those involving special scenery or effects as for the comedy '*The Steward*' and the melodramas, '*The Antiquary*' and '*Tekeli*', were hinted at from time to time but often took several weeks to prepare. '*Tekeli*', for example, had a plot which included the hero being transported inside a sack across a practical bridge, a scenic device which caught the public's imagination and was served up in other dramas. Although this sounds tame by present standards, it would have been a draw at the time. Attendance figures were not recorded, but this particular season was hot and such weather is not generally conducive to mass attendance in a sizzling and sticky theatre. In July, a girl working in a hay field at Berkswell, just outside Coventry, dropped dead with heat exhaustion. The inquest verdict was "*Death suddenly by the visitation of God.*"

> "*The Managers beg leave to return their most grateful thanks to the public in general of the City of Coventry and its vicinity for the generous patronage and support during the short season the theatre had been open and assure them every exertions and assurity shall be used to merit their future favours.*"

Beneath this advertisement was another giving similar thanks from Mr Salter for the patronage at his benefit. All had gone well, despite the heat, and the season ended on July 28th with the '*Midnight Hour*' and, considering performances often took four to five hours to get through, it may have lasted that long.[8]

In August 1820, R.W.Elliston placed an advertisement in the *Coventry Herald* that London's Drury Lane Theatre was about to reopen with Edmund Kean, possibly the most famous actor of this period. For whom was this notice intended? Coach journeys to the capital were available but expensive and the appeal is unlikely to have galvanised the working classes into walking there and back over several days, yet the cost of newspaper space was obviously expected to yield results, possibly from the gentry who had the time and possibly a residence in town.

Edmund Kean, the noted tragedian and regarded as second only to the great David Garrick, paid a flying visit to the Midlands for six nights in September 1820 presenting '*Richard III*' and '*The Merchant of Venice*' on alternate nights at the Northampton Marefair Theatre, Leamington Bath Street Theatre and the new Coventry Smithford Street house.[9] Such was Kean's standing that admission prices were more than doubled and, at Leamington, the pit was swathed in green baize and re-titled pit-boxes in order to justify the increase. This reflected Kean's worth at the time and similar happenings occur in our age when successful 'stars' appear before the public. One only needs to look at Covent Garden prices on the occasions Pavarotti has been in residence. Most of the principal families in Coventry and the neighbourhood were present to see Kean in the main pieces and Elliston in those which followed, such as '*The Deaf Lover*' and '*The Liar*'. "*His (Kean) astonishing performance was received with the most unbounded applause by a fashionable and numerous auditory.*"[10] Elliston also enjoyed rapturous applause. It was a good evening. Kean went to London where he played '*Richard III*' at Drury Lane before embarking on a tour of America. Small of stature and with an expressive face, this unconventional actor took London by storm in the role of Shylock in 1814, after struggling for years on the provincial circuits where he learned his craft during periods of destitution.

Two lectures were given at Coventry's St Mary's Hall in early June; one on the 'Safety of Gas Lighting' and the second, how to apply to Mr Hands, superintendent, between the hours of 10 and 12 noon at the company's works if one wished to be connected. On September 15th, 1820 there appeared an advertisement in the *Herald* inviting builders to submit estimates for the construction of a local gas works. Was this the cart coming before the horse, thereby making the application to Mr Hands seem a little premature? Many playhouses in the country changed to gas in the 1820s and 1830s, so it seems this new form of energy came to Coventry quite early for a provincial town. Being close to Birmingham where this lighting revolution was inaugurated by William Murdoch at the works of Boulton and Watt may have been a factor. The existence of local collieries and a canal must have been significant. It is not known whether the Coventry Theatre opened using candles or oil for lighting, but the changeover to gas is likely to have occurred during the early 1820s. In 1819 Mr Clarke, from the London Lyceum Theatre, appeared at the Warwick Theatre to demonstrate '*Philosophical or Gas Light Fireworks*', with danger, smell and smoke carefully expunged from the performance.

Alterations

Penley, together with two of his three daughters, returned for his third, and last, season on February 23rd 1821, opening with '*Virginius*' or '*The Liberation of Rome*' and the comedy '*Riches*'. It is not known why he gave up the lease after so short a period of three years; possibly he found the distance between Coventry and his other outlets too inconvenient. However, before he returned,

> "*the internal arrangement has undergone an entire change since the last season and every part has been rendered extremely commodious and elegant. . .the boxes have been rendered more circular with free access behind them, the pit has been elevated with due regard to convenience and proportion and the whole has received every embellishment in the power of art to bestow.*"[11]

In the absence of newspapers for the period, this article would aptly describe what we know of the Ipswich Theatre Royal interior at that time. It is not unknown for faults to be discovered after theatres have opened. Accounts of our own National Theatres on the South Bank prove that the art of making mistakes has not been entirely lost. These lessened when architects like Phipps, Matcham and Sprague became responsible for designing playhouses for a living, as they tended to get it right first time more often.

The Coventry auditorium no doubt began as an oblong with straight edges. (see Figure 11, page 15) That the pit had to be elevated suggests it was only slightly raked initially (it is unlikely to have been a flat floor) which failed to give clear uninterrupted sight lines. Owing to the fact that the pit at Coventry was longer than in other theatres, it is difficult to see how a highly elevated slope could be achieved: it is possible the rear part was raised a little more than the rest. It has to be assumed that "*free access behind the boxes*" referred to the installation of an access corridor behind each set of side boxes, since those in the middle already had a generous vestibule to the rear. This alteration would suggest some loss in seating capacity as the 'free access' is likely to have displaced the back most benches.

If the impressions of the alterations are correct, there would have been an overall loss of seating in all parts of the house, except the gallery. The new figures are calculated thus: pit 203; first tier centre boxes 69; the two first tier side boxes 64; the two second tier side boxes 86 and gallery 198. This makes a new total of 620, a loss of 185 places. It may be assumed that the original capacity was rarely achieved and that greater comfort afforded by the alterations would generate more goodwill.

It is not known whether these structural alterations occurred in 1820 or 1821, when Penley re-opened for his third and last season on February 23rd with '*King Lear*' and '*Whittington and His Cat*' as the afterpiece. There followed a fair proportion of classical pieces including: '*Virginius*', '*George Barnwell*', and '*King Henry II*'. Pantomime was not neglected, there being two. That in February was entitled '*Three Wishes*' or '*Harlequin and the Fair*' whilst the March offering was '*Perouse*', complete with new scenery and dresses. Penley finally retired from Coventry on March 23rd 1821. It is not known if he leased any other provincial theatre following his departure from the city, although he re-appeared in Newcastle-upon-Tyne managing the Theatre Royal, Mosley Street, from 1830 until his brother Montague succeeded him in 1835. Penley rarely appeared in Newcastle being unhappy there, partially due to the great distance from London which took thirty two hours to reach by coach.[12]

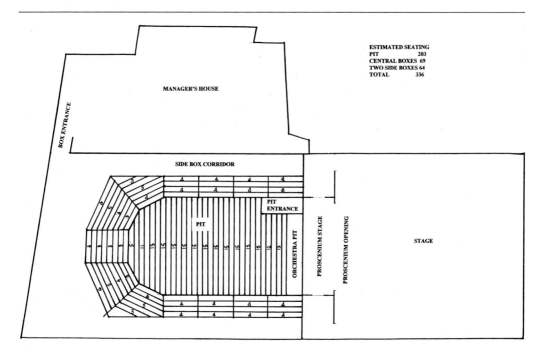

Figure 16 Impression of the alterations made to the pit and first tier of boxes of the Coventry Theatre in 1820/21

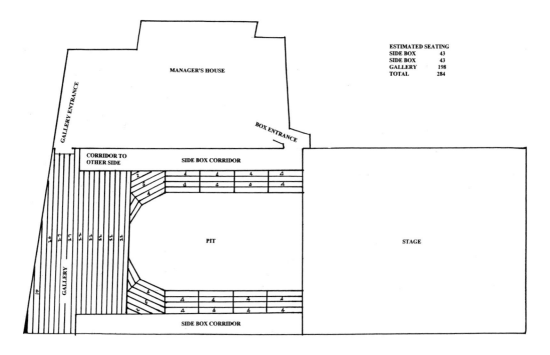

Figure 17 Impression of the alterations made to the second tier of boxes and gallery of the Coventry Theatre in 1820/21

Charles Mathews [1803–1878], later the husband of Madame Vestris (1838), presented *'Budget of Budgets'*, a series of Welsh, Irish and Scottish recitations accompanied by comic and appropriate songs, as part of a whistle stop tour of the area. He played the theatre in Leamington but gave his presentation on June 11th, 1821, at the Craven Arms Hotel Assembly Rooms in Coventry. It is likely that the transfer of the lease from Samson Penley to Robert William Elliston on July 6th, 1821 prevented this performance taking place at the theatre. The new regime was marked by Elliston's personal appearance on July 9th.

The son of an actor, Mathews first appeared at the London Olympic Theatre in 1835 in the year of his father's death. He trained as an architect and began his theatrical career on amateur stages. He was later successful at appearing in his own comedies.

On October 8th, 1821 Mons. Alexandre, ventriloquist, gave two performances at the theatre. His act included a sketch comprising three characters, the imitation of nailing and sawing of wood and the frying of an omelette. Another sketch involving a drunken servant and a man walking to and from the cellar, the voice appropriately expanding and receding. He also demonstrated the ability to drink and sing simultaneously and finally he imitated the interior of a nunnery with seventeen different characters. There was no half price admission and the audience went wild, as it would today.

[1] Poole, "History and Antiquities of Coventry", 1870.
[2] Paul Ranger, "Under Two Managers", Society for Theatre Research 2001.
[3] Poole, "History and Antiquities of Coventry", 1870.
[4] Poole, "History and Antiquities of Coventry", 1870.
[5] Warwickshire General Advertiser, 28 September, 1822.
[6] Angus MacNaghten, "Windsor and Eton in Georgian Times", Angus MacNaghten 1976.
[7] Coventry Herald, 9 June, 1820.
[8] Coventry Herald, 28 July, 1819.
[9] Lou Warwick, "Theatre Un-Royal", Lou Warwick 1974.
[10] Coventry Herald, 22 September, 1820.
[11] Coventry Herald, 4 March, 1932.
[12] Harold Oswald, "The Theatres Royal in Newcastle-upon-Tyne", Northumberland Press Limited 1936.

Chapter 4

Robert William Elliston [1774–1831]

Figure 18 Robert William Elliston (1774-1831).
Portrait by G. H. Harlow c. 1808
National Portrait Gallery, London

Robert William Elliston was originally intended for the church but he turned to the stage instead. His first appearance was at the Bath Theatre Royal in 1792, and later he became a leading actor and manager having connections with most of the country's leading provincial theatres at one time or another. He was a favourite of King George III and Queen Charlotte. His Midland interests concerned theatres in Birmingham, Leicester, Northampton, Shrewsbury and Worcester as well as Coventry, which he added to his circuit in 1822. He was described as: eccentric, extravagant, having a passion for management and was fond of the bottle, occasionally going beyond the state of being 'bon vivant'. An actor both on and off the stage, he championed the cause of the minor theatres against the oppressive regime of the patent houses, a situation not resolved until 1843.[1] He was known as the 'Napoleon of Drury Lane' controlling that theatre for some time. He ruled his employees with a firm discipline instituting a range of fines for being late at rehearsal, refusing to play a designated role, being imperfect with the text and other misdemeanours. He was not beyond the same degree of firmness with his audiences but occasionally they got the better of him by voting with their feet.

He was not beyond employing the art of deception if he thought it would fill his treasury. Business had been very bad in Birmingham for some while and the playbills announced the appearance of a Bohemian of extra-ordinary strength who would toss a stone weighing a ton as though it were a tennis ball. The crowded house fidgeted their way through the play awaiting the promised extraordinary event but then Elliston went before the curtain and with great emotion said the Bohemian had deceived him, and the audience, by not appearing. He pulled several letters from the elusive gentleman out of his pocket and offered anyone in the audience an opportunity to read them, so long as he understood German. No! he offered to translate but the mood of the assembly was such that he desisted and offered to show them the stone instead. A wink to the orchestra brought forth strains of "*The Battle of Prague*" and up went the curtain to reveal the huge sand rock labelled "*This is the stone.*" And he got away with it, just.

At Worcester he announced a grand expensive fireworks display inside the theatre for his annual benefit. The landlord forbade such foolhardiness in so small a building, but the announcement was not rescinded. Addressing the packed audience he subtly planted the idea how terrible it would be if an accident occurred and the theatre caught fire, as though he had just thought of it. In the end the audience was grateful to Elliston that the fireworks were not ignited and they had escaped with their lives. Then he announced a treat to make up for their disappointment. "*The Band (it consisted of three very vile fiddlers) will strike up 'God Save the King'.*"[2]

Elliston was declared bankrupt in December 1826 having lost his money running London's Drury Lane Theatre, although later he recovered some of his former fortunes by staging the ever popular 'Black Ey'd Susan' which always brought him good houses. The piece played the London Surrey Theatre in 1829 and ran 400 consecutive nights – a record run for those times. The play was another version of '*A Lass that Loved a Sailor*' used, it will be remembered, by W.S.Gilbert in '*H.M.S.Pinafore*' but was more dramatic with triangular passions, an assault upon an officer and a threatened hanging. Elliston's last stage performance was on 24th June, 1831 in "*The Jew*" and "*Black Ey'd Susan*". Within a fortnight he was dead.

Patent and Licensing

It may be helpful to describe the way theatres were licensed as this will explain why companies only stayed for a relatively short period of time in any one town.

During Cromwell's Commonwealth, all theatres were closed by order. On the restoration of the monarchy, King Charles II [a devotee of the theatre during his period of exile] issued patents to two theatres, Drury Lane Theatre and the other which eventually ended up at Covent Garden. The London Haymarket Theatre had a licence from Queen Anne, later converted into a patent, but this only enabled that building to open for drama during the summer recess when the other two were closed and their resident performers, not on tour, were out of work. The two theatres holding patents had the sole right to present plays throughout the year; other theatres had to apply for a temporary licence which, if granted, was for a limited period. The law did not take into account the rapid expansion of London and that people outside the city centre wanted their own local theatres. Surprisingly, the provinces were treated no differently.

Up to 1737, strolling players outside the capital had to apply to the local magistrates before being granted permission to play in assembly rooms, barns or wherever was suitable. The Act of 1737, introduced by Sir Robert Walpole, stated that no plays could be legally presented, including the provinces, without a patent issued by the monarch or the Lord Chamberlain. Between 1768 and 1788 only six of these were issued, namely to theatres in: Bath, Bristol, Edinburgh, Ipswich, Norwich and York. The London Minor theatres were permitted to present dancing, tumbling, riding and any activity in which music played a greater role. Those who transgressed these requirements were deemed rogues and vagabonds and liable to be punished by the law to terms of imprisonment. Managers were as cunning as anyone else and tried various ways around the difficulty, one solution being the evolution of the burletta, which was a dramatic entertainment in rhyme but sung with plenty of action. Legally any three act play had to include five or six songs to qualify as a burletta and it was common for Shakespeare to be staged in this fashion. There were other occasions when audiences were charged for attending a concert but were offered plays, performed during the intervals, for nothing.

In 1788 the House of Commons passed an Act in favour of the two Patent Houses but also allowed any theatre, outside a radius of twenty miles from London, to open after managers had made a formal representation to the magistrates at the Quarter Sessions. The University cities of Oxford and Cambridge were not included. This was the green light for theatre building to take place. By 1805 there were 279 theatres, or other places of entertainment, in the country. The ensuing licence, rarely withheld, entitled the company to play for sixty days in any one town as long as the period taken occurred within a four month period, but there were local variations to this ruling. In theory a company only required a circuit of six good towns to tide it over for a year, but in practice more outlets were needed as few habitations had the population to support an eight week period of continuous drama every year.[3] Some theatres were only open once every other year for this reason. Coventry seemed well able to give support for two months annually, as did most other theatres on the Worcester circuit.

After the allotted sixty days, the company would remove itself, together with props and scenery, to the next theatre in the circuit where the pattern would be repeated. In the following year the company would return to the first theatre with a new set of plays and begin the routine all over again. Even after the passing of the 1843 Act, little change was seen at first for a number of reasons: the product was becoming less acceptable to a larger proportion of educated people, the habits of the upper classes had changed and some magistrates were prone to hinder applications. The patent houses had occasional influence with members of the Bench in refusing the appearance of visiting companies. This applied more frequently to portable theatres, few of which were ever recorded in the Coventry press.

The same degree of intolerance reappeared in the twentieth century when the legitimate theatre brought court actions against the music halls for putting dramatic sketches into twice nightly bills. The repeal of the Theatres Act in 1843 was influenced largely by William Macready and Edward Bulwer-Lytton, a dramatic author of the period.[4]

The Patent theatres, fearful of losing their monopoly, were not always slow to challenge rival concerns in the courts.[5] William Robert Copeland, manger of the Liverpool Royal Liver Theatre, was taken to court by Robert Sanford Robinson of the Liverpool Theatre Royal over the presentation of '*The Pet of Petticoats*' at the former establishment as late as December 1842. The law stated that comedies, tragedies, operas, farces and plays were not to be given in unlicensed premises (the Royal Liver Theatre was not licensed) for hire, gain or reward. As Copeland was not in the theatre as a philanthropist, he charged customers for admission and was fined £50 for his trouble.[6]

Trouble at Coventry

It was important to rigorously observe the length of the permitted season in order to keep within the law. In 1821, Elliston had permission to open for sixty nights at Coventry, which he took literally, but which the Bench interpreted as sixty consecutive evenings. The lessee, during his season at the Leamington Bath Street Theatre, took the company to Coventry each Wednesday which, in theory, spread the load, but this eventually put him outside his allotted allocation of time and the company was arrested inside the Smithfield Street theatre while dressing for the evening's performance of '*Venice Preserved*'. Penley, recorded as the manager, was summoned before the mayor for an interview which delayed the start of the entertainment until 9.30 p.m. That Penley was involved comes as a surprise since he had already yielded the lease to Elliston; perhaps he had been recruited to be in charge of this company at this time. Maybe the vision of a newspaper advertisement with the wording "Come and see the Actors who were sent to Coventry Prison" was too much for the magistrates. In the end the play was permitted to go ahead as scheduled.[7] There is no such thing as bad publicity in the theatre.

The Coronation

At the time, Coventry was a fiercely radical town. King George IV had recently been crowned and Elliston organised a facsimile of the coronation into a ninety minute stage performance. In it were included exact copies of the original costumes, accoutrements and paraphernalia used in the procession to and from Westminster Abbey, the crowning inside and the ceremony in Westminster Hall. Coronations had appeared on stage before but they had been within the context of a play, such as Shakespeare's '*Henry VIII*' or '*2 Henry IV*'. This was the first occasion in which the event was the sole purpose of the performance. The piece, with Elliston as the King, ran for over 100 nights at Drury Lane, a phenomenal run at that time, and which no doubt added much to his financial well being. Elliston must have reasoned that such a success would also accrue additional profits in the provinces and therefore arrangements were made for Mr Lee, stage manager at the London Royal Adelphi Theatre, to take it around the country with Samson Penley in the leading role of George IV, as Elliston was not available.[8] At York Theatre Royal it was reported that one hundred assistants were engaged, an organ erected, and a military band employed, with the king making his way to the Abbey via a platform constructed over the pit, as at Drury Lane.[9] The theatres at Coventry and Leamington were leased by Elliston at the time and the stock company from the latter did the honours at both theatres and at Northampton Marefair's Theatre too.[10] It was regarded as one of the most spectacular events seen on any stage. In every town the piece passed off without incident, but at Coventry the characters, whom the audience identified as being politically offensive, had a rough time with hisses, cat calls and deafening noises which greeted their every appearance. Even the entry of the King did not pass off quietly, the townsfolk siding with the Queen (who was barred from the coronation) as a wronged woman.[11] At Drury Lane '*The Coronation*' was sandwiched in-between two other plays and it can be assumed an identical arrangement existed at Coventry.

A similar representation of a royal event had taken place at the time of King George III's illness. The temporary abatement of porphyria, with which he had been suffering, was marked by a special service of thanksgiving in St Paul's Cathedral in 1789. This event, together with the procession of the royal family in full regalia, the Horse Guards, the Police and Lord Mayor, all went on the stage in a truncated version and is known to have toured Thornton's southern circuit.[12] Now we see such events live on television.

The Stock Companies

All the characters portrayed every evening during the season were played by members of the resident stock company, rather reminiscent to the weekly repertory companies of the twentieth century. From time to time well known performers from Drury Lane and Covent Garden patent theatres were invited to appear as guest artists, a practice more common at the close of the London season when such 'stars' were freely available for hire. They were often expensive to engage but managers optimistically hoped to make something out of the venture through increased activity at the box office, although financial returns depended largely on the capacity of the house. Henry Thornton, manager of the southern circuit, found it difficult to make money in some of his smaller theatres since a full house would yield so little, possibly £30 or thereabouts.[13] The Coventry theatre was better suited to attract a flow of well known artists, especially in the earlier years.

The methods of acting and production were so stereotyped that little variation existed between the same plays performed in different theatres, hence the ability of visiting 'stars' to act major roles after little or no rehearsal with the rest of the cast before the opening night. This unvarying static presentation no doubt contrasted badly with newer and freer methods being developed in the up and coming London minor theatres and must have contributed partially to the demise of the provincial theatre in the 1840s and 1850s. Although companies were limited by law to a short stay in any one place, it is reasonable to assume that a stock company, with the same actors and actresses performing a different play each evening, would find it difficult to sustain the interest of the playgoing public over a long period of time. If the patent law had not existed, it is likely companies would have had to move on after a few weeks anyway.

In August 1822 Mr Braham, the celebrated vocalist, performed in 'Tom and Jerry' and 'Rob Roy'. John Abraham, shortened to Braham [1774–1856], the son of a Portuguese Jew, became a renowned tenor whose compass from A in the bass to E in the alto was contrived by his ability to access the falsetto range. He was described as an angel of a singer but a beast of an actor,[14] but the *Herald* did not pass an opinion either one way or the other.

> "We regret to hear that some dissatisfaction arose in the City in consequence of the price of admission being raised. We say "regret", to hear it, because it would seem to deny that advantage for mental superiority, which would not be withheld in any other cause, for we believe it cannot be denied that when a superior article of any nature is brought to market, a superior price is attached to it . . ."[15]

The desire to obtain the best for next to nothing is not only a facet of our own generation. The management bowed to public demand and reduced the price of tickets. Braham financed the building of the London St James's Theatre in 1835 but this, together with his other venture into the property market, the Regent's Park Colosseum, caused him financial embarrassment. The St James's was demolished in 1957 for office redevelopment but not before an outburst by Vivienne Leigh in the public gallery of the House of Lords, an unusual but dramatic intervention which highlighted the need for theatre protection.

In early November Adam's Circus came to the Bull and Anchor Yard although it appears they travelled with no animals other than horses and humans. Circuses throughout the Victorian era, although not frequent visitors, had a habit of staying in a locality for around six weeks at a time which often interfered with theatre attendances if the dates clashed.

The 1823 season opened on December 1st with Mr Chamberlain as company manager; Elliston (the lessee), with his many irons in theatrical fires, did not appear. The comedy 'John Bull' opened the season, the 'Irish Tutor' being given as the afterpiece. Elliston's next recorded visit was in November 1826 in the play 'Heir at Law'.

Although Samson Penley had long given up the lease of the theatre, his three daughters, Miss Penley, Miss R. Penley and Miss E. Penley, the last not being with the company initially, took their farewell benefit in May 1828 playing in '*The Serjeant's Wife*', it being reported this was their last appearance upon any stage.[16]

Death of Sir Skears Rew

Rew died in 1828 and the theatre, along with other of his properties, was left in trust to George Eld and David Shakespear (sic) Waters until Henrietta Turland either reached the age of twenty one or married. Henrietta was the illegitimate daughter of his deceased servant and would have been aged between thirteen and fourteen at the time of Rew's death. Married, but apparently childless, Rew brought up the girl as his own daughter who, apart from a few bequests, inherited his entire estate. Shortly after Rew's death, Mr Carter, Rew's solicitor, received a letter dated August 3rd, from T.P.Cooke [1787–1864] then performing at the Cheltenham Theatre Royal.

> "*Sir, I have been informed that the Theatre Coventry is to be lett (sic). I have not seen the advertisement therefore I do not know who to apply to but knowing you were the solicitor of Sir Skears Rew, I conjecture I am not wrong in addressing you – If you have letting of it – you will let me know the Terms by return of Post and would willingly oblige Your most obedient servant, T.P.Cooke.*"[17]

He was unlucky. T.P.Cooke, known as the nautical actor since he had fought on the high seas with Nelson, was well known as William in '*Black Ey'd Susan*', a part in which he appeared over 200 times at the London Surrey Theatre.

Madame Vestris, later to make her mark as lessee at the London Olympic, ventured to Coventry for two nights during Race Week in August 1829.[18] Born Lucy Elizabeth Bartolozzi (1797–1856) she had a short but disastrous marriage to Armand Vestris, a French ballet dancer, and which ended in 1820. Blessed with a fine contralto voice she was destined for the operatic stage but preferred burlesque and comedy, to which she was introduced by Elliston at Drury Lane. She leased the London Olympic Theatre in 1830 where she met and married her second husband, Charles Mathews, in 1838. In addition to her singing she was celebrated for her interpretation of breeches parts, being blessed with a good pair of legs. She proved an innovator, having original ideas on decoration and stage management, insisting on using real rather than fake properties. There is some dispute as to whether she invented the box set seen at the Olympic in 1832.[19] A box set is one which represents an inner room. Traditionally this would have been presented in the form of a series of flats, parallel to the stage opening, a cloth, or wide shutters, at the rear of the stage and borders above to mask the flies. The box set Vestris used had two side walls which angled upstage and contained working doors and windows. Above was suspended a ceiling from which working chandeliers were hung, carpets were laid on the stage floor and real furniture adorned the set – an arrangement expected now, but which took audiences by surprise in the 1830s.

As the terms of the licence only permitted venues to open a few weeks in the year, provincial theatres were closed more than they were open and in the winter months empty buildings suffered recurring problems of damp. It was customary to insert the phrase *"Good fires constantly kept in the theatre"* into advertisements to assure the public that the place was properly aired and free from condensation. The form of heating at Coventry is unknown. In the nineteenth century theatres the size of Drury Lane and Covent Garden incorporated stoves beneath the pit stalls which warmed the air that circulated the house through flues – rather like the Roman under floor system. On the other hand smaller theatres, like Richmond Georgian Theatre Royal, Yorkshire, and Leicester Theatre Royal, had coal fireplaces in the pit, box corridors and at the back of the stage and the Coventry theatre probably mirrored these arrangements.[20]

The season at Coventry began around Boxing Day and lasted until the end of February or the beginning of March. Occasional lettings to other companies, performers, light entertainers or lecturers occurred at other times of the year but these would have required a separate licence from the magistrates.

It was not unknown for the pit in earlier and smaller theatres to be boarded over to provide a floor which became an extension of the stage, an arrangement useful for balls, banquets or other fashionable functions. As Coventry theatre was relatively narrow compared with other nineteenth century buildings, it is likely such an arrangement was possible, although no records of this happening have yet come to light.

Infant Prodigies

Readers familiar with the works of Charles Dickens will recall the actor manager Vincent Crummles in '*Nicholas Nickleby*' and the stock company in which many members of his family took part. One of the more unusual performers was the

Figure 19 The Infant Phenomenon (centre) as depicted by the artist F. Barnard
Author's collection

Infant Phenomenon, a young person capable of mature dramatic interpretation and who was intended to appeal to a wide audience. Dickens' characters were frequently based on real people. Crummles was a caricature of T.D.Davenport [1792–1851], manager of the Norwich circuit and who, before that, was responsible for the London Westminster and Olympic theatres.[21] It is believed the Infant Phenomenon was an actress, later known as Mrs Lander. The accuracy with which he described a provincial touring company led Edward Leman Blanchard to maintain that Dickens had, in fact, been a member of Davenport's company.[22]

Infant prodigies were not rare and Master Joseph Burke was the first to visit the Smithford Street house, as far as existing records show. W. Clark Russell described his acting as extraordinary, even though children are natural mimics and can be taught by rote. Master Burke, born in 1818, took part in the musical play 'The Haunted Tower' on January 30, 1829 and this was followed by the 'Red Barn' or 'The Dream of Death' in which he took a major role.[23] He appeared again in the middle of February and then the advertisements disappeared, probably because he went elsewhere, until his benefit on May 8th when he took the stage in the musical drama 'The Prize', 'The Irish Tutor' and 'The Life and Death of Tom Thumb'. He took the part of Lord Grille whilst another Master Burke, brother to the same and only six years old, played Tom Thumb for the first time on any stage.[24] The third week of September saw Joseph in the title role of 'Richard III' at the Wakefield Theatre Royal[25] and in the following year he acted the part of Shellac and Richard II at the Cheltenham Theatre Royal.[26] His London debut was at the Surrey Theatre in 1827, then under the management of R.W.Elliston, when he was described as being between the ages of eight and nine years but looking younger. In the following years he was seen 'effectively' at the Newcastle-upon-Tyne Theatre Royal, so he saw much of the country and the country saw much of him.[27] At Coventry no age is mentioned, except that for the younger sibling, who is curiously absent from any other known reference. A native of Galway, Ireland, it was reputed he could sing songs at twelve months and play the fiddle at three years. At the age of six he took the part of 'Tom Thumb' at Dublin's Theatre Royal and two years later he appeared at Liverpool Theatre Royal in 'Heir at Law' and 'The Irish Tutor' (billed as a 'clever Dublin boy'), before embarking on an English provincial tour ending up at the London Haymarket Theatre.[28] Eventually he left for America on October 3, 1830 and played the theatres there before becoming a concert violinist in later years. He remained there until his death in New York on January 19, 1902.[29]

In 1825 advertisements appeared in the Birmingham Gazette[30] for the appearance of the 'Infant Roscius' at the Birmingham Royal Hotel Assembly Room and George Hotel, Walsall before venturing north to Manchester and Liverpool. This anonymous creature, labelled seven and a quarter years of age, was billed for 'Richard III' and 'Rollo' (from the play *Pizarro*) with "*The whole of the scenery and machinery adapted to the performance will be exhibited*", which probably means that the set was altered in scale to make the lad appear bigger than he really was. This seven year old would have been born in 1818, the same year as Joseph Burke and it would seem reasonable to assume it was he but, according to Derek Forbes,[31] another infant prodigy, Master William Grossmith, was also showing off his thespian prowess at the time and there exists a playbill to show him at this Birmingham Venue in May 1825. Later in August he provided a full evening's solo programme at the Shrewsbury Theatre, giving a series of character studies from the classics and everyday life. One interesting inclusion was a 560 feet diorama roll showing scenes of Italy and which was displayed during the interval.[32] We shall meet Master Grossmith on Coventry soil later.

There was no animal rights movement to disapprove of Mr Wood and his two dogs, Bruin and Hector, who performed for three nights at Coventry from March 16th, 1829. Bruin appeared in the play 'Knights of the Cross', based on Sir Walter Scott's 'Tales of the Crusaders', a drama which the bills mentioned had seen a hundred performances at Drury Lane. In one scene Bruin seized a lighted torch with which to burn the cords tied around the wrists of his mistress. Brave mistress! An afterpiece was 'The Grateful Lion' in which one of the dogs was dressed in a suitable skin for the part.[33]

A second infant prodigy, Miss Jane Coveney [1824–1900], vocalist and later actress, travelled from the Birmingham Theatre Royal to perform at Coventry on March 23rd, 24th and 25th, so she was sandwiched between the two appearances of Joseph Burke. Jane Coveney performed, with a full military band, in the comic opera 'Love in a Village', a piece written by Isaac Bickerstaffe with music by Thomas Arne which was staged as far back as 1762, but it remained popular with early nineteenth century audiences. Large houses, astonished at her performance, demonstrated great approbation. She was described as 'about' twelve years of age at the time but, according to William Knight, could only have been five. He records that she appeared the year before as Emmelina in 'The Swiss Family' at the London Surry Theatre, a venue she frequented throughout most of her working life.[34] As we shall see, she cropped up some years later still in the first flush of youth.

Competition appeared at two other venues in the town. At the Draper's Hall on May 5th, 1829 the Lord Mayor granted permission to Thomas Hudson for a musical entertainment of his favourite songs which he called 'Rhyme and Reason'. This was a 'one off' occasion but regular musical evenings were put on at St Mary's Hall, a place which featured as an entertainment outlet for the whole of the Victorian period and, indeed, much beforehand, probably back to Tudor days.

In our time, it is customary for seats to be reserved, either in person at the box office, via the telephone, post or Internet. In the 19th century only box seats were bookable in advance using the services of an agency rather than the theatre itself. In 1829 the box plans were held at Rollason's and Reader's and reservations had to be made there. As late as 1873 W. Chater's Music Warehouse acted as the ticket agent for the Theatre Royal. Patrons of the pit and gallery paid their money, usually in exchange for a metal token, at the theatre as they attended the performance.

Madame Vestris returned for two nights on August 31st and September 1st in 'Home Sweet Home' and 'Sublime and Beautiful' and she also sang during the intervals.[35] Her sister, Miss Bartolozzi, played supporting roles and the joint engagement attracted full houses.

Coventry was to experience the third of its infant prodigies during November 1829 in the form of William Robert Grossmith, billed as the 'Young Roscius of the

Age' who, at the age of eleven, performed major roles in Shakespearean plays. We met him at Birmingham in 1825. The term Roscius referred to Quintus Roscius, (c120–62 BC), a famous Roman comic actor whose success resulted from his thinking out and practising every gesture before using it on stage.[36] Probably the best known young English '*Roscius*' was William Betty, whose years as a child actor were over before the Coventry Theatre was built although his son, Henry, played there in 1848. The title '*Roscius*' was seen as an accolade of virtuosity when conferred on those of tender years.

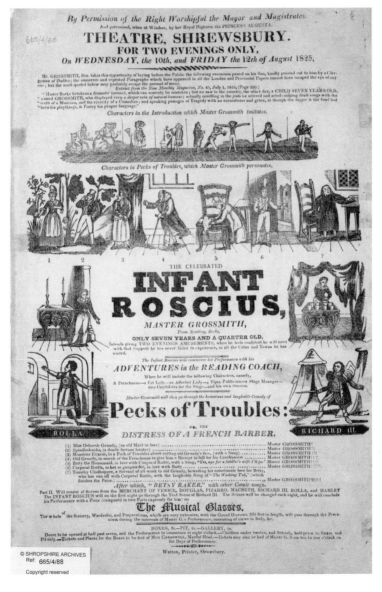

Figure 20   Various cuts of Master William R. Grossmith
at the Shrewsbury Theatre (10th August, 1825)

Reproduced with the permission of Shropshire Archives [Reference SA 665/4/88]

Young William Robert's father, William Grossmith, made looking glasses, picture frames and artificial limbs at his London workshop. He had an interest in the stage and encouraged his two young sons, William Robert and Benjamin, to display their undoubted talents on the boards. The third son, George, father of George Grossmith the Savoyard, was not stage struck but became a journalist and lecturer. Young William Robert Grossmith had toured many towns, including Birmingham in 1825, and in the south on Edward Barnett's circuit of Reading, Newbury, Hungerford and Salisbury in 1826, then back to the Midlands including Northampton, Leicester, Banbury, Reading and Sheffield acting in his father's specially built portable theatre, at least for the first couple of years. After this he played in purpose built theatres. At Northampton his representation of Shylock was deemed above all praise.[37] To some extent he was later 'upstaged' by his younger brother Benjamin who made his debut at an earlier age and was to appear at Coventry in 1839. The breed of young performers was not confined to a previous age. Before the Second World War, Jack Hylton and Bryan Mitchie toured the country with a show replete with 'child discoveries' among whom were the future Morecambe and Wise, and since then we have had child vocalists and, of course, young film personalities as seen in the films of '*Harry Potter*'.

A typical evening's programme would usually consist of two full-length plays and a farce; or alternatively a full five act drama and a couple of comedies, the intervals being occupied with songs and dances performed by individual members of the company. The whole programme might last four to five hours and unless a piece proved popular it was not repeated within the season. This necessitated players to be quick studies and well versed in a wide ranging number of parts, possibly thirty or forty in a season. Penley once gave his audience both '*King Lear*' and the pantomime '*Dick Whittington and His Cat*' on the same evening.[38] Mondays, Wednesdays and Fridays were now the days of performance, unless the assizes, races or other public events brought an influx of visitors into the town. The intervening days were taken up with rehearsals. At this distance in time, and with the lack of film or video footage, it is difficult to compare the standards offered then with those of today; one can only say they must have been different.

In twentieth century days, when every city or town had its own Repertory Theatre, members of the resident company would find themselves performing one drama during the week, rehearsing a second for the following week and learning their lines for the third the week after. Kenneth More illustrates his experiences at the Newcastle Byker Grand Theatre, in-between the two world wars, playing one drama twice nightly from Monday to Wednesday and a different piece for the remainder of the week. From his narrative one gathers that the scripts were in-house, short and fluid which meant most of the dialogue spoken on stage was frequently made up as they went along.[39] The situation was probably more rigorous for actors and actresses in early and mid Victorian stock companies. John Coleman, in his autobiography, often recalls how he, and others, would join a new company only to find they were billed to play a major role, and frequently one they had never seen before, the following night. Late nights, wet towels, strong coffee and a natural gift for memory often saw them through this ordeal. However, established performers would occasionally find areas of a script, with which they had been familiar for years, escape them at a moment's notice. Coleman cites a lovely example of where the famous Charles Kean forgot his words during a performance of '*Macbeth*' in Liverpool, a part he must have played hundreds of times, but on this occasion the prompt came not from the wings but from someone sitting in the gallery *"in the euphonious dialect of the district."*[40] Kean had the graciousness to walk to the footlights and bow his gratitude.

[1] Percy Fitzgerald, "A New History of the English Stage", Vol 11, Tinsley Brothers, 1882.

[2] Henry Barton Baker, "Our Old Actors", Richard Bentley and Son 1878.

[3] Cecil Price, "The English Theatre in Wales", University of Wales press, 1948.

[4] John Coleman, "Players and Playwrights", Gebbie & Co, Philadelphia 1890.

[5] Elizabeth Grice, "Rogues and Vagabonds" or "The Actor's Road to Respectability", Terence Dalton 1977.

[6] The Era, 29 January, 1843.

[7] Lou Warwick, "Theatre Un-Royal", Lou Warwick 1974.

[8] Christopher Murray, "Robert William Elliston", Society for Theatre Research 1975.

[9] Sybil Rosenfeld, "The York Theatre", Society for Theatre Research, 2001.

[10] Theatre Notebook, Volume XXV No 1. Autumn 1970, "Elliston's Coronation Spectacle", Christopher Murray.

[11] Lou Warwick, "Theatre Un-Royal", Lou Warwick 1974.

[12] Paul Ranger, "Under Two Managers", Society for Theatre Research 2001.

[13] Paul Ranger, "Under Two Managers", Society for Theatre Research 2001.

[14] W. Clark Russell, "Representative Actors", Frederick Warne & Co.

[15] Coventry Mercury, 2 September, 1822.

[16] Coventry Herald, 11 May, 1828.

[17] Coventry Archive Office. Document 14/6/53.

[18] Coventry Herald, 21 August, 1829.

[19] Martin Banham (ed), "Cambridge Guide to the Theatre", C.U.P. 1992.

[20] Richard Leacroft, "The Development of the English Playhouse", Methuen 1973.

[21] T.L.G.Burley, "Playhouses and Players of East Anglia", Jarrold and Sons, 1928.

[22] John Coleman, "Fifty Years of an Actor's Life", James Pott 1904.

[23] Coventry Herald, 30 January, 1829.

[24] Coventry Herald, 8 May, 1829.

[25] C.M.P. Taylor, "Right Royal" – Wakefield Theatre 1776–1994, Wakefield Historical Publications No. 35. 1996.

[26] Theodore Hannam-Clark, "Drama in Gloucestershire", Simpkin Marshall 1928.

[27] Harry Oswald, "The Theatres Royal in Newcastle-upon-Tyne", Northumberland Press 1936.

[28] R. J. Broadbent, "Annals of the Liverpool Stage", Benjamin Blom 1908 (Re-issued 1969).

[29] Christopher Murray, "Robert William Elliston", Society for Theatre Research, 1975.

[30] Aris Birmingham Gazette, 23 May, 1820.

[31] Richard Foulkes (ed), "Scenes from Provincial Stages", Society for Theatre Research 1994, "The Earliest Grossmiths and their Pictorial Playbills", Derek Forbes.

[32] Derek Forbes, 'Illustrated Playbills', Society for Theatre Research 2002.

[33] Coventry Herald, 13 February, 1829.

[34] William G. Knight, "A Major London Minor", The Surrey Theatre [1805–1865], Society For Theatre Research 1997.

[35] Coventry Herald, 21 August, 1829.

[36] Phyllis Hartnoll (ed), "Oxford Companion to the Theatre". O.U.P. 1965.

[37] Lou Warwick, "Theatre Un-Royal", Lou Warwick 1974.

[38] Coventry Herald, 1 February, 1821.

[39] Kenneth More, "More or Less", Hodder & Stoughton 1978.

[40] John Coleman, "Players and Playwrights", Gebbie & Company, Philadelphia 1890.

Chapter 5

Henry Bennett [1791–1868]

Henry Bennett was to oversee the fortunes of the Coventry house as lessee until Hall and Pitt bought him out in 1851. His circuit included Wolverhampton (opened 1779), Worcester (1822), Loughborough (1823), Ashby (1828) and Shrewsbury (rebuilt 1834). Worcester, Shrewsbury and Wolverhampton had been within the same circuit during James Miller's managership in 1788.[1] Reputation paints Henry as an autocratic, irascible miserly man of average acting ability but, unlike many of his contemporaries, he kept his theatres open and solvent.

The Coventry theatre was closed from August 1829 until Bennett re-opened it on 17th November, 1830 after putting into effect the necessary repairs and cleansing. The inaugural season lasted two months and offered a range of Shakespearean plays, classics and what one recognises as frothy productions such as the '*Bottle Imp*', which appeared several times as a Christmas piece. Bennett made an immediate impact, his scenery, costumes and decorations being considered of a higher standard than witnessed before. "*. . .if he [Bennett] does not succeed in Coventry, certainly no one else will. . .*"[2] The Christmas Eve offering was Matthew Gregory Lewis's popular tragedy '*The Castle Spectre*' complete with new dresses, scenery and decorations. It was a spectacular moral piece, where virtue triumphs over evil, set in Conwy Castle and employing machinery, moving portraits, sliding panels, an oratory, subterranean passages, transparencies and an escape in which the actor climbed a wall and jumped through a Gothic window while his black guards played dice. The final scene, with all the characters on stage, was climaxed by the appearance of the ghost of Evelina. It had everything and revolved around a plot similar to those exploited by Hollywood in the twentieth century. '*The Castle Spectre*' was part of a generation of Gothic dramas, a breed of play which depicted ruined castles, sea shores lashed by storm waves, midnight scenes in inky blackness, dark forests, mists and fogs and anything at all relating to unease, mystery and tragedy. It first saw the light of day at London's Drury Lane in 1797, and earned its author a lot of money, being frequently revived well into the mid Victorian period. However fashions changed and when Buckstone resurrected it at the London Haymarket Theatre in the late Victorian era, the audience regarded it as a light burlesque and laughed heartily from beginning to end – rather like the behaviour of some when witnessing a silent film classic for the first time in our day.

Stage effects were sufficiently advanced at the time to produce the right atmosphere for Gothic dramas. Mists were created by using a gauze between the audience and actor and the use of suitable lighting so that some parts of the stage were faintly illuminated while others were plunged into inky blackness. Lightning relied upon the ignition of small quantities of nitre, charcoal, sulphur and barytes. Wind and gales were done with the time honoured machine which had silk or canvas in varying degrees of tautness placed over a revolving drum complete with wooden slats. The faster the revolutions the stronger the gale. A thin metallic thunder sheet provided the added dimension of a storm. Not every theatre had its own thunder run where a canon ball rolled along a wooden trough in the roof to descend by a series of sudden drops into the flies or even lower still. Mechanical devices lasted until the use of recording machines in the early part of the twentieth century and occasionally a few wooden relics may still be discovered in the cellars or dark corners of a fly gallery.

Madame Tussaud's waxworks, not seen in Coventry for eight years, lodged itself at St Mary's Hall for a month and at the King's Head Rooms in the High Street there was a musical entertainment on offer, even though the theatre was dark at the time.

Performances in the theatre continued to be given on Mondays, Wednesdays and Fridays. The 1831 season began in early November with plays announced through weekly block advertisement in the *Herald* which was published every Friday. Not occasionally the phrase '*a play and farce*' would be announced for the Wednesday or following Friday indicating that the actual play had yet to be chosen or rehearsed. Christmas saw several performances of '*The Lilliput Army*'.

"*We may add the Green Room Report speaks very favourably of the high state of discipline in which the Lilliputian Army was found at the last rehearsal.*"

Good attendances were maintained. The festive season was dominated by news that Newcastle and Sunderland were in the midst of a cholera epidemic and there were fears of it spreading south.[3] Samson Penley wished to postpone the opening of his season at the Newcastle-upon-Tyne Theatre Royal because of it.[4]

Benefits

The end of every season was heralded with the announcement of a series of benefits organised for senior members of the company. Benefits, which were an integral part of the profession between the 1660s and 1880s, were a means by which individual players, most of whom were not over paid, could enhance their financial standing depending on their popularity with the public. A clear benefit was accorded only to the top 'stars' when they would take the entire box office receipts, leaving the management to pay all sundry expenses. The next most rewarding was a half benefit whereby the performer shared the profits and expenses with the manager. A joint benefit occurred when several of those lower down the cast hierarchy joined as recipients of a whole or half benefit and there were other variations on the theme. The receipts could be very good but those relying upon their benefit emoluments might encounter occasions of: inclement weather, infectious disease, recession and other discouragements on the night resulting in their being out of pocket after paying the manger the necessary expenses for the evening. Beneficiaries would spend much time walking the area and knocking on doors trying to sell tickets to as many people as possible to ensure a good house. If members of the nobility could be encouraged to give support so much the better. Since the recipient for the evening had the power to choose the play, it is not surprising that a large number of comedies were aired on these occasions. It must be remembered that the benefit system also gave the recipient the opportunity to display his or her talent in roles which, under normal circumstances, the management had not seen fit to provide. In this way some hoped that by being seen in a different theatrical light, preferment in some other company might follow.

In January 1832, Mr Clarke advertised in the *Coventry Herald* for three grand concerts at the Birmingham Theatre Royal where the virtuoso Paganini was to appear. The prices of admission reflected his high professional standing – boxes 7s. pit 5s. and gallery 3s.[5] It was not known then that the famous violinist would perform at the Coventry St Mary's Hall, the following August on two nights for 7s. 6d, a seat.

Travelling

From 1832 Bennett began most of his seasons on Boxing Day, or a day or two after. This poses the interesting speculation by which route the company reached the city and just how much of their properties and scenery were transported from one theatre to another. Little of this common 'nitty gritty' has been written down although some detail is available from the work of Moira Field on the Fisher Circuit in East Anglia. With a dozen or so theatres in this circuit the only permanent fixtures in each house were the act-drop and stage curtains, everything else moved with the company and this necessitated the employment of substantial carts to traverse what, in those days, passed for roads but which were, in reality, dust tracks in the summer and muddy byways in winter.[6] Theatres on the Fisher Circuit were relatively close together in a mainly flat countryside. Just how much scenery and properties were permanently left in each of Bennett's theatres is open to speculation but since they were only used once a year, excepting Worcester which had two seasons, much capital would have been tied up multiplying flats and cloths, so it is safe to assume most of it was carted around, possibly taking several days to complete the respective journeys.

Bennett, like Penley, instituted a limited number of season tickets which were exclusive of Benefit Nights. His block advertisements did not appear regularly every week as reliance, no doubt, was made on the effectiveness of fliers and word of mouth.

The 1833 Season included Weber's musical drama '*Der Freischutz*', or '*The Demon of the Wolf's Glen*', first produced in Berlin in 1821. As this was an afterpiece it is difficult to imagine the whole work being performed. It was common practice to present only the Wolf's Glen, or Incantation, scene, which lent itself to tense drama by demonstrating the manufacture of seven magic bullets using supernatural powers. So popular was this work that in 1824 London, it was possible to see eight different adaptations of it ranging from crude melodramas with *'horrible music'* borrowed from Weber, to those which more faithfully represented the composer's intentions.[7] The bullets were formed from a concoction of glass stolen from a church, quicksilver, the right eye of a lapwing, the left eye of a lynx all melted into a crucible and after that a series of monsters, ghouls, reptiles, serpents, phantoms, huntsmen and skeletons greeted the casting of each bullet whilst a storm with thunder, and a few meteors thrown in for good measure, added to the scene. It was the nineteenth century equivalent to a 'horror movie'. One wonders how the Coventry musicians managed with Weber's score.

> *". . .(the) exertions of our spirited manager, Mr Bennett, are becoming more appreciated by the inhabitants of this city and that the performances are better attended than they were some weeks ago."*[8]

Another attempt at opera came with the Grand Scene from Rosinni's *'Cinderella'* in February 1834. It is possible these musical dramas, like some of Shakespeare's plays, were subject to editing or simplification.

'Robinson Crusoe' formed part of the evenings entertainment in the 1835 season and was paired with a different play most nights. More opera in the form of *'The Devil's Bridge'* and a comic ballet, *'The Village Apothecary'*, were served up in January. Local patronage from Lt Col Molynieux and Vicountess Hood must have guaranteed well attended performances of the comedy *'The Belle's Stratagem'* and *'Black Ey'd Susan'*.

The attempt to deceive is not entirely new. March 1835 saw a block advertisement for the Coventry Craven Arms Assembly Rooms where *Pacanini* was due to appear. However this entertainer, with a 'c' not a 'g', was expert at ventriloquism and conjuring, rather than the fiddle, and he only charged 2s. and 1s. respectively.[9]

Pantomime did not always appear at Christmas and the seasonal offering for December, 1835 was J. R. Planche's *'The Vampire'* for which a new trap was introduced to the stage. The play, first seen in 1820, heralded the vogue of presenting the supernatural within melodramas and it required the invention of a new stage trap. This consisted of a couple of spring leaves in the stage floor permitting the character (in this case the Vampire) to suddenly disappear, after being struck by a thunderbolt, whereupon the trap door closed immediately behind him. The principle could be applied horizontally and was sometimes incorporated into upright scenery enabling the body of an actor to pass like that of a spirit through a solid. There was no mention of this specialist vampire trap in the *Coventry Herald*, but it is difficult to conceive the play being done without it.

The First Americans

One of the first American actresses to visit Coventry was recorded at the beginning of 1836. Josephine Clifton, [1813–1847], who had appeared at Covent Garden and Drury Lane, acted in 'The Stranger'. The season included 'The Jews', a drama translated from the French by T.H.Lacy and first staged at Drury Lane in 1835. Bennett took a whole column advertisement which highlighted, in detail, each scene and what happened therein.

> "In consequence of the very enormous expense in attending the production of the above ['The Jews'], nothing under full price will be taken to any part of the house."

Mr Phillips painted the special scenery, and

> "the arrangements of the troops, was managed much better than could have been expected from the limits of the stage,"[10]

an interesting observation highlighting the handicap of the stage area which presumably referred to the narrow width. All this in a season which included the operatic drama 'Gustavus', or the 'Masked Ball' also titled 'Carnival of Venice', which was 23 years before the version written by Verdi, so whose music was it? Members of the audience were invited to join the masquerade on stage but only if dressed in appropriate costumes. This is reminiscent of the BBC television series 'The Good Old Days', broadcast from the Leeds City Varieties Theatre in the 1960s and 1970s and where it became obligatory for members of the audiences to attend in period dress. Two years beforehand, 'Gustavus', with scenery painted by Newnum, had been specially licensed for York and Hull. It would, indeed, be a coincidence if there was no connection between the two productions.

In May there were two astronomical lectures at the theatre given by D.F.Walker entitled 'The Eidouranion'. One was held in the evening and the other at 3.00 p.m. the following afternoon for the benefit of schoolchildren and the 'neighbourhood'. The Eidouranion was a large transparent orrery, named after Charles Boyle, Earl of Orrery, and consisted of a mechanical device, about fifteen feet square, with which it was claimed to make the varying lengths of days, twilight, movement of the planets and their satellites, comets and other heavily phenomenon, perfectly intelligible to ordinary people. This performance had toured the country for some years, Mr Walker junior having taken it to the York Theatre in 1784, 1796 and the Wakefield Theatre in 1805. Whether the same Walker had toured for fifty two years is not made clear, but it obviously generated a good living for the family.[11]

The announcement of the 1836/7 season, for which a new drop scene had been painted, was greeted by a press announcement that "Mr Bennett [manager] has the honour to inform the nobility, gentry and the inhabitants in general..." This standard sentence heralded the opening of almost every new season at the theatre. The press critic, who could not always have been in attendance, frequently prefaced his comments with the phrase 'we understand that the house was well filled' or similar passages. Lack of personal knowledge did not prevent him eulogising over Henry

Bennett's management and praising the players who, *'with scarcely an exception'* were above mediocrity. Dickens' work went on stage in the form of *'Sam Weller'* and the usual mix of popular culture and classics followed. *'The Spectre Bridegroom'*, or *'A Ghost in Spite of Himself'* by W.T.Moncrieff, was a farce written in two acts and first seen at London's Drury Lane in 1821, and probably appealed more to the pit and gallery. Mrs Julia Glover (1781–1850) appeared *'positively for one night only'* but managed two more the following month. Christened Julia Betterton, it is thought she was a descendant of the great Thomas Betterton associated with the Restoration stage, the London Lincoln's Inn Fields Theatre and the first London Haymarket Theatre. She was considered one of the ablest actresses of her time, dressing well with a commanding figure although *"monstrously fat."*[12] Known as *'Mother of the Stage'*, owing to her long time on it, she had a fine voice and was described by Macready as a thinking actress.[13] On March 16th, *'Hamlet'* was put up for her benefit but it is not recorded whether she took the leading role, as she had at the London Lyceum in 1822, and where the great Edmund Kean, who witnessed the performance, had gone round to congratulate her afterwards.[14]

The numerical strength of Bennett's Company is not recorded. The Fisher group of players often consisted of twenty or more thespians in addition to musicians, carpenters, scene painters, stage hands, candle and lamp handlers, bill posters, wardrobe women, money-takers and door keepers. One assumes other provincial companies followed in like fashion. A new company was engaged for the Coventry season which began on December 21st. One wonders what befell the former players, whether they dissipated to new theatres or were dismissed. Full houses were on record. Following in the wake of the *'Vampire'* in 1835, the seasonal fare for 1837 was *'The Monster Frankenstein'*. Bennett and his company received high praise from the *Herald*: *"a better company is not often to be met with on the boards of a provincial theatre and we trust the manager will meet with the encouragement and success he deserves."*[15] The 1838/9 season opened with *'Ellen Wareham'* and a new vaudeville *'The Dancing Barber'*. The word vaudeville is often associated with American style variety but the origin of the expression is French and referred to plays of a light or satirical nature, often interspersed with songs. In France this form eventually led to light or comic opera. A mixture of classics and frothy entertainment followed for the remainder of the season with Julia Glover making another appearance in *'The Love Chase'* and *'Popping the Question'* in February and *'Hamlet'* in March. Towards the end of the season Mr Hughes played *'The Rent Day'* for his benefit for which *"the orchestra will be considerably enlarged and perform the overture 'Tancredi'."*[16]

'The Lady of Lyons' made one of its first appearances at Coventry since the opening night at London Covent Garden in 1838. It was written by Bulwer-Lytton, a contemporary of Charles Dickens, who was so horrified to see his novels dramatised by hack authors, that he resolved to beat the pirates at their own game. He studied the methods used by the French Romantic theatre so it is not surprising his stage work emerged with a tinge of the Gallic about them. This, and his *'Richlieu'*, were costume historical dramas which became highly popular during the mid to late Victorian period.[17] Further ventures into opera took place on February

15th, 1839 with '*William Tell*' written ten years earlier. It was a popular play, added, '*altered and improved*' by the author J.Sheridan Knowles and aided by the powerful music of Rossini which "*must prove a high treat to the lovers of the drama and ensure a full and fashionable audience*".[18] One wonders how a provincial theatre orchestra at that time coped with the score.

William Robert Grossmith's younger brother Benjamin (b.1827) appeared at St Mary's Hall on August 9th 1839. He first performed at the age of three with his brother and was now a veteran actor at the tender age of eleven, engaged on a busy whistle stop tour, with Birmingham the following night and Wolverhampton the day after. He was billed as having already appeared at London's Drury Lane Theatre as well as the main houses in Dublin and Edinburgh. His brother William, who had visited the Coventry Theatre in 1829, was due to appear with him but unfortunately there was no write up in either the *Herald* or the *Standard* for this unusual performance. Benjamin was labelled a mono-dramatic actor, that is he appeared alone and probably with the sets and equipment used for his command performance at Windsor Castle before King William IV and Princess Augusta. As with other infant prodigies it is more than likely the scenery was set to a scale which made the boy appear larger and more adult than he was, a kind of Alice in Wonderland setting. Usually both boys worked on their own but William Robert did occasionally appear with adult actors, which was not usual for child performers. In the 1840s he took an apprenticeship with the family firm whilst Benjamin gave up the stage in February 1843, became a missionary and disappeared in Africa where it was thought he was eaten by a lion.[19]

Sheridan Knowles

'*Guy Mannering*' was seen during January 1840 with the now ageing Mr Braham as the lead vocalist. It was fashionable not only to adapt novels for the stage – this one was from the pen of Sir Walter Scott – but to turn them into operas or, more correctly, straight plays with songs and interlude music and this was called opera. A week of classics was seen in late January including '*Othello*', according to the Act of Parliament, whatever that meant.[20] This was given on the same evening as "*The Heart of Midlothian*" or "*The Lily of St Leonard's*" and, unless abridged, must have lasted until a late hour. Dramatisations of Dickens' novels were a regular feature and this season saw two, '*Nicholas Nickleby*' and '*Oliver Twist*'. Sheridan Knowles [1784–1862] and Miss Elphinstone [1807–1888] appeared at the end of January in a four night engagement which included '*The Hunchback*' and '*Love Chase*'. The players were husband and wife; the disparity in their ages is explained in that she was his former pupil. Knowles (related to Richard Brinsley Sheridan, an Irish dramatist), wrote '*The Hunchback*', '*Love Chase*', '*Virginius*' and many other dramas. His first appearance was at Cork in 1784 but then he dabbled in the militia, medicine and teaching before returning to the stage as a comedian and singer at Dublin's Crow Street Theatre in 1807. His acting was described as natural, as though he were behaving in real life, which was not in accord with the rantings and histrionics frequently witnessed on the boards at that time. Two years previously, the *Northampton Mercury* opined that he was not surpassed by any living actor. In later life he spurned the theatre and became a Baptist Minister denouncing the stage, possibly with thespian vehemence, whilst appearing to accept royalties from his plays.[21] It is not known whether Knowles' wife was a member of the Elphinstone family who, later in the century, were involved in the running of theatres in the Potteries, South Wales and Stafford, but it seems possible.

The fall of dates being what they were, the theatre opened on Shrove Tuesday and closed Ash Wednesday. In later years theatres would frequently close for the whole of Holy Week or organise sacred concerts in place of the usual fare. Such observances were probably an attempt not to arouse more criticism from churches and chapels than already existed.

Easter week 1840 brought forth Mr Distin, who played the trumpet and French horn, along with his four musical sons in a series of concerts. The family was to make frequent re-appearances at the theatre over the years.

In September 1840 Franz Liszt appeared at the Draper's Hall in Coventry, playing his Hungarian March, and other compositions. Tickets were 6s. each or 21s. for a family of four. Again the vacant theatre was by-passed.

The 1840/41 season began on December 28th with the '*Merchant of Venice*' together with a full and complete orchestra, and '*King Lear*' followed, an infrequently performed play then as it is now. An evening which saw '*The Wonder*' was patronised by Colonel Vandeleur and the 10th Royal Huzzars, as they had done over many years. Patronage, especially by the military, was a common occurrence being a practice by which a person, or organisation, promised to support the performance, the Victorian equivalent to a block or party booking.

In February there was staged a Grand Representation of the christening of the Princess Royal, the first child of Queen Victoria and Prince Albert. There were no anti-Royal sentiments this time round and '*The Princess Royal*' appeared several times during the season. February 12th saw a special benefit performance of '*Othello*', and a concluding farce, with music provided by the band of the 10th Royal Huzzars, organised for the distressed artisans of Coventry. The amount raised was £28 3s. 3d..

The 1841 season included '*Dick Whittington and His Cat*' which was played in addition to '*Romeo and Juliet*' on the same evening. The pantomime would probably be unrecognisable as such now.

John Vandenhoff

John Vandenhoff (1790–1861) and his wife Mude, together with Mr Henrie from Liverpool Theatre Royal, played the tragedies '*Richlieu*' and '*Ion*' on January 17th and 18th, 1842. From Flemish stock and destined for the catholic priesthood, Vandenhoff was educated at Stoneyhurst College where he saw a performance of '*Oroonoko*' and this spurred his ambitions towards the stage. He decamped from Stoneyhurst and briefly taught classics in his youth making his stage debut as

Osmond in '*The Castle Spectre*' at Salisbury in 1808 at the age of eighteen, and modelling his acting on the Kemble school.[22] After learning his trade touring provincial theatres he was taken on by the stock company at Liverpool Theatre Royal in 1814 at £3 per week.[23] He had a fine voice and commanding features being most popular in the north, especially Liverpool and Manchester and although he acted in London between 1820 and 1838, he never made a 'top liner' there. The Vandenhoffs re-appeared at Coventry in '*As You Like it*' a few days later in January. '*The Flying Dutchman*' became a common afterpiece to a number of different main dramas. One assumes this was a play since Wagner didn't write the opera until 1843. As with '*Der Freischutz*', the main attraction would have been the supernatural element portrayed by the ghost ship and her crew led by Captain Vanderdecken. New scenery was prepared by Mr R. Smith.

On February 11th the '*Clandestine Marriage*' was given in aid of the distressed artisans of Coventry.

Mazeppa and the Ducrows

Ducrow's National Establishment of horses and fairy ponies interrupted Bennett's season with a week of equestrian activity, the main attraction being the play '*Mazeppa*' (February), a popular dramatisation of Byron's poem of the same

Figure 21 '*Mazeppa*' – a backstage view created by Tenniel and published in Punch, Volume XXI, 1851. The illustration gives a fascinating insight into the backstage workings of a mid Victorian theatre. The rudimentary wolves were operated by two crouching stage hands, then called stage carpenters, hidden behind a groundrow and the effect would have given a degree of realism acceptable to the audience. The carpenters are depicted wearing their traditional paper hats which are also illustrated in Richard and Helen Leacroft's "*Theatres in Leicester and Leicestershire*", published by Leicestershire Libraries, 1986

title, first produced at the London Coburg Theatre (present day Old Vic) in 1823, and later revised for London Astley's Amphitheatre in 1831. Later the play gained a degree of infamy on Broadway in the mid-1860s by the American actress Adah Isaacs Menken, who brought her own interpretation to the role. The climax of the play occurred when Mazeppa, a male role usually played by a woman, was tied 'bound in nature's nakedness' to the back of a wild horse which was chased across precipitous mountain terrain by 'ravening wolves' as a punishment for making up to his master's wife.[24] It is interesting to speculate the nature of such a chase on so small a stage. Maurice Willson Disher in his book 'Blood and Thunder' (Frederick Muller, 1949) writes that the horse clambered up a rake to the back of the scenery, but how the interpretation of a pursuit over difficult countryside was done has to be left to the imagination, along with whether the concept of nakedness was achieved realistically with fleshings, or toned down with something more substantial for the moral good of the pit and gallery. However there must have been an imposing display of pageantry, beautiful scenery and extra-ordinary equestrian feats, "to which nothing of the kind hitherto brought forward in this city can bear comparison."[25]

Earlier in the century the play 'Timour the Tartar' was staged by Andrew Ducrow, the great horseman and acrobat. The drama included processions of horses, combats and attacks and whereas this might be imagined in the larger circus theatres of the day, it is another matter to visualise such a scenario played on the small stages as they were of Thornton's southern circuit of theatres.

> "...having witnessed the Equestrian Performances in London, we had no idea they could have been given with any possible effect in a provincial theatre. It is really astonishing to see them go through the self same manoeuvres with the self same effect as if they had a larger space for action, indeed the smallness of the scale so far from lessening our delight increases our wonder and admiration..."[26]

No evidence has come to light that 'Timour the Tartar' ever played Coventry, but the review suggests that dramatic equestrian dramas worked on small stages.

The new season starting December 1842 not only began with a considerable embellishment to the interior of the theatre by Mr Conner and his assistant, but also marked the appearance of Mr and Mrs Charles Kean for one night only on January 2 1843 in 'The Lady of Lyons', the house being exceedingly full with a delighted audience.[27] Charles Kean [1811–1868], son of the legendary Edmund, was married to Ellen Tree. He reached the head of his profession while at the London Princess's Theatre (1851–1859), where his classical plays were researched in precise detail regarding historical accuracy. His Coventry appearance occurred in the years of his theatrical ascendancy. Two operatic pieces, 'Rural Felicity' and 'The Loan of a Lover' brought the Misses Smith to Coventry. They were nieces of the Countess Dowager Essex, better known as Miss Stephens – a vocalist of the 1820s. After their engagement the ladies held a concert in St Mary's Hall on 20th January.

Dion Boucicault

Figure 22 Dion Boucicault at the age of thirty four.
A lithograph by F. D'Avignon, once owned by the dramatist Pinero
Boucicault Collection at the University of Kent

February 1843 saw Boucicault's '*London Assurance*' staged as a modern comedy, a work which had seen the light of day under Madame Vestris' management of London's Covent Garden in February 1841. The plot revolved around a father who fails to visually recognise his son, a rather thin tale one supposes and it consisted of a rag-bag of ideas 'borrowed' from Restoration comedy, Boucicault's favourite dramatic period, yet his skill at inventing dialogue made the piece an instant success. Indeed, the London National Theatre, on the South Bank, revived it in 1979. It was the author's sixth play from over 150 dramas written during the course of his life, and this was one of his more successful achievements. A number of plays by Boucicault entertained Coventry playgoers over the years.

The 1843/4 season opened on December 22nd with three Shakespearean productions: '*Macbeth*', '*Hamlet*' and '*King Richard III*' although there may have been more, but Bennett did not advertise in the *Herald* every week, neither were there regular reports of performances. One supposes the *Herald* editor only provided column inches for reviews if the lessee stumped up cash for an advertisement.

'*Don Caesar de Bazin*' or '*Love and Honour*' adapted from Dumanoir and D'Ennery's French melodrama by Dion Boucicault in collaboration with Benjamin Webster, opened on December 27th, 1844 only two months after its first night at the

London Adelphi Theatre. It turned out to be a popular drama that was served up many times in Coventry during the following years.

The visit of the dancer Mademoiselle Marie Taglioni [1804–1884] in October 1845, occasioned the doubling of ticket prices with no reductions at half time. She was the most celebrated ballerina of her day and one for whom her father wrote '*La Sylphide*' in 1832. This should not be confused with the Chopin/Fokine '*Les Sylphides*' [1908] although this used similar costumes to those worn in Taglioni's period. On this occasion she was partnered by Mons Silvani, of the Italian Opera House, in '*the Grand Ballet of Nathalie ou la Laitiere Suisse*'. In his autobiography John Coleman described her as "*the poetry of motion incarnate*" as her dancing was not confined to her body but to her very soul.

Reduction of prices

At the beginning of his 1845/6 season

"*Mr Bennett begs to add, that in deference to the wishes of his patrons, and following the example of other towns, he has reduced the prices of admission to: Boxes 2s. 6d, second price 1s. 6d, pit 1s. Gallery 6d. No second price to pit or gallery.*"

Such reductions were "*made with the prevailing spirit of the times*", in other words the economy was bad.[28] The old prices had held since the opening of the Theatre but in the following year there was more news to come;

"*visitors of the theatre this season will find a very agreeable effect from the altered arrangements as to the prices – that being relieved from the noise and annoyance of that tremendous rush into the gallery which formerly attended the half price admission.*"[29]

This rude interruption, accompanied by shouts and yells together with the noise of these late comers clambering over the wooden benches to obtain the best vantage points (all in the middle of a performance), did not endear the theatre to those who would normally occupy the box seats and wished to take the drama seriously. However, as will be seen later, the second price admission was re-introduced later in the century.

Sir Walter Scott, like Dickens, was a popular novelist whose works were translated for the stage. '*The Heart of Midlothian*' opened in January but much of the season was not publicised in the press.

J. Ridgeway brought thirty six infant female dancers to the Theatre for one night on July 13, 1846 introduced by Mercer Simpson of the Birmingham Theatre Royal and which included the *infant* prodigy Miss Jane Coveney amongst the supporting artists. It will be remembered that Jane Coveney was a child artist when she first appeared in Coventry during 1829 some seventeen years earlier; perhaps she wore better than others for if she was then five but looked twelve, one's arithmetical powers can calculate she was now in her early twenties but presumably did not look thirty. Like other companies beforehand, Mr Ridgeway managed to squeeze a further night the following week and two more in September.

The 1846/7 season began on December 26th with J. B. Buckstone's melodrama, *'The Green Bushes'*, a play set in North American Indian country, and which was performed for several nights, but the remaining evenings were not marked with anything out of the ordinary. Bennett's benefit on March 26th was *'A Bold Stroke for a Husband'* which heralded the end of the season.

A vocal concert organised by Henry Russell of America took place in May 1847 when the box seats were numbered, an interesting statement which may suggest that although boxes were normally booked in the name of the hirer, the actual seat was not. In Kathleen Barker's book *'The Theatre Royal Bristol 1766–1966'* (Society for Theatre Research 1974), there is a copy of a sheet from one of the early box books which shows a plan of box seats with names inserted.

Distin together with his four sons returned in July to present a musical concert with silver sax horns and sax tubas.

'Othello' was the sole Shakespearean representative of the 1848 season which included a three-day visit from Mr Donald King [vocalist and actor 1812–1886] and his wife in February when *'The Beggar's Opera'* and *'William Tell'* were offered. The season included another of Buckstone's melodramas, *'The Flowers of the Forest'* and an adaptation of Scott's *'Guy Mannering'*.

The Theatre Royal

Up to now the venue had always been referred to as the Theatre, but Mr Henry was advertised to give a lecture on astronomy at the 'Theatre Royal' on 20th April, 1848, when a display of Chinese fireworks was promised. Few of the Theatres Royal that exist now, and the many that have gone, were strictly Royal in that most did not hold a Royal Patent; they were honorary Royals. The word was added presumably because it was thought to elevate the venue in the mind of the public. Using the word 'Royal' would not be strictly legal without authority; whether this was the reason the name vacillated between 'Theatre' and 'Theatre Royal' for a few years, or whether it was habit, it is not possible to verify. In keeping with usual practice, Mr Henry performed for possibly one night but managed a return visit some months later.

Mr Jacobs, magician and ventriloquist, was a frequent visitor over the years and printed a long column in the *Herald* detailing his act. Madame Warton's Walhalla Establishment was another frequent visitor (this time in October 1848) with the living tableaux, or living pictures, representing personages and events in history taken from well known sculptures and paintings. Close attention to classical accuracy and appropriate scenic illustration was taken in each of the fifteen to twenty illustrations presented at every performance. Fears of impropriety were expressed in the *Herald* beforehand, presumably with the notion that various forms of apparent nudity would be on view but Victorian sensibilities were not outraged on this occasion. The company's permanent home was at the Walhalla Gallery in Leicester

Square, a building which started out as Saville House and then Winwood Gallery before Madame Warton took it over. Afterwards it became the Royal Living Marionette Theatre.

Henry Betty [c. 1819–1897] appeared in *'Richlieu'*, *'The Country Squire'* and *'Sea Bathing'* on December 29th, 1848. This was the son of William Henry West Betty, probably the best known child prodigy during the past two hundred years, born in 1791 and taking the stage by storm in the early 1800s. It is unlikely he ventured to the barn at Spon End; his itinerary being carefully stage managed to play the more lucrative dates in the country but he did appear in *'The Earl of Warwick'* and *'Alexander the Great'* at the small Warwick theatre in 1822, some time beyond his prime. This was a reappearance on the boards after a three year gap and following an attempt to commit suicide. He finally retired in 1824. His star faded after reaching puberty but his later years were spent in training and directing his son, this Henry Betty, as another child actor although he never achieved the fame of his father. Born around 1819, Henry retired in 1854 to look after the ailing William and was never seen on the stage again.[30]

In January 1849, Mr John Baldwin Buckstone [1802–1879] and Mrs Edward Fitzwilliam [1802–1854] appeared in the *'Lady of Lyons'*, a play commanded by Queen Victoria at Windsor, intelligence which made its way into the advertisements to hopeful advantage. Buckstone, actor and dramatist, worked in a solicitor's office before taking to the stage first at Wokingham [1821] and then on to the south coast circuit. Encouraged by Edmund Kean he eventually became manager of the London Haymarket Theatre which his ghost is said to haunt still.[31] The Coventry theatre had been re-fitted and re-decorated and now sported a light and cheerful appearance. The year included more treats from the magicians and musical concerts. A Grand Concert given by G.H.Lake in August 1849 was excellent but not well attended. The *'Flying Dutchman'* became a regular feature in the 1849/50 season but there was a general lack of classical drama and the *Herald*, wrote at some length on the subject in January 1850.

> *"If the drama has not actually declined since the days when the theatre was the principal Court Amusement, and has certainly not advanced in popular estimation and the little theatre of Coventry is hardly so mighty in its attractions as the shows and plays for which this city was once so famous. There are many reasons for this, the most obvious being the increase in other modes of amusement; and the circulating novel, the improved homes of the middle classes, the popular lecture, the cheap concerts, and the Mechanics Institutes are all powerful rivals to the stage. Nevertheless with the increase in the population of our large towns, it is a matter of surprise that theatres do not flourish, for theatre must be a large class to whom amusement must be almost a necessity, and we know of no amusement, when properly conducted, if so refined and inspiring a character as the acted drama."*

> *"Much has recently been said of the management of the Coventry Theatre, but a due allowance has hardly been made for managerial difficulties. Actors of a high class are not quite so plentiful as in the times of Good Queen Bess, or the merry Charles, and the days when the highest known cultivation was deemed essential to*

the education of the actor, and when the managers of the stage were the pattern for society, appear to have passed. Nevertheless the stage is still attractive to the working classes, who might be greatly benefited by judiciously selected representations. Unfortunately in the metropolis, which is, of course, the manufactory of new plays, the tendency to write down to the mass, and hence the inefficiency of the modern stage as a means of moral elevation."

"In the provinces, however, the genuine drama does stand some character of being presented, and even on the too much neglected Coventry stage, some of the best productions of comedy are, considering all unavoidable drawbacks, not adequately performed. We may instance the sparkling comedy of 'The Honeymoon' performed on Friday last, as a highly respectable presentation, and one which would not have done discredit, in its principal actors, to the metropolitan stage. The same may be said of the performance of 'The Cure for the Heartache' on Wednesday. Of the performance of 'Macbeth' we cannot speak so positively, not having been present during the entire performance, but we fancy, from what we saw, that Mr Shelley would do better if a little less anxious to create strong effects. Taken altogether we think the Coventry Theatre entitled to a larger share of box patronage, but must candidly confess that we do not expect it will be obtained, unless at considerably reduced prices of admission. We perceive the upper boxes are reduced to 2/- and 1/- at half price, this is some improvement, but we fear it will be hardly sufficient."[32]

Much of the above could be written today or, one supposes, in any age. Life was always more perfect in yesteryear when the stage, without unwarranted competition, adequately performed its role as the moral instructor of the working classes. It would seem that drama occupies a permanent place on the nation's 'sick list' and as for other attractions, they are always legion.

Feathers of the *Herald* critic were still ruffled.

"Mr Shelley treads the stage with conscious professional pride and he rarely lacks stage tact or personal energy. He has, however, genius enough to forego the spasmodic physical force exhibition of passion and should trust his success to those truer, but less glaring exhibitions of feeling which evidence the genius of the genuine artist."

Mr Macfarren was dealt with more quickly.

"Mr Macfarren had talents of various kinds but his elocution through carelessness, is too often of the monotonous common place character."

The plays in which both were criticised were not named. The ladies were left relatively unscathed.[33]

Novel attractions continued with Mr Childs who, for one night on February 26, 1850 presented a Victorian planetarium and leviathan oxy-hydrogen microscope capable of magnifying seven million times; this performance was followed by a painting of Adam and Eve in Eden and their expulsion from paradise. Conclusion came with a dissolving cyclorama of remarkable places in the world together with Storm at Sea and Thunder and Lightning – a feast of entertainment indeed. In

April Mr Crowther gave a microscopic exhibition and lecture which was *"highly amusing but instructive"* and which had been supported by the high clergy of the cathedral cities of: Canterbury, Chichester, Lichfield together with the University of Oxford. Respectability was always paraded with an eye to publicity and business.

The London Haymarket Company brought drama back to the theatre in July 1850 with a series of non-classical plays *and "large and respectable audiences"* were attracted. After *'Lavater, the Physiognomist'* and *'Lend me Five Shillings'*, *"(the) applause did not terminate until the curtain drew up and revealed the whole company on the stage."*[34]

The stage director of the 1850–1 company was John Coleman, later to assume the lesseeship of the Royal. He was nineteen and had been promised a winter season at Bristol and Bath but a mis-understanding with Mrs Macready, the stepmother of the famous William Macready and in charge of the theatres in those towns, led Coleman to be dis-engaged at a time when the better companies had filled their posts. Fortunately he was able to join Bennett on the Worcester, Shrewsbury and Coventry circuit. He became a very credible actor of his day – we shall meet him several times – and always acknowledged the importance of Macready in teaching him his profession. The company opened in Coventry at Christmas, 1850 to houses crowded to overflowing with girls from the ribbon factories. On January 21st, 1851, John O'Ryan Coleman took a train to Kegworth in Leicestershire where he married Maria Jane Davies, daughter of a local lawyer, and returned to Coventry for the evening performance.[35] Coleman but briefly refers to his own nuptials in his autobiography but never mentions his wife's name or anything about her, save she was a friend of his sister whom, we are told, engineered the match making process.

This was Henry Bennett's last season whence he retired from the stage to lead a prominent public life in Worcester. He became a city councillor on three separate occasions and assumed the role of churchwarden at St Michael's Church, where he presented a stained glass window. Bennett had always enjoyed a warm and sympathetic press in Coventry and now he disposed of his interests to Henry Hall [1808–1858] and Thomas Spencer Pitt [1825–1856] in 1851 thereby ending the most stable and constant regime until his namesake, William Bennett, acquired the theatre in 1880. The intervening thirty years were to witness tempestuous times with more troughs than crests in the fortunes of the Royal, but unlike so many other provincial theatres, it survived.

There were signs of economy. Weekly block advertisements were not as regularly inserted in the local press as before; announcements were only placed at the beginning of each season or on the occasions of important benefits. Greater reliance was made on the circulation of small bills posted in every part of the town. In-between seasons a greater diversity of entertainment was provided in what were termed ballets and operas, but closer inspection suggests these entertainments consisted of plays, performed by the stock company, with the insertion of songs or dances performed by visiting artists.

1   Theatre Notebook, Volume XXVIII Number 1, "John Hodgkinson in the English Provinces 1765–1792", Billy J. Harbin.
2   Coventry Herald, 24 December, 1830.
3   Coventry Herald, 23 December, 1831.
4   Harold Oswald, "The Theatres Royal in Newcastle-upon-Tyne", Northumberland Press Limited 1936.
5   Coventry Herald, 27 January, 1832.
6   Moira Field "The Fisher Theatre Circuit 1792–1844", Running Angel, Norwich 1985.
7   Theatre Notebook, Volume 35. No 1. 1981, "Of Der Freischutz, Ducrow and His Stag Salamander", Alan Hughes.
8   Coventry Herald, 17 January, 1834.
9   Coventry Herald, 20 March, 1835.
10 Coventry Herald, 5 February, 1836.
11 Sybil Rosenfeld, "The York Theatre", Society for Theatre Research 2001.
12 W. Clark Russell, "Representative Actors", Frederick Warne & Co.
13 H. Chance Newton, "Cues and Curtain Calls", John Lane the Bodley Head Ltd 1927.
14 R.J.Broadbent, "Annals of the Liverpool Stage", Benjamin Blom, 1908. (Re-issued 1969).
15 Coventry Herald, 19 January, 1838.
16 Coventry Herald, 30 March, 1838.
17 George Rowell, "The Victorian Theatre, A Survey", OUP 1956.
18 Coventry Herald, 15 February, 1839.
19 Richard Foulkes (ed), "Scenes from Provincial Stages", Society for Theatre Research 1994, "The Earliest Grossmiths and their Pictorial Playbills", Derek Forbes.
20 Coventry Herald, 24 January, 1840.
21 Lou Warwick, "Theatre Un-Royal", Lou Warwick, 1974.
22 John Coleman, "Fifty Years of an actor's life", James Pott 1904
23 R.J.Broadbent, "Annals of the Liverpool Stage", Benjamin Blom, 1908. (Re-issued 1969).
24 Russell Jackson, "Victorian Theatre", A & C Black 1989.
25 Coventry Herald, 18 March, 1842.
26 Hampshire Telegraph, 10th February, 1814, from Paul Ranger, "Under Two Managers", Society for Theatre Research 2001.
27 Coventry Herald, 6 January, 1843.
28 Coventry Herald, 19 and 26 January, 1845.
29 Coventry Herald, 2 January, 1846.
30 Giles Playfair, "The Prodigy – The Strange Life of Master Betty", Secker and Warburg 1967.
31 W. Clark Russell, "Representative Actors", Frederick Warne.
32 Coventry Herald, 11 January, 1850.
33 Coventry Herald, 15 February, 1850.
34 Coventry Herald, 2 July, 1850.
35 Leicester Record Office.

Chapter 6

The Start of the Troublesome Years

Henry Hall [1808–1858] and Thomas Spencer Pitt [1825–1856]

The new lessees, who had connections with the New Street Birmingham Theatre Royal, took over the Worcester Theatre Royal, Shrewsbury Theatre Royal and the Ashby Theatre from Bennett and it was their company which opened a short season at Smithfield Street in August 1851. The Coventry theatre was entirely refitted from the stage to the rear of the gallery giving the appearance of a new theatre. Brunton carried out the decorations and Osler, of Birmingham, provided specially-made chandeliers. A new curtain adorned the proscenium opening and Lennox repainted the proscenium and act-drop and provided new scenery. Every part of the building was considered to have been tackled in excellent taste. This was the period before the elaborate plaster decorations of the Phipps and Matcham periods so the interior embellishments would have looked comparatively plain when compared to later buildings of the Victorian and Edwardian eras. Smoking was strictly banned from the auditorium, those contravening the instruction were *"to be given into custody"* a threat, curious by today's anti-smoking standards, but which was much applauded by the *Herald*.[1] The endurance of fumes from the gas lighting was probably bad enough. Bennett was careful with his money and except for 1842 and 1849 it appears little had been spent on the interior of the theatre during his tenure, which may have led to the need for drastic action now. Pitt, a native of Walsall, had studied medicine at Birmingham General Hospital but always nursed a passion for the theatre. A sizeable inheritance enabled him to indulge his obsession and he teamed up with Henry Hall, an established actor and specialist in rustic and Irish parts, who had appeared at the London Strand and St James's theatres.[2] The number of playing nights was extended from three to five not including the week-end. Mr Wybrow was appointed treasurer and all appeared well.

The first season, starting on August 11th 1851, commanded good houses at the beginning and excellent notices throughout, especial comment being made on the dressing and costumes with *"few imperfections in acting."* The new company was 'carefully selected' and drilled after the fashion of Mr Phelps at the London Sadler's

Wells Theatre and who believed in high standards and proper dramatic training for actors and actresses. The Birmingham Company passed muster.

On 8th and 9th September, singer and composer Henry Russell gave his American Entertainment revolving around Negro life in both slavery and freedom and this was accompanied with panoramas, stories and anecdotes. Negro entertainment was very popular for most of the Victorian period, and Russell was not an infrequent visitor to Coventry, but his material would not be 'politically correct' in this part of the twenty-first century.

Theatre in recession

The 1840s and 1850s saw an acceleration in the decline of the provincial theatre. The deterioration was felt at Coventry but permanent closure, that befell so many other playhouses, was avoided. As far back as Boxing Day 1842, Henry Bennett re-opened the season stating that *"business has not been of a very brilliant description but it is expected to improve."*[3] The problems were multi-fold, but had as much to do with recession and poverty as with the staleness of the product and its execution which failed to attract the box clientele, those who paid the highest prices and therefore kept the theatre in profit. The social habits of the middle and upper classes were changing; they now dined between 8 p.m. and 10 p.m., a time previously spent in the theatre, and they found alternative amusements which took preference over the play. Reading three-volume novels, sometime out loud to other members of the family, became popular. The upper classes found that the preponderance of melodramas lacked sufficient intellectual meat to satisfy them. Here was a chicken and egg situation whereby if the managers gratified the artistic expectations of the box and dress circle patrons, those in the pit and gallery would rebel, and if they pleased the gods the rest would be driven from the theatre. Working class audiences were largely illiterate and managers had to make allowances for labourers not relishing 'highbrow' material after physically working hard during a twelve hour shift. Even presentations at Drury Lane and Covent Garden, the pinnacles of British drama, were becoming tawdry and mediocre. As the standard of the dramatic masterpieces fell, managers pandered to a lower common denominator in order to attract greater audiences, after all they had huge auditoriums to fill. The accusation of 'dumbing down' is frequently levied against television companies in our own age and so the problem is not new. Managers begot more spectacular productions, the expenses of which necessitated larger audiences to pay for them. Consequently the quality of drama suffered.

The torch of improvement was led by the growing number of 'fringe' or minor theatres, whose innovative approach towards drama left the Patent houses increasingly in the cold. Drama of quality was frequently seen at these minor houses, which blossomed after 1843 when the Patent theatres could no longer legally prevent rival performances through the courts, although it represented but a drop in the ocean. It did not help that some provincial theatres were situated in what had become slum areas which did not encourage members of the upper classes to visit, however Smithford Street was not in this category, being an area of high class retailers right through to the blitz of 1940.

It was the less discerning occupants of the pit and gallery who enabled the theatre to carry on although there were rumbles of discontent there. Many of these loyal people felt aggrieved by the manner in which managers were keen to take their money but give little by way of comfort in return. The Theatrical Journal in the mid 1850s carried numerous letters itemising sources of complaint. Narrow backless benches placed two feet apart may have been acceptable in the past but they were out of place now and those which had perpendicular wooden backs were torture to sit on. People blessed with long legs had to endure cramp; the lack of adequate ventilation on the one hand gave discomfort due to excessive heat, yet *'villainous draughts'* gave others a stiff neck. Women frequently brought their shopping with no place to put it, movement in and out of the rows caused feet to be trodden on, people consumed ginger beer from bottles the corks of which were permitted to fly in all directions and there was no place to put one's hat. Many correspondents threatened to withdraw their custom until something was done. Dissatisfaction with the auditorium was one thing, but antagonism with the product was another. A combination of the two spelt disaster for many a manager and his circuit.

The early 1850s was a period when several 'wizards' visited the town with a complete evening's entertainment, many returning within the year. Our ancestors would have revelled in the performances of Paul Daniels and appreciated the magic of 'Harry Potter' as much as this generation.

Another novelty was a gentleman identified by the name Young Hengler, regarded as the best equilibrist in Europe, and a member of the well known equestrian family who earned their living running circuses. In later years many cities had permanently built Hengler's Circuses, the London Palladium was built on the site of one in 1910. Young Hengler delighted the Coventry audiences who showered him with redoubled applause for his equilibrist prowess but, like boxers, weather men and TV soap characters in some modern pantomimes, the management expected the poor chap to act as well. He played the role of Claude Melnotte in·'*The Lady of Lyons*' in February 1852, where his performance evidenced some "*slight misconception of the character.*" Later in the week he played '*Hamlet*' for his benefit to an uncomfortably crowded house, except for the boxes. Criticism of his performance was like the curate's egg, good in parts, but sometimes the "*text was delivered with an affectation which destroyed all illusion and the melancholy Prince was forgotten in the imperfect actor.*"[4] He combined his '*Hamlet*' and rope dancing act at the York Theatre in 1850.[5]

Young Hengler moved to pastures new and Mr Raynor, of the stock company, appeared in '*Macbeth*' in February 1852. The *Herald* critic rarely expected to see good Shakespearean acting in London so he made generous allowances for like productions in the provinces, but he found this play "*performed to the full (with) as much spirit as could be expected*".[6] Praise indeed, but he recommended that the management should rely more on other plays such as domestic dramas. It was becoming increasingly common for classics in general to be beyond the capabilities of resident stock companies. They may not have performed the classics any worse than in previous years but the public were becoming better educated and more critical in what to expect than in former times. A similar situation occurred in the twentieth century when the standard of television drama sometimes highlighted the shortcomings of provincial repertory. On April 9th, 1854 Mr Noel gave a lecture at the Mechanics Institute at which he claimed that Shakespeare's plays were better acted in Germany than in England.[7] The *Coventry Herald* responded,

> "*This is a minor national disgrace and we hope it will soon yield to a better taste which will not allow the "gods" in the galleries any more than the "select circles" to be content without good plays and good acting.*"[8]

A benefit performance of '*The Wife*' was given on March 3rd 1852, for those caught up in the Holmfirth catastrophe. Holmfirth, the well known setting for the '*Last of the Summer Wine*' television series, was inundated when a nearby reservoir burst killing eighty inhabitants. The sum raised throughout Coventry was £250 but, to the regret of the *Herald*, the box patrons did not show up in large numbers for this event either, even though the company was "*more effective by recent additions.*"[9]

In March 1852, full houses greeted Mons. Devani, the human contortionist whose feats baffled Birmingham medics to find anything abnormal about his body; such disappointment! The following week John Coleman succeeded in filling the boxes with '*Richlieu*', starring Agnes Kemble and Macready. The season ended with what were described as well attended houses, but this trend was not common place.

Henry Hall, along with Messrs Atkins and Barton of the Birmingham Company, presented the '*Travestie of Macbeth*' in August 1852 which invoked a continual roar of laughter, but this was short lived as the death of the Duke of Wellington in late September, brought a temporary cessation to all amusements. Perhaps this was a different twist to the alleged curse of the Scottish play.

Long waits for scene changing were a feature of the Victorian theatre and such occasions gave a reason d'être for the theatre band to supply overtures and entr'acte music. Hall and Pitt were strongly advised by the *Herald* to curtail long intervals and they suggested that the "*ear piercing piccolo might also be subdued with advantage. It is frequently too loud and quite out of harmony with other instruments.*"[10] Theatregoers in the current age consult their programmes for details of the performance, but these were not available in the mid nineteenth century, audiences having to make do with copies of small playbills for which the charge of 2d, was made.

A visiting Exhibition of Royal Entertainment of the Overland Route to California was brought into the theatre by George Payne on 25th October 1852. This was a purely panoramic presentation with Payne standing on the stage and giving a rapid explanation of the scenes as they rolled by from one side of the stage to the other. It conveyed the audience over a journey of 4500 miles from St Louis to San Francisco taking in the gold mines and American Indian life on the way. The performance drew crowded houses as it had done in Birmingham and Manchester previously. Prices were reduced for the occasion to Dress Circle 1s. 6d, Boxes 1s. pit 6d, and gallery 3d.

Hall and Pitt ran the theatre along similar lines to Bennett but were more adventurous when booking London names and novelties, which must have been expensive. Sims Reeves and Julia Harland appeared in a repertoire of operas in December 1852 which were much appreciated by the pit and gallery.

> *"The lessees have spared no trouble or expense in improving the theatre and rendering it almost everything that can be desired in a provincial city, they present the attraction such as a singer as Mr Reeves, aided by a highly talented lady, the least they have a right to expect is full houses."*[11]

Hall and Pitt raised the price of first tier box seats to 4s. and upper box seats to 3s. for the Reeves and Harland engagement, which the *Herald* thought an error as previous attempts had never succeeded. They thought it better to keep the old prices and have bumper houses.

Fanny Kemble [1809–1893] performed in 'Othello' in January 1853 for which the *"orchestra is very greatly improved."* Fanny was a member of the large and well-known Kemble acting family being a daughter to Charles and sister to Henry and John. Her talents and fame filled the Covent Garden theatre for three years in the early 1830s and she was equally competent in both tragedy and comedy. Her marriage to Pierce Butler, a southern planter in America, in 1834, was dissolved in 1845.

Gallery behaviour

Theatre etiquette in the first half of the eighteenth century was much freer than would be accepted today. The most lively part of the house was the gallery. The tastes of the 'gods' did not always coincide with those occupying the boxes and they had a more forthright manner of expressing their disapprobation. It offered the cheapest admission and was very much a lower working class area. Workers would arrive in working clothes from their place of employment bringing such refreshment, in solid and liquid form, to sustain them until late in the evening. On popular nights they would be encouraged to sit closer together, adding to the discomfort caused by a continual flow of hot air which rose from the naked gas jets below. The 'gods' were frequently noisy and not averse to disposing of unwanted orange peel, nut shells and the like over the balcony front to those who had the misfortune to sit in the pit directly below. Their wit could be harnessed into making jokes among themselves or quips at the expense of the 'swells' in the boxes, especially if the latter did not display the decorum expected of their class. They certainly added to the atmosphere and could be amusing and entertaining but also, at times, infuriating.

A description of the gallery at the London Victoria Theatre (now the Old Vic) in the nineteenth century gives a flavour of what one might expect.

> *"The gallery of the Victoria was a huge amphitheatre, probably containing about fifteen hundred perspiring creatures; most of the men in shirt sleeves, and most of the women bare headed, with coloured handkerchiefs round their shoulders . . . This "chickaleary" audience was always thirsty – and not ashamed.*

It tied handkerchiefs together – of which it always seemed to have plenty – until they formed a rope, which was used to haul up large stone bottles of beer from the pit, and occasionally hats that had been dropped below."[12]

Figure 23   Fred Barnard's illustration of a mid Victorian gallery audience. There could, on occasions, be as much drama in that part of the theatre as on the stage

University of Bristol, Theatre Collection

Barracking an incompetent actor was considered fair game, and it can be argued this helped to weed out the incompetent, but smothering professional performances just for the 'fun of it' antagonised the rest of the house and was sometimes only controlled with the presence of the law. On February 1853, during the benefit performance of Mr and Mrs Clifford, the whole of act one of Lytton's '*The Lady of Lyons*' was reduced to a dumb show due to the crowded and unsettled state of the gallery. *"We may suggest that a remedy for this nuisance would be the employment of a policeman or two on benefit nights."* Owing to the enormous crowds on this occasion, people were obliged to stand in all parts of the house, except in the boxes, several of which were unoccupied. Benefit nights were also highly-charged affairs and matters easily got out of hand – often. The box clientele, for their part, complained of the draughts from the doors which appeared not to close properly.[13] No one was happy. The rowdy conduct of the 'gods' was another facet in the disappearance of the box patrons which put the management in a cleft stick, for the former were loyal in their attendance and a heavy hand would not necessarily have guaranteed the middle and upper classes returning on a regular basis.

John Buckstone, Mrs Fitzwilliam, Mr Ben Webster, Mme Celeste and Julia Maitland all journeyed from their London theatres to Coventry during the short term of Hall and Pitt's lease. Benjamin Nottingham Webster [1797–1882], a versatile character actor and dramatist, leased both the London Haymarket and Adelphi Theatres in the 1830s and 1840s and was, for a time, associated with Madame

Vestris at the Olympic. Madame Celeste [1814–1882] was a French dancer and pantomimist who spent some time in American before settling in London. Rather slow to learn English, she did not undertake dramatic roles until late in the 1830s. The entire Haymarket Company played Coventry again in October 1853 although they were rewarded with poor houses, unlike their previous foray into the city.

April 25th and 26th, 1853 were reserved for another astronomical entertainment. C. Popham F.A.S demonstrated the working of the heavens using thirty nine moveable transparent diagrams including a dissolving diorama of sacred, classic, alpine and arctic scenery. The stage was dominated by a suspended transparent globe twenty two feet in circumference, surrounded by clouds upon which were reflected the rays of the rising sun. Ships were seen to cross the oceans and the revolving earth demonstrated day, night, the seasons and eclipses. The events were attended by an enthusiastic but less than full house on each night.[14] The globe would have occupied almost half the width of the stage.

The local amateur dramatic society tried their luck in May 1853, with Richard B. Sheridan's 'Pizarro', the beneficiaries being the Coventry Seniority Fund. After expenses, sixteen pounds was handed over but, again, the boxes were virtually empty. The play, adapted in 1797 from the German, proved a money spinner for John Kemble, it being a spectacular piece beloved by theatre goers of all ages, even when the topicality of a French invasion had receded. It portrayed the Spanish conquest of the Incas in South America and usually involved spectacular sets, massed groups of soldiers, priestesses and mourners. The mortally wounded hero secured himself by a pendant branch over a chasm, then managed to stagger amongst the rocks to be seen a little later disappearing into the distance. This perspective was created by a smaller duplicate person appearing upstage.

The London Haymarket Theatre Company played a return visit for five nights in August 1853. "We should be glad to think they have come willingly to Coventry and that they should not have cause to feel, now they are here, that they have been sent." Attendance was generally rather poor, perhaps because their second visit followed too soon after their first.[15]

On September 8th and 9th 1853, Harry Lee Carter presented a moving diorama depicting the routes to Californian and Australia. The apparatus consisted of a long canvas roll. Musical entertainments added to the evening's programme.

An Italian marionette novelty came to Coventry on October 10th, 1853 using full size dolls. They gave a parody of common stage gestures of the day, all of which were instantly recognised by the audience. The popular vaudeville 'The Swiss Cottage' and selections from Bellini's opera 'Norma' were offered. The vocalists in the company were ranked as first rate, as was the concert music which was deemed worth hearing in itself.

Sims Reeves, the celebrated tenor, visited Coventry several times during the 1850s. Box tickets for his musical evening on 4th November 1853, were in such demand that the management abolished the 'pit' and annexed the ground floor accommodation to the respectable dress circle, calling the new area 'stalls' and taking the opportunity to increase the prices at the same time. The normal seating of 200 people on wooden benches was reduced to 144 reserved cushioned seats and, to prevent confusion, they were numbered. Pit benches were never numbered. The alterations cost £5,[16] which would have yielded a profit. Entrance to the new stalls (the old pit) on this occasion, was through the dress circle of boxes. Since the pit floor rose almost to box level it would have been a simple matter to remove a front panel and create a gateway with a few short steps to connect the two. It must be remembered that the theatre, until the middle of the twentieth century, rigidly mirrored class demarcation within society. Each class had its separate part of the house and its own entrance. It would have been unthinkable for a box patron to use the same doorway as his butcher, tailor or the man who mended his drains. It was more usual, later in the century, to bisect the ground floor into stalls at the front with chairs, and the pit behind with benches, and to separate the two with a wooden barrier.

Figure 24   The pit barrier was usually an adjustable fence that divided the stalls from the pit. This example was re-introduced into the Gaiety Theatre, Douglas, Isle of Man, during the major refurbishment of 2000. Originally the pit accommodation on the furthest side of the barrier would have been provided by benches

Photo – Author

The ratio of stalls/ pit accommodation could be varied by the simple expedient of moving the barrier either forwards or backwards and installing the appropriate number of chairs/ benches.[17] On the occasion of Sims Reeves' visit, the gallery was curtailed owing to the fact that on a previous visit this part of the house was only half filled. From this it can be assumed that as he appealed more to the 'educated classes', the front part of the gallery was re-classified into something like an amphitheatre with an improvement in comfort to justify an increase in prices. This location was possibly that area which was later converted into the central tier of boxes, most likely in 1857. Anyway, the attraction was a musical concert in which

Mrs Reeves, Farquharson Smith [buffo], George Case [concertina] and Emile Prudent [piano] took part.

In the November 4th edition of the *Coventry Herald* there appeared a notice to architects to submit plans for a proposed new Corn Exchange to be built in Hertford Street. The interior room was to be designed for: a corn exchange, a music hall and for general purposes and had to be lit partially from roof windows. The cost had to be kept within the limits of £6000.

From November 30th to December 3rd 1853 inclusive, Coventry was treated to a performance of Hoffman's Organophone Band straight from the London St James's Theatre. The clarionet, cornet, drums, musical boxes, trombone and bagpipes were all relayed to the audience using only the human voice and without any kind of mechanical aid. The programme was changed each evening and the engagement brought forth crowded houses and much unbounded applause.

'The Corsican Brothers'

A production of *'The Corsican Brothers'* in January 1854, included Mr Gomersal (whose son William became lessee and manager of the Worcester Theatre Royal in 1880) just before the connection of Coventry and Worcester theatres was broken. It was well brought out *"so well as to deserve more encouragement than Mr Clifford has hitherto received."*[18] It is speculative to wonder whether the stage was fitted up with the special Corsican trap but it is quite likely. The story used in the play originated from the elder Dumas and was adapted by Eugene Grange and Xavier de Montepin

Figure 25 A model of the Corsican trap reinstated into the Gaiety Theatre, Douglas, Isle of Man in 2000 for their production of *'The Corsican Brothers'*. The inclined wooden 'railway' raises the actor to stage level as the platform is pulled from one side to the other

Photo – Author

and translated by Dion Boucicault, being first seen in this country at the London Princess's Theatre in 1852. The plot involves the ghost of a twin, killed in a duel, appearing before his brother, both characters being played by the same actor with a substitute where necessary. Unlike spectres used in Pepper's Ghost, this one rose out of the stage as it travelled from wing to wing. The character stood upon a small square shaped platform, complete with wheels, which ran upon an inclined wooden railway from below to stage level. With subdued lighting, a suitably placed groundrow and a row of bristles to conceal the gap, the ghost appeared to emerge from a solid stage. The device was used in no other stage play, yet so popular was this drama that almost every theatre adapted one of its bridge traps for the purpose.[19] As the popularity of the play declined so the accompanying machinery was dismantled, that is, until 2000 when it was re-created at the Douglas Gaiety Theatre for the centenary celebrations of the theatre's opening. The machinery remains for future use at this theatre.

'Hamlet' and the 'Iron Chest' were seen at the end of January 1854. "*Miss J. Reynolds as Ophelia gave the 'mad scene' with some sweetness and feeling but otherwise showed little conception of the part of the gentle and court-bred maiden.*"[20]

'The Sea of Ice' was presented at the end of March 1854 with special effects, although these were not detailed. "*Mr Lacy made a most respectable captain. . . but he cannot play villains; his face is not made for it, it is far too open and John Bull like.*"[21] 'The Wife' was little better, "*Mr Clifford, no doubt, has much to do but he should know that the effect of a part is slightly marred when as loudly spoken by the prompter as himself.*"[22]

Mr Jacobs, magician and ventriloquist, attracted but scant audiences despite humour and comedy, during his engagement in May 1854, an unusual state of affairs in Coventry for this type of entertainment.

The Coventry Amateur Dramatic Society hired the theatre on May 15th to raise funds for the Lady Godiva Procession. The offering was '*The Lady of Lyons*', a piece which is "*deeply pathetic; its effect depends entirely upon the 'nicest' possible acting and perhaps it was rather daring of the Coventry Amateurs to undertake it.*"

J.Harris

On June 16th, 1854 J. Harris was announced as the new lessee, there being no reference to Hall and Pitt, both of whom quit Worcester around this time. Whilst Pitt was liberal with his money, he apparently did not know how to run a theatre efficiently. With a treasurer on hand and Hall, who was experienced in the ways of the theatre, it is surprising neither put Pitt on the straight and narrow to curb his extravagances. After three years Pitt's fortune had gone. With his theatrical and medical careers in tatters, he settled in Birmingham where he drank himself to death in 1856 at the early age of 31.[23] Harris came at the right time, for it was Fair week and he opened the theatre every night, there being a different set of plays each day.

Madam Vestris' London Lyceum Company played for five nights to very thin houses and yet the following month (August) crowds attended G.V.Brooke's

'Othello', although the *"behaviour of [the] gallery did little to the credit of Coventry. Desdemona was smothered with hootings and altercations going on. On Wednesday police preserved the peace."*[24] Gustavus Vaughan Brooke [1818–1866] first appeared in Dublin at the age of fourteen being described as the Hibernian Roscius and slowly he made his mark, being at one time manager of the Kilmarnock Theatre. This was a simple place of entertainment situated above a stable but which was unable to provide him with enough remuneration to buy decent board and lodging, so he lived in his dressing room instead. John Coleman had a similar experience at the same theatre. Brooke eventually became the idol of the provinces although he did have his successes at the London Drury Lane and Haymarket theatres. He should have been a wealthy man, despite entering into one or two disastrous managerial appointments, but his life was governed by the bottle and debt. There are many recorded instances where he missed, or curtailed performances, as the result of drink. One, at Northampton's Marefair Theatre[25], Brooke began his greatest role, 'Othello', but dried after a few lines and had to retire to hisses from the house. He attempted to start afresh in Australia but drowned when the 'S.S.London' taking him there foundered in the Bay of Biscay in 1866. Brooke's performance at Coventry was well praised but the police were in evidence the following evening although there was no trouble.

Lectures on the Aztec Lilliputians, together with a troupe of these foreigners, drew crowded houses for three nights in October 1854. The Aztecs were people around two and a half feet in height and were worshipped as Gods in the City of Iximaya in Central America. Other novelties included further lectures on astronomy by Frederick Grafton, closely followed by Professor Anderson, the 'Wizard of the North', who took the theatre for a week commencing December 1st. He paid for a half-column advertisement in the *Herald*, itemising his entertainment which included natural magic, clairvoyance and spirit rapping, which would be exposed as fraudulent. He let it be known that his performances had been presented before Queen Victoria at Balmoral and many crowned heads of Europe. Testimony indeed. These out-of-season novelties were probably more remunerative than the regular dramatic seasons.[26]

The new year (1855) did not bring improved attendance figures. Taglioni's performance in February only attracted six patrons in the boxes.

> *"Genius here, if it comes at all, is always 'sent to Coventry', and from the reception it meets with, it is never likely to come of its own accord. The Aztecs, or any other specimen of the idiot kind, would draw crowded houses for a week."*[27]

This forthright statement followed an evening's musical entertainment given by Miss P. Horton who rendered works by Purcell and Handel, portraying around a dozen different characters, all in the appropriate costume, to a comparatively empty house. Miss P. Horton was, in fact, Mrs German Reed and her husband accompanied her on the occasion. Before her involvement in the musical world, she had acted in drama and was Macready's leading lady from 1837 and an occasional actress at Covent Garden, which then operated as an outlet for plays rather than opera. During the 1870s, the German Reeds ran the Gallery of Illustration in Lower

Regent Street, London, which was, in all purposes, a small theatre but the name permitted patronage from those who thought the 'theatre' rather common and a place of ill repute, a fancy fostered by many religious denominations of the period. The word Illustration was a pseudonym for playlet. So successful was the venture that Reed took the St George's Hall and re-named it the St George's Opera House where larger scale productions were seen. He staged several pieces of musical theatre written by Arthur Sullivan and a number of straight plays from the pen of W.S.Gilbert, hence the old adage that the Gilbert and Sullivan operas were *'cradled in the Reeds'*.[28]

John Coleman [1832–1904]

Figure 26   John Coleman, one of the stalwarts of the provincial touring scene
Author's collection

Grand Opera made a visit to the Royal in April 1855 with *'La Sonnambula'*, *'The Bohemian Girl'*, *'Lucia di Lammermoor'*, *'Maritana' and 'Fra Diavolo'* on the menu. The chorus was limited but efficient – on the whole. The principal tenor was Elliott Galer who became lessee of the London Royalty Theatre in 1862. From

September 1877 he opened and ran the Leicester Royal Opera House and became proprietor of the Reading Theatre Royal in 1884. Galer was also a dramatist and architect, these latter skills being employed in the designs of the Leicester Opera House along with the main architect Charles Phipps. *"The theatre (Coventry) has passed into new hands and have considerable reason to congratulate ourselves upon this first fruits of it."* There was the announcement of a new lessee but the name was withheld at the time. In June John Coleman, who later added Stamford, Sheffield and Wolverhampton theatres to his circuit, was cited as the responsible manager at Coventry and Worcester, thereby replacing J. Harris. Mentioned as living at High Broughton, Manchester, he was granted a licence for a period of twelve months by Mayor T.H.Merridew, Alderman Caldicott and Alderman Newsome. In a statement Coleman said his first venture as manager in Coventry was financially guaranteed by his old employer Henry Bennett, an interesting piece of intelligence since the former manager, who died a wealthy man, was considered to be 'careful' with his money.

Coleman belonged to a newer and different school of acting which did not rely upon ranting, raving or wild gesticulations to portray a character.[29] His first task was to engage the comedian Charles James Mathews for two nights on June 23rd and 24th, 1855 and whom we met when he first appeared at the Coventry Craven Arms Assembly Rooms back in 1821. Mathews (1803–1878), a trained architect, took to the stage in the year of his father's death, marrying Madame Vestris in 1838 and later assuming the managership of the London Covent Garden and Lyceum theatres. Coleman was one of the nation's best light comedians of his age and could command a respectable salary, although his managerial positions frequently left him in straightened circumstances. He was not as prudent with his money as Bennett, but no doubt achieved greater artistic success.

> *"In consequence of the enormous expenses connected with this engagement – Mr Coleman having guaranteed Mr Charles Mathews a fixed and heavy remuneration regardless of receipts, the prices of admission will necessarily be increased."*[30]

One need only recall the last week's variety bill at London's Chiswick Empire in June 1959, when the engagement of the internationally famed Liberace necessitated raising the prices of admission by about 100 per cent to realise everything has been done before.

In July the *Herald* announced the last night of Thorne's Theatre in the Bull Field, Coventry.[31] This is likely to have been one of an increasing number of portable theatres which travelled from town to town with a prefabricated structure capable of being erected or dismantled within hours rather in the manner of a circus tent. Few portable theatres were recorded at Coventry. The most modern example of this type of structure is the wooden Century Theatre which was built in Hinckley, Leicestershire, after the Second World War. Most of its working life was spent as a static structure in Keswick, Cumberland before finally moving to the Snibston Discovery Park, Coalville in 1997 where it continues to function as a small community theatre and cinema.

Panoramas and Dioramas

August 13, 1855 saw a two weeks engagement of Mr Hamilton with his historical moving panoramic display of the war with Russia. The country was in the middle of the terrible Crimean conflict and in the days before cinema and television footage, panoramas were offered to the public to explain what was happening, or what had happened, on the field of conflict. They were known in various forms from around 1790 to the beginning of the cinema age and were sufficiently popular to warrant special buildings in which to house them. Originally they were static scenes painted in special perspective on the inside of a domed cylinder to be viewed from the centre. The pictures would often represent events about which people had previously read in their newspapers; the modern equivalent would be the television newsreel which portrays a story also available in the press. This domed 3-D picture gave way to the flat panorama which was viewed by audiences looking down a tunnel, thirty to forty feet in length, the pictures being painted on opaque and translucent materials and illuminated by daylight.

Theatre managements, with their expertise in showmanship, developed the idea still further with the moving panorama which created an atmosphere that could be enhanced with words, music and lighting. There were scenes of great accuracy painted onto very long stretches of canvas which were unrolled out from one wing and rolled up in the one opposite. The unwinding gave the impression of a sideways moving picture. One in America was 3,600 feet long and took two hours to unroll. These moving cloths were often placed upstage to enable them to be bordered by a fixed frame such as a cut cloth. Sometimes the positioning of groundrows (shallow pieces of scenery) placed downstage would give a 3D effect. The idea was milked at every turn and was employed to visually enhance pantomime, melodramas and even Shakespeare.[32] At Coventry, Hamilton accompanied his moving panorama with swords, muskets and helmets taken from the enemy on the battlefield, or so he said.[33] The engagement proved most popular and terminated prematurely due to a prior booking in Birmingham. As far back as 1824 a diorama, which to all intents and purposes was synonymous to the panorama, had been introduced into the *"Harlequin and the Flying Chest"* pantomime at the Birmingham Theatre Royal in June.[34]

In October the local amateurs presented 'Charles II' and 'The Illustrious Stranger', with full band, but thin houses. *". . .and this is almost universally the case when an attempt is made to raise the prices."*[35]

November 1855 saw more touring opera including 'The Beggar's Opera' which *"was divested as much as possible of all that was coarse and objectionable."*[36] A comic opera written by John Gay at London's Lincoln's Inn Fields Theatre in January 1728, it had the good run of sixty two nights and was revived many times, a more up to date season being seen at the London Hammersmith Lyric Theatre in the 1920s. It brought the displeasure of the church around its ears when Dr Herring, later Archbishop of Canterbury, censured it for seeming to encourage vice and portraying a highwayman as an unpunished hero.

In this same year the Eagle Concert Room, supposedly capable of holding 1,000 people, opened in Coventry for dancing. There was a proposal that the premises should be used as a concert venue but nothing came of it, presumably because it was eclipsed by the Corn Exchange opening the following year.[37] The exact location of the Eagle is a mystery for in 1855 there were no licensed premises by that name. Even more tantalising is the information reported in the November 25th edition of the *Era* that a Coventry Music Hall had opened on November 17th to a densely crowded audience of a thousand people to witness Madame Aldini and Messrs Randall, Collins and Russell, for this cannot be located either. As both venues opened within three weeks of each other it is possible the reports refer to the same building, which may have been of a temporary nature.

Coleman's first season ended on March 14th 1856, the *Herald* being of the opinion it deserved higher appreciation from ranks above the working classes. He was a popular manager but occasionally blotted his copy book in that he was wont to 'puff' visiting companies and stars beyond their capabilities. "*. . .he must not come the Mr Barnum or Mr Bunn over us. . .*"[38]. Alfred Bunn [1796–1860] was manager of the Birmingham Theatre Royal before and after its destruction by fire in 1820. He had a flair for spectacular productions but was always in debt and by the end of 1821 owed £13,000, a huge sum for the time. "*There was no money even for scenery, and Bunn [himself] made three horizontal flats and a tomb.*"[39] He would do almost anything to get people into his theatre.

This was but a temporary blip upon Coleman's character for he usually generated a warm response from the press. It was wondered why the London stage had not snapped up Coleman, though it was said he may have found filling the large theatres of the metropolis with sound more difficult than the small theatre at Coventry. This must refer to an alleged story of a 'collapsed lung' when still a young man but, according to his autobiography, this did not prevent his filling the largest theatres with his voice. Once at Sheffield's Theatre Royal, during Coleman's 'Othello', Huntly May Macarthy (the eccentric Irish manager) exclaimed, "*lost one lung has he? Lord be praised for small mercies then for devil a theatre in the kingdom would be safe if he'd got two o'them. It's afeared I am, even now, that he'll bring the roof down about our ears this blessed night . . .*"[40] Coleman's illness as a teenager was probably no more complicated than a chest infection. Perhaps he was not right for the capital because "*his figure is, unfortunately, too stout for youthful parts.*"[41] From Coventry Coleman took his company to Worcester and then to Wolverhampton in September.

The Corn Exchange

March 1856 saw the opening of the Corn Exchange in Hertford Street. Constructed on the site of the King's Head Hotel, the stables of which remained in the cellar, it measured 110 feet in length, 55 feet across and 47 feet in height. There were roof lights and three interior sunburners. Designed by James Murray, it was built by Pratt of Coventry for £8000, a quarter more than the stipulated figure of

Figure 27   Exterior of the Corn Exchange, Hertford Street, Coventry (1856)
Coventry Local Studies, Central Library

1854. Although principally intended as a unit where farmers, corn merchants and maltsters could ply their trades during the day, the provision of an open platform stage enabled the building to be used for entertainment at night. Whilst not fitted up for the presentation of plays, the Exchange was booked for concerts, lectures, and other one night stands which, in previous years, would either have gone to the

Figure 28   Interior of the Corn Exchange, Hertford Street, Coventry (1856). This is an early illustration taken from the Mander Collection. The artist's drawing includes an organ which was never built
Coventry Local Studies, Central Library

Theatre Royal, St Mary's Hall or may have bypassed Coventry altogether for want of a suitable venue. There had been an earlier Corn Exchange run by Thomas Grimmitt in Smithford Street, but there was no provision for entertainment there. The new Exchange was the first serious competitor in the life of the Theatre Royal.

The London Dramatic Company did not desert the Royal in July 1856, playing there for five nights direct from the Nottingham Theatre Royal (in St Mary's Gate) before moving onto the Leeds Theatre Royal which was part of Coleman's circuit. The Friday evening's performance was given patronage by Captain Murray and the officers of the 10th Huzzars.[42] One of the plays was 'The Lady of Lyons' which the critics said was played too often in the town. It seemed almost every visiting troupe included it. In the company was James Rogers (sometimes spelt Rodgers) who had taken brief control at Coventry from Coleman only six months previously, an event kept rather quiet at the time.

On August 7th, 1856 'The Honeymoon' was played under 'distinguished' patronage, which appeared to give the patrons airs and graces above their station.

> "*Cigars were smoked, the talking (was) louder than the actors, and brandy and soda-water was handed to the centre dress box as a fit and worthy example, we presume, to the gods above.*"[43]

Before the main play, '*Romeo and Juliet*' was given, the latter part being interpreted by Miss Augusta Clifton, the nom-de-theatre of a local girl who made good.

Another child prodigy came along, not an actor this time but a talented infant pianist, aged four, by the name of Master Blakemore, but there was no record of his performance in the local press.

John, aged 9, and Marie, aged 11, another in the line of child performers, portrayed characters of England, Scotland, Ireland and South America in October 1856. Although competent, John was thought to have the exaggerated mannerisms of an adult, where Marie's acting came from within, yet "*we disapprove entirely of such exhibitions as a mis-use and perversion of early precocity; and we wonder that any amusement can be found in that which really is so sad.*"[44] One could argue that some children found the precocious theatrical life preferable to sweeping chimneys or working in factories or down the mines.

By mid October 1856 James Rogers was mentioned as lessee and manager at the Worcester Theatre Royal, which would automatically include Shrewsbury, Wolverhampton and Coventry, all on the same circuit. In early November the company moved to Shrewsbury before opening at Coventry at the beginning of the Christmas season which they did with '*Dred*'. "*The scene in the dismal swamp being most effective*", which doesn't sound very Christmassy at all.[45]

Coleman's Problem

> "*We are glad to perceive that the dispute as to the future of the lesseeship of this establishment (Coventry Royal) has been amicably arranged. Mr Coleman, of*

the Sheffield circuit, has waived his right for the current season, and then holds to a lease of ten years on the building. Mr James Rogers is now the sole director for the winter Campaign."[46]

So said the *Era Magazine*. The *Herald* made similar noises indicating Rogers would be in charge until the end of March. In the meantime the season progressed with '*Rob Roy*', '*Romeo and Juliet*', complete with new scenery and dresses, '*Belphegor*' and a host of similar plays. Roger's leading lady was Agnes Burdett.

Unlike today's press, which delights to seek out salacious details of public figures on the 'right-to-know' principle, the problem surrounding Coleman was not aired in public but it almost certainly involved an incident at Worcester about money. As a manager, Coleman found it difficult to make ends meet.

"A touring company had lost money in Worcester, leaving Coleman with debts which he had somehow forgotten about. Returning to Worcester to perform during the race week, he was rather surprised to be arrested for debt. He had to endure an awkward and embarrassing night in the city gaol before the affair was sorted out."[47]

He owed £150 but after suffering heavy losses on a recent concert tour of his Midland theatres, he was further out of pocket. Whether he had incurred similar debts in Coventry is not known, but the reaction of the Board of Directors on hearing their lessee was a gaolbird can be imagined. Being in trouble over money probably contravened various clauses in his lease, anyway he was dismissed before time had elapsed for any explanation. Communication was slower then, confined to a letter or a personal journey from one place to another, now-a-days an e-mail or telephone call would be employed immediately. Once the facts were known, Mabbatt seemed willing to reconsider Coleman's position, but by that time a rival had been given the theatre in a legally binding agreement.

Under both Coleman and Rodgers, the season remained confined to the first few months of the year and followed the practice of Pitt and Hall by performing each weekday. The short sixty day seasons, enforced by the Patent theatres' monopoly, were theoretically abandoned in 1843 and this gave greater freedom to all other managements to operate for any length of time they chose. In practice it took many years for any noticeable change to be effected, possibly through habit, though more likely due to the lack of public response to what was on offer. Stars of the London stage continued to appear though not always in the classics, probably in the hope that lighter material would prove a greater box office draw. This did not placate the *Herald* critic who deprecated the idea that such talent should be seen in anything but legitimate drama and, although he chortled as much as the others at the antics of Charles Mathews in *"Married for Money"*, he was *"ashamed to laugh at such horrid nonsense."*[48]

The new season opened on Boxing Day 1856 still under the management of James Rogers [1816–1890]. *"Rogers is a stranger to Coventry but theatres at Shrewsbury and Worcester have been run by him."*[49] It seems the *Herald* correspondent had forgotten his short appearance the previous January. Rogers (sometimes better known as Jemmy Rogers), had also run theatres in Newcastle-under-Lyme, Liverpool (the Liver in Church Street), Douglas, Isle of Man, Tewkesbury and Hanley. Here, in July 1857, he converted the People's Hall into the first Theatre Royal, successors of which existed until 1998 when it was forced to close due to the reopening, after an expenditure of several millions of pounds, of the nearby former Regent cinema as a number one touring house. Later Rogers associated himself with theatres in Sheffield, Chesterfield and Glasgow. He is probably best remembered for successfully operating the Birmingham Prince of Wales from 1876 until his death. Rogers' Coventry season attracted acceptable houses, with the exception of the boxes. 'The Hut of the Red Mountain', "*did not afford Miss Agnes Burdett a fair opportunity of displaying her ability as an actress. She has not mastered the ability to stand still on the stage – she is too demonstrative and gesticulative.*"[50] Ludovew and his performing dogs were sandwiched in-between 'Othello' and 'Flowers of the Forest', a perennial favourite concerning gypsy life, fortune telling, duels and a suicide.

The celebrated tragedian Charles Pitt [1819–1866] performed in 'Ingomar', 'The Corsican Brothers' and 'Macbeth' in February 1857. Of his Shakespearean performances his *acting "[was] too much of the artificial school – we admire his skill but he failed to give the impression of the dramatic character as whole.*"[51] He rolled his eyes throughout, uttering his speeches as if giving a school oration and poor Agnes Burdett, as Lady Macbeth, was "*physically incompetent for the part and want of dignified composure*", her tremulous voice in emotional scenes being overdone and distressing to hear.

Ira Frederick Aldridge [1807–1867]

Ira Aldridge, billed as the '*African Roscius*', only attracted superlatives for his acting the following week beginning February 23rd. Marked by a strong physique and a powerful voice, he did not rant, exaggerate or employ stage tricks but acted with feeling, energy and intelligence, managing to succeed in tragedy, comedy and farce. At Coventry he performed in 'The Black Doctor' and 'Othello', his greatest role. "*Nothing could have displayed the pathetic and physical powers of this gentleman to greater advantage*", however the *Coventry Herald* thought he could have done with better parts in the non Shakespearean plays.[52]

Ira Frederick Aldridge is an interesting character in that he was one of the few black actors to rise to the top of his profession, apart from James Hewlett. The popular story of his origins is that he was born in Senegal with aristocratic parentage going back to the Fulah Princes in French West Africa. This may have been useful for publicity purposes but it is a romantic tale. It was intended that he should follow his father as a preacher, but the stage called louder. Adopting the name Keene (a pun on Edmund Kean), he assailed the Black Theatre in his native city, but with little success. Owing to racial prejudice in America, he emigrated from New York to Britain where he learned his craft for nearly thirty years in the provinces and was exceedingly popular, yet the patent theatres in London seemed wary of booking him,

Figure 29   Ira Aldridge in his most famous role of
Othello taken from a lithograph by S. Bühler in the
Theatre Museum, Munich

Author's collection

although he did appear at the minor theatres with regularity. His colour gave him
novelty appeal (as did the 'Nigger Minstrel' shows later in the century) but his skill
ran much deeper than that. This is the only appearance that has come to light of
Aldridge in Coventry, although he spent the best part of his acting life touring, and
he played neighbouring Northampton and Cheltenham several times. The number
of leading roles available to a black actor was limited and he tended to keep to the
same ones over a thirty or forty year period, which is probably the reason the *Herald*
critic thought better parts, rather than dated plays, would have done him greater
justice. John Coleman had a great admiration for Aldridge's skills and had the
opportunity of acting with him on occasions.[53]

The pantomimist Edward Leman Blanchard [1820–1889] played in the '*Dumb
Boy of Manchester*' and the '*Slaves Revenge*' at the beginning of March 1857. He is
best remembered as a successful author of farces, burlesques and pantomimes by the
score; most of his Christmas offerings were seen at Drury Lane, Astley's, The
Olympic or at the Surrey theatres. He wrote articles on theatrical matters for the
Era was also retained as a critic on the staff of the '*The Daily Telegraph*' for many
years. His work was topical and as such has not survived outside the period for
which it was written.[54]

In May John Coleman was back in harness as the sole lessee at Coventry having
nineteen years of a twenty one year lease yet to run and he returned to the boards
for six nights, managing to attract good houses which gave him a warm welcome.
According to his autobiography, he found the smaller theatres on his circuit

impossible buildings in which to play the 'heavier' and more spectacular pieces as he would wish to stage them. The confines of these playhouses restricted him to the standard works. However Coleman was the boy who could do no wrong in the eyes of the *Coventry Herald*.

> *"We were sorry that during the last season under other management (James Rogers), a set of performers should be brought that played to pit and gallery alone."*[55]

Madame Warton's Pose Plastiques and Tableaux Vivans Company returned in June *"with good acrobatic feats by Master Wilder."*[56] Like their counterparts at the London Windmill Theatre, which specialised in nude tableaux in the 1930s, 40s and 50s, these artists, half clad but not naked, were required to pose with absolute stillness. Madame Keller had a similar troupe on tour around the same time. The posters advertising the event at the Daventry Theatre in January 1858, were what we would now describe as misleading, the result being the assembly of an excited audience which was *'sorely disappointed'*.[57] Sam Cowell returned on the 26th with a concert of comical songs. Originally booked for one night, he came back for another evening in July and managed a couple of other occasions the following year.

Just as James Rodgers' Hanley theatre was to open, Coleman engaged Charles Mathews for Coventry for one night, on the 20th July, supported by the Birmingham Company playing in *'Married for Money'* and *'Cool as a Cucumber'* – nothing too dramatic.

1   Coventry Herald, 8 and 15 August, 1851.
2   Suz Winspear, "Worcester's Lost Theatre", Parkbarn 1996.
3   Era Magazine, 8 January, 1843.
4   Coventry Herald, 13 February, 1852.
5   Sybil Rosenfeld, "The York Theatre", Society for Theatre Research 2001.
6   Coventry Herald, 13 February, 1852.
7   Coventry Herald, 13 April, 1854.
8   Coventry Herald, 13 April, 1854.
9   Coventry Herald, 5 March, 1852.
10 Coventry Herald, 6 September, 1852.
11 Coventry Herald, 10 December, 1852.
12 Gilbert B Cross, "Next Week – East Lynne" Domestic Drama in Performance 1820–1874. Lewisburg Bucknell University Press London 1977, also John Booth, "A Century of Theatre History, 1816–1916: The "Old Vic" London, Steads Publishing House 1917.
13 Coventry Herald, 18 February, 1853.
14 Coventry Herald, 29 April, 1853.
15 Coventry Herald, 5 August, 1853.
16 Coventry Herald, 4 November, 1853.
17 Russell Jackson, "Victorian Theatre", A & C Black 1989.
18 Coventry Herald, 27 January, 1854.
19 David Anderson, "Forgotten Theatre Machinery: The Corsican Effect or Ghost Glide", Theatrephile Vol 1 No 4. September, 1984.
20 Coventry Herald, 3 February, 1854.
21 Coventry Herald, 7 April, 1854.
22 Coventry Herald, 31 March, 1854.
23 Suz Winspear, "Worcester's Lost Theatre", Parkbarn 1996.
24 Coventry Herald, 11 August, 1854.
25 Lou Warwick, "Theatre Un-Royal", Lou Warwick 1974.
26 Coventry Herald, 28 November, 1854.
27 Coventry Herald, 2 February, 1855.
28 Leslie Baily, "The Gilbert and Sullivan Book", Cassell & Company Ltd 1953.
29 Coventry Herald, 12 October, 1855.
30 Coventry Herald, 29 June, 1855.
31 Coventry Herald, 13 July, 1855.
32 Michael R. Booth, "Victorian Spectacular Theatre 1850–1910", Routledge and Kegan Paul 1981.
33 Coventry Herald, 10 August, 1855.
34 Aris Birmingham Gazette, 7 June, 1824.
35 Coventry Herald, 12 October, 1855.
36 Coventry Herald, 2 November, 1855.
37 Era Magazine, 4 November, 1855.
38 Coventry Herald, 21 September, 1855.
39 J.E. Cunningham MA, "Theatre Royal, Birmingham" George Ronald 1950.
40 John Coleman, "Fifty Years of an Actor's Life", James Pott & Co 1904.
41 Coventry Herald, 14 March, 1856.
42 Era Magazine, 13 July, 1856.
43 Coventry Herald, 8 August, 1856.
44 Coventry Herald, 17 October, 1856.
45 Era Magazine, 4 January, 1857.
46 Era Magazine, 11 January, 1857.
47 Suz Winspear, "Worcester's Lost Theatre", Parkbarn 1996.
48 Coventry Herald, 25 August, 1854.
49 Coventry Herald, 26 December, 1856.
50 Coventry Herald, 9 January, 1857.
51 Coventry Herald, 13 February, 1857.
52 Era Magazine, 1 March, 1857.
53 Herbert Marshall & Mildred Stock, "Ira Aldridge – The Negro Tragedian", The Macmillan Company New York 1958.
54 Phyllis Hartnoll (ed), "Oxford Companion to the theatre". O.U.P. 1965.
55 Coventry Herald, 8 May, 1857.
56 Coventry Herald, 12 June, 1857.
57 Theatrical Journal, 6 January, 1858.

Chapter 7

Rebuilding

On 11th June 1857 a meeting took place between John Dell (wine merchant), John Henry Prosser (chief constable), William Mabbatt, (hairdresser and perfumer), John Scampton (grocer and cheesemaker), Stephen Knapp (printer), Ralph Smyth, Henry James West, Oliver Minster (solicitor) and John Coleman who resolved unanimously to form *"The Coventry Lessee Company"* (limited liability) to purchase the lease of the New Theatre Royal and after enlarging and re-decorating it, make it available for operatic and dramatic performances. The Company was to have fifty shareholders, each of whom would subscribe £20 for a share.[1]

On 22nd June it was resolved to make those at the initial meeting, with the exception of John Coleman the lessee, directors of the new company which appointed the Coventry Union Banking Company as its treasurer. Oliver Minster had a meeting with Thomas Dewes, a fellow solicitor, about Coleman's position. Dewes pronounced that Coleman had no title to any position due to his insolvency. Perhaps not everything had been forgiven after all. The new company displaced him as lessee, a situation he appeared reluctant to accept, but they were not prepared to sub-lease the building to him on a permanent basis. Neither were Mr and Mrs Shepheard of Napton on the Hill, owners of the property, willing to re-lease the theatre unless the rent could be guaranteed. Mrs Henrietta Shepheard was, in fact, Henrietta Turland who had inherited the theatre from Sir Skears Rew. In the late 1840s she married Edward Shepheard who farmed 158 acres of land at Frankton near Rugby. The 1851 census shows that they had two children, Philip Edward and Henrietta. Unless they had other male children it would have been Philip's descendants who donated the oil painting of Sir Skears Rew to the Coventry Art Gallery in 1926. It has to be assumed that the theatre remained in the family until William Bennett purchased it in 1881.

> *"At the Police Office on Monday last [20th July], Mr W. Mabbatt applied for, and obtained, a licence for the Coventry Theatre for six months from the 20th inst. Mr Prosser and Mr J. Bell were accepted as sureties."*[1]

Thomas Pratt (of Exchange Chambers, Coventry) was appointed architect and his plans for the alterations were agreed within the week. An advertisement appeared in the 31st July edition of the *Herald* giving notice to local builders that plans and specifications were available for inspection on August 5th and that tenders were to be submitted, sealed and addressed to Mr Mabbatt, of 20 Hertford Street, by no later than 4.00 p.m. the following Monday, the 10th.[2] The proprietors pledged themselves not to necessarily accept the lowest bid. Mr Howe was duly appointed as the official contractor, his estimated costs being £185, not including gas for which he was charged during the alterations. He was paid £20 on account at various times during the following months. In addition to re-fashioning the auditorium, new dressing rooms were to be developed from two adjacent dwellings. The manager's house at the front of the building was unaffected. Although the Minute Book reveals Howe's costs of £185, Poole states the total charge to the directors was £1000, a sum which is difficult to reconcile with twenty first century prices and costs.

It would appear that Mabbatt leased the theatre from the Shepheards and, in turn, sub let it to various managers. This probably suited the farming family as they were neither theatre entrepreneurs nor on the spot. How long the hairdresser and perfumer had been speculating on the theatrical scene is not known but on the 10th August, a group of directors resolved that he should be paid £325 for the purchase of the fixtures and goodwill of the theatre and the £1,000 be deposited with Mr and Mrs Shepheard as security. The lease from Mabbatt to the new company began upon payment of the rent, rates, taxes of the current quarter.

One hundred new chairs for the dress circle were ordered from Hussey, of High Wycombe, with the stipulation they were to be the same design as supplied to the Corn Exchange in 1856, so it can be assumed they gave satisfaction. They were destined to replace all the benches in the centre lower boxes. Assuming each chair had a width of two feet, this number of chairs would have been sufficient for the entire tier except for the side boxes, which would have retained the benches.

William Mabbatt, who had been nominated Honorary Secretary for the new company, went to London to arrange for Mr Simpson to redecorate the house.

Mr Howe was allowed £8 for building a side wall within the excavations of the side boxes.

In September thirty five silver tickets, each costing 4s 9d were ordered for the purpose of allowing shareholders free access to the theatre.

Coleman's finances must have improved, as his offer of £40 to reopen the theatre until Christmas was accepted, so long as the sum was paid in advance. However the building work took longer than anticipated, so the figure was reduced to £30 to cover a shorter season. The minutes show that Coleman was expecting to have the theatre from year to year, as opposed to a long lease, for £150 per annum, subject to conditions as laid down by the company solicitor. In return, the company expected him to supply an entirely new act-drop.

The exact nature of the work undertaken is not detailed in either the Minute Book, the local newspapers or the *Era*, which was the only regular theatrical publication at that time. Benjamin Poole's "*Coventry, it's History and Antiquity (1870)*" suggests that the gallery was made more commodious and the boxes were enlarged by extending them backwards, thereby forming a new dress circle which was fitted out with chairs in place of benches. This would have been achieved by removing all or some of the box partitions and opening out this level into the rear vestibule thereby making the area resemble circles in later theatres. Since this was before the age of the cantilever, the wooden pillars placed to support the upper tier, and to which the box partitions would have been attached, remained and would have interfered, to some extent, with the sight lines.

> *"A new stage was erected at reduced height; the pit was also lowered three feet six inches, so as to permit of its extension under the boxes; thus procuring an enlargement whereby it was made to accommodate about four hundred and fifty persons."*

Unfortunately Poole gives no sources for this information, neither have details of these alterations been uncovered elsewhere. Lowering the ground floor and extending beneath the boxes was not an unknown alteration at this time and it also occurred later into the century.

In the 1850s there was a move nationally to substantially improve the quality of theatre buildings as a means of reversing the negative trend in patronage. Since there was uncertainty as to whether the theatrical fortunes could be restored, the emphasis was often placed on the less expensive renovation than the more costly replacement. Demolition and rebuilding, or drastic reconstruction, occurred at: The Effingham Saloon (1855), The Grecian, The Adelphi and The Britannia (1858) – all London venues. Nottingham Theatre Royal, in St Mary's Gate, was reconstructed by John Faucit Saville in the summer of 1854. Similar rebuilding occurred at Sheffield Theatre Royal in 1855 and Newcastle Theatre Royal in July 1857. In all these provincial examples the pit was lowered and taken beneath the dress circle boxes. It was not unknown for dress circles to be raised from their mezzanine position leaving the pits at the same level but capable of being extended backwards. Enlarging the ground floor accommodation by burrowing beneath the first circle was carried out at the Glasgow Tivoli as late as 1903, the Kings Lynn Royal in 1904 and London Haymarket in 1905.

Exactly what Poole meant by accommodating about 450 people is not clear. Did he mean the new pit held that new number? In 1853 this area accommodated 200 people. Extending beneath the boxes would not have yielded more than about

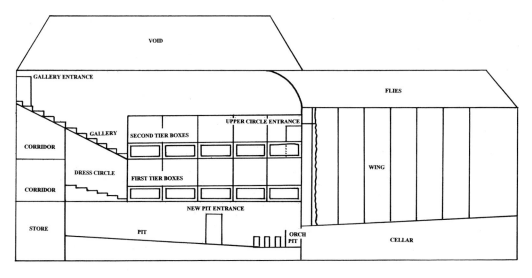

Figure 30   The Coventry Theatre: Impression of auditorium and stage after the alterations of 1857

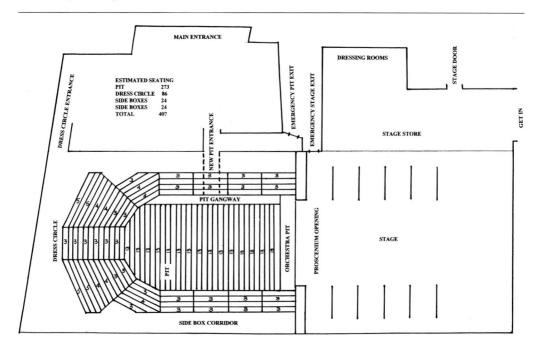

Figure 31   The Coventry Theatre: Impression of pit and first tier of boxes after the alterations of 1857

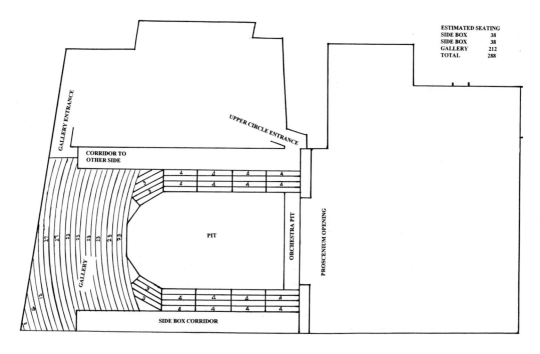

Figure 32   The Coventry Theatre: Impression of the second tier of boxes and gallery after the alterations of 1857

seventy additional seats at best. If he meant that the house held a new total of 450 people then it still isn't right, as the gallery probably held just over 200 people and the new dress circle may have seated around 86 (a reduction since chairs took up more room than benches). The upper boxes (still with benches) possibly accommodated 76 persons. Added together, this gives the house a rough total of just under 700. It is difficult to accommodate the figure of 450 into any plan.

An impression of the new seating accommodation can be summarised as follows: pit 273, dress circle 86, two first tier side boxes 48, second tier of boxes 76 and gallery 212 making a grand total of 695. This figure most certainly will have been reduced in the following years with the introduction of stalls seating and the completion of the second circle of boxes, which would have resulted in the loss of some gallery accommodation. More reductions are likely to have taken place as further degrees of comfort were introduced and attempts made to take into account the greater demands from the local magistrates for additional safety.

In constructing a plan of the reconditioned theatre, a number of assumptions have had to be made and for which no evidence exists. Decisions have been taken using knowledge of what occurred in other theatres of the period. The new pit entrance has been placed in the side wall beneath the manager's house. Its usual position by the side of the orchestra pit is not shown on the only photograph of the interior, therefore it is assumed it was moved either in 1857 or later. The year 1857 is the most likely date since the lowering of the stage would have interfered with the original passageway. It has been postulated that the usual scramble of patrons over the pit benches may have been eased by a narrow gangway near the entrance, a move which would have offset some of the gains in seating capacity by burrowing beneath the dress circle.

Lowering the stage would have necessitated a complete new set of traps and machinery and it is likely that the rakes of the boxes and gallery would have needed re-adjusting to maintain the correct sight lines. The opportunity to remove, or cut back, the proscenium stage and doors is likely to have taken place at this time, although there is no evidence for it. The Ipswich Theatre Royal retained its proscenium doors into the mid-1880s yet, on the other hand, the Leicester Theatre Royal opened in 1836 without any. Benjamin Wyatt initially disposed of proscenium doors in his new Drury Lane of 1811 but they were restored in a later rebuild, however, they were generally on the way out. By 1840, proscenium doors were becoming increasingly old fashioned in the capital; those at the Olympic had already been converted into private stage boxes.[3] During the rebuild of the London Haymarket in 1843, both the proscenium doors and forestage were eliminated thereby permitting additional, and more expensive, stalls seating to be incorporated into the vacant area. If such a move took place at Coventry, this would have represented a move which was apparently not common in the provinces at that time. No semblance of proscenium doors are visible in the only available interior photograph and it has been assumed they were removed, probably in 1857 but certainly before 1889.

In September it was reported that Mr Howe was to be paid £12, in place of the £20 agreed, on August 27 for alterations to the lower boxes; no reasons were given, neither was the nature of the work explained. Later in the month he was paid £23 for altering the arches over Mr Whittems' Vaults and a further sum for unspecified alterations to the upper boxes. It is possible that this was an attempt to connect the two rows of side boxes on the second tier with new additional boxes in the centre, a move which would have eliminated the front two or three rows of the gallery. Mr Whittems ran a wine and spirit shop in Smithford Street and had recently rented from Mr Shepheard, owner of the Theatre Royal, cellars beneath the theatre, together with an adjacent shed, for storage purposes. The City Record Office holds the original lease which was signed by Edward Shepheard and his wife Henrietta.

Money was obviously becoming tight as on 2nd October an application was made to the bankers for permission to overdraw the account by £150.

The alterations were a major undertaking and would have changed the Georgian appearance of the interior bringing it more into line with Victorian practice.

In the following two decades sufficient confidence in theatre viability lead to the construction of brand new theatre buildings which left the older ones, like Coventry – despite modernisation, increasingly at a disadvantage. Some areas of rapid population increase were able to sustain more than one theatre.[4] Coventry had not quite reached this point, although the conversion of the Corn Exchange into a Temple of Thespis was not far behind.

Extensions to the right hand side of the stage (if looking into the auditorium), took place at this time, along with new dressing rooms fashioned out of two adjacent dwelling houses, which brought this part of the theatre outside the building and afforded a safer means of escape in the event of fire. The houses were owned by Mr Mabbatt and it was resolved, on 3rd September, that he be paid an annual rent of £6 for them on top of "£17. 16s. 6d, for balance of rent and rates."[5] The 1888 Ordnance Survey map makes it clear that scenery and properties were unloaded in Vicar Lane and man-handled along the north side of the Congregational Chapel, although the two right angle bends would have made negotiating long cloths, and other pieces of scenery, difficult. It is likely that the stage door entrance led directly from Smithford Street down what is termed Court 2 to the dressing rooms. Before 1857, the dressing rooms were most likely placed beneath the stage and access to them gained from a doorway in the Theatre Yard.

By December it was minuted that Coleman had broken the terms of an agreement (the exact nature of his crime was not detailed) and the building was to go out to tender via the Coventry newspapers and *The Sunday Times* for a new lessee. Coleman's autobiography makes no mention of his tenure of the Theatre Royal, so the mystery is unsolved, although it is probably safe to suggest money was at the bottom of it. The advertisement yielded four replies from: Mr Chute, J.B. Clifford, who later ran the Workington Theatre Royal, Mr Hewlitt and Henry Nye Chart of the Brighton Theatre Royal. The last named gentleman was chosen to be the lucky lessee on the following conditions: his tenancy was to be from 26th December to the end of May for the sum of £120, to be paid: £50 forthwith and two bills of exchange for £35 each, to be drawn at two and three months each. He was to be given the opportunity to take the theatre from 2nd May to 1st November for £40. The Holding Company was to be responsible for all rates and repairs.[6]

Henry John Nye Chart [1821–1876]

In the meantime, hundreds were turned away on 9th November, 1857 for the re-opening of the theatre. The production was 'Hamlet', which had its share of stage mishaps, but such phenomena are common to a first night production even now. Some scenes failed to work properly and the lights either flared up or went out leaving the audience in darkness; auditoriums were not then dimmed during a performance. The *Herald* critic enjoyed the play, but rounded on the citizens of Coventry for only applauding the blood and guts actions and greeting the more subtle and finer scenes in stony silence.[7]

> *"The band is numerous and efficient – too numerous and too noisy. . . but please, Mr Conductor, however excellent your music, we do not want our ears stunned, or the roof of our little theatre blown off."*[8]

Instead of commenting on the changes within the auditorium, the drama critic of the *Herald* vented his spleen on the new act-drop. Whether this is the one demanded from Coleman is not made clear. The writer produced a considerable amount of copy exclaiming his personal disgust with the new drop which showed Lady Godiva and her husband, the Earl Leofric. His summary was thus expressed, *"this wretched daub is beneath criticism and contempt"* and it *"is a good idea villainously carried out."*[9] One wonders whether he thought it rude.

Coleman was still officially the lessee, but his tenure lasted only until the beginning of the winter season on 28th December, 1857. After a short while, the novelty of a 'new' theatre began to wear off and more and more empty seats were in evidence. Coleman did everything to please, *"but times are bad and money, as everyone knows is scarce."*[10]

Henry John Nye Chart took charge on December 28th, 1857[11] He was born Henry John Chart adding Nye, the surname of a friend who was an amateur actor, later. Starting life as an apprenticed piano manufacturer, he later became a professional actor with what was described as a rich and racy humour, and was later the leading managerial light at the Brighton Theatre Royal (which he bought in 1866) from 1854 until his death.[12] His stay in Coventry, however, was only of two years duration, ending on May 9, 1859. Finding a suitable second theatre was probably important to Chart so that he could keep his stock company together when the season finished at Brighton. The alternative was for the performers to seek employment elsewhere leaving the manager to begin from scratch the following year, an unenviable task especially if his last company was a good one. The dead season at Brighton was usually between the beginning of the year and July, which fitted in reasonably well with the available dates at Coventry.

The English Opera Company, a recurring visitor to Coventry, opened the new 1858 season with a variety of works with Elliott Galer as the leading tenor. On January 2nd, during a performance of '*The Beggar's Opera*' at Coventry, Galer had cause to complain, whether from the stage or privately is not known, "*of the carelessness and want of attention on the part of the orchestra, which in some measure marred the effect of the piece.*"[13]

Whereas in the earlier part of the century, the normal bill of fare consisted of two main plays, or one main drama and a couple of shorter and lighter pieces, together with songs and dances in-between, the pattern was now changing which, in effect, reduced the length of the theatrical evening. Charles Kean at the London Princess's Theatre led the new fashion, which was to present a main play preceded by a curtain raiser, or '*levers de rideau*', which was often a one-act play, of little consequence or value, by way of an *hors-d'oeuvre* to the main course. Frequently patrons missed the curtain raiser and only arrived for the main play. It is interesting to compare this with current practice where theatre goers seem intent on enduring as short an evening as possible, which is aided by productions frequently having but one interval only.

Attendances, not noted for being large, were becoming progressively thinner and the severe depression within the silk and ribbon industry, the main employment in the town, was largely responsible. The demand for ribbons had altered, along with changes in ladies' fashions and cheap imports from the far east, China and India, did not help matters. Later, in 1860, a treaty with France enabled many articles, including foreign ribbons, to be imported duty-free which worsened the situation. The ensuing depression within the town was severe and long lasting, the former levels of production and employment never fully recovered and, although additional industry in wool, cotton and elastic was brought in to fill the vacuum, the situation remained grim.[14] This was to have a serious and lasting impact upon the fortunes of the theatre, especially in view of the rising number of emerging alternative cheaper entertainments. The immediate effect was a reduction in bookings, shorter seasons and frequent changes of lessee. Unemployment among manual workers can explain the meagre attendances in the pit and gallery, but one has to look elsewhere for the regular pattern of empty boxes. Except for a short fillip in the spring of 1858, their patronage was beggarly.

The half yearly accounts, presented by the Coventry Lessee Company in February 1858, showed a loss of £61 11s. 8d, which may explain why Chart was offered, and agreed, to take the theatre for £180 – £60 more than was originally asked.[15] This figure was later raised to £200 from 1st May and included the dwelling house and dressing rooms which were customarily let separately, although how companies could have managed without the latter is difficult to understand. It is like going into a restaurant and being charged extra for use of the table. Chart was also required to pay for the licence and allow the Company a Benefit in the winter season.

Chart may have recouped something from staging his Brighton pantomime, which he presented at the beginning of March, to good houses. Transporting properties, scenery and costumes from the southern watering hole would have been made easier with the developing railway system, as opposed to toll roads. The 1858–9 season only lasted six weeks, contained fewer classical productions and more 'popular' plays. March saw the pantomime, '*Little Red Riding Hood and Baron Von Wolf or Harlequin Little Boy Blue, Dame Durden and Old Gammer Gurton*'. Victorian managers delighted in creating pantomime titles of inordinate length, which included the characters of Harlequin, Columbine, Pantaloon, Punchinello, Scaramouch et al from the Italian Commedia del Arte, and from where our native pantomime originated. The production would be unrecognisable as such today and was short enough to share the evening with a full length drama or comedy.

March 1858 saw one of the frequent renderings of '*The Corsican Brothers*'. The ghost scene was well brought out *"but if light had been thrown on the countenance of the ghost of Louis dei Franchi, it would have added materially to the effect, as the majority of the audience scarcely knew that the same person who fought the duel represented the ghost."*[16] This was before the advent of electric follow spot lights and the lighting effect called for could only have been achieved using the highly dangerous limelight. [see page 117]

On April 21st 1858, Nye Chart secured a twelve month lease of the Theatre Royal, Clemens Street, Leamington Spa from the local magistrates, being bound by the sum of £200 and supported by Mabbatt and John Dell of Coventry. His Brighton Company opened a three week season there with Sheridan's '*The Rivals*'.[17] His stay was successful and it is possible he may have seen Leamington as a safety net, should the Coventry season turn 'pear shaped'.

Chart was back at Coventry in May with '*Belphegor*' on the menu.

"We should be inclined to give Miss Seton a word of praise for her Francois, did not this lady show rather too much an inclination to appear in male habiliments, at least if we may judge by the frequency of her appearances in such attire. It is a custom we cannot approve of, but whether the lady or her manager is most to blame we have no opportunity of ascertaining. Miss Seton shows excellent taste in dressing the characters of her own sex, that we would wish never to see her in any other."[18]
Oh dear!

On Chart's admission the season had not been a financial success. Plays which failed to pass muster did not help fill seats. His 'Nicholas Nickleby' came in for heavy criticism.

"To those of the audience who had not read the original, the drama must have been perfectly unintelligible; while to the rest it was tiresome and unsatisfactory".[19]

In May 1858 there were problems with water under the stage and the directors ordered Howe to make suitable repairs to the drainage system for £3 5s. 6d.

Chart was obviously a popular actor manager and in May was offered a ten year lease at £200 for the theatre without the former manager's house or £215 with it included. The theatre's accounts showed a profit of £3 17s. 3d. The place was just ticking over.

Queen Victoria and Prince Albert paid an official visit to Coventry and Stoneleigh Abbey on June 14th, 1858. Special events took the form of a concert at the Corn Exchange and a performance of the comedy '*The Queen's Visit*', subtitled '*The Peasants journey from village to court*', followed by the '*Queensbury Fete*' at the Theatre Royal. It would appear the monarch brought with her a heat wave which thinned down the numbers at both events, neither of which the royal party attended.

Chart booked Miss Goddard, the Australian tragedienne, and Mr Swanborough for three nights from July 26, 1858, one of the plays being '*Hamlet*', although it was not Swanborough who took the title role. Female Hamlets, including Mrs Glover, had been seen before and have been known since. Despite favourable press coverage in other towns on her tour, this interpretation did not impress. Her false, inflated and unreal style, together with her attempt to assume a masculine voice with vowels stretched out long enunciations and were roundly condemned.[20] However, the lady did not stay long as she was booked at the Worcester Theatre Royal on the 29th July during Cavalry week, where her performances were given 'loud' praise in the local press.

In September certain unspecified alterations were carried out to the lower boxes for which Mr Needham was paid £13 10s. Fifty dress circle chairs were sold to defray the cost. Money was in short supply and one of the directors (Mr Lutyens) offered the company a loan of £250 which was accepted.

Mons. Desarais stayed six nights from 27th September with his Parisian troupe of performing dogs and monkeys, which attracted better houses than the normal dramatic fare.

Individuals from the developing music halls occasionally called at Coventry for one or two nights. Sam Houghton Cowell [1820–1864], a fugitive from opera and 'straight' plays, made an appearance covering 15th and 16th December 1858.[21] His father, Joseph, had been a member of the York Theatre Company. Sam was born in London but reared in America where he picked up Negro melodies from the 'deep south' and made them his own. At thirty eight years of age, and with a national reputation of singing the Music Hall songs of the day, he graduated from Evans' Supper Rooms in London and was chosen for Morton's inaugural bill at the Lambeth Canterbury Music Hall that year.[22] His frequent tours took in Coventry on a number of occasions in the 1850s. His life was cut short after contracting a virulent form of consumption in 1864.[23]

On Tuesday February 22, 1859 Mr D'Oyley (not to be confused with D'Oyly Carte of Gilbert and Sullivan fame) transgressed too near the naked gas jets, which set his costume afire. Misses Delafield and Conway, on stage at the time, managed to extinguish the conflagration and the performance continued without injury.[24] This was by no means a rare event in any theatre and was the reason wire guards were placed in front of the footlights, and the bunch lights in the wings, though such precautions did not always prevent serious injuries or fatalities during the era of gas lighting. The season ended around this time and the *Herald* expressed doubt as to whether Chart had made any money out of it.

The Mayor gave patronage to a performance of '*Sweethearts*' in April 1859 which was well attended, except that other members of the Town Council were noticeably absent. A stinging attack came from the *Herald*.

> "*We are sorry. . . .because the theatre is now most respectably conducted, and if it is to be supported only by the gallery and pit, the performances which are now of the most unexceptional character, will eventually be lowered in tone to suit the lower morale of the uneducated class. . .*"[25]

The 'educated' classes continued to ignore such comments with predictable regularity.

It would appear that Chart only hired the theatre building in May 1859 as it was reported that a Mr Harrison had been accepted as a suitable tenant for the former manager's house at an annual rent of £15.

Nye Chart brought his Brighton Company to play a part of the season which ended on May 9th. His short stay was recorded an artistic success, but financially disappointing.

No matter how popular Chart was with the directors, he wasn't making any money and indicated a wish to terminate his tenancy. The directors permitted him to have the theatre for seven nights from May 2nd for five guineas to help him recoup his losses, but they later agreed to waive all fees. Chart's venture to Coventry was described thus ". . .*houses as bare as Lady Godiva with nothing to wear.*"[26]

Towards the end of May, Chart's Company tried their luck by opening for a season in the Doncaster Theatre Royal, a building he had not acted in for seven years.[27]

To help reduce mounting losses at Coventry, free access previously ascribed to the directors was curbed, instead their silver tickets permitted half-price admission to most sections of the house.

In June 1859 Henry Powell, of Leicester Theatre Royal from November, 1858 to August, 1859 was accepted as the new tenant to replace Chart for twelve months from 4th July, 1859; £100 to be paid forthwith and two sums of £50 at various intervals. In March, 1860, when Powell assumed the lesseeship of the Leicester Theatre Royal, he was offered a seven year lease at Coventry for £200 per annum, he being responsible for both internal and external repairs. The manner by which the rent increased and the burden of repairs was shifted to the tenant, illustrated a declining financial stability. The Company Minutes recorded the wish of several directors to sell the property. This was temporarily reversed by suggesting each shareholder should lend the company £2 at 5% interest to keep things going.

Henry Powell

Powell spread his interests far and wide for he was already in charge at Leicester Theatre Royal and the Theatre Royal, North Shields and he was later to be associated with theatres at, Durham, Whitby, Swansea, Wolverhampton, Oldham, Bolton and London Sadler's Wells. He opened in Coventry on October 31st. The

Herald correspondent could never understand why the Coventry season always began after Christmas, considering the nights beforehand were just as long and dark. Historically the season occupied the first three months of the year, since the company played in other towns for the rest of the twelve months, but by 1859 the circuit system had virtually disappeared, and there was no reason why the theatre could not be opened at other times of the year, except that the national touring system had not developed sufficiently to fill the gaps. There had to be a question as to whether sufficient local patronage existed to keep the theatre open for longer.

The pantomime, '*Puss in Boots*' or '*Harlequin and the Family of the Golden Palms*', emerged on Boxing Day and lasted several weeks, being well supported, except for the boxes. During the overture, the curtain, which either rose in a series of festoons or was rolled (there being no fly tower) revealed an act-drop covered with advertisements. The act-drop would have been a rolled canvas with a scene, often local in character or something depicting classical art, and was raised and lowered at the beginning and end of each act – hence the name. The main curtain would have been used only at the beginning and end of the play. Powell would have gained revenue from such advertisements, which were familiar to the theatre going public in later years through the cloths organised by Stilwell and Darby, and which were on view both before the performance and during the intervals. The quality of scene painting of '*Puss in Boots*' caused such an uproar of approval that the entire pantomime opening went on in a dumb show.

John Coleman, the former lessee, paid several visits, as guest actor, to Coventry where he received a warm and rapturous welcome, even during the height of the recession. J. Robinson took his benefit on January 31st. The boxes were all but empty, but many were turned away from the pit and gallery. In '*Hamlet*', "*the ghost was effective until he spoke – he was imperfect in his part.*"[28]

On February 23, 1860 John, or James Townsend, the ex-Liberal member of parliament for Greenwich, decided to impart his skills as a tragic actor on the unsuspecting playgoers in Coventry. He was an ex-member of parliament due to a declared bankruptcy. Originally an auctioneer by profession, he decided to go on the stage owing to a surfeit of auctioneers in the market place. The experiment seemed to be somewhat unwise for "*he may have been a good auctioneer or a useful legislator, but he was certainly never intended by nature for an actor...*"[29] Townsend had entered into a brief management at the Leicester Theatre Royal from the autumn, 1859 to March, 1860 but suffered pecuniary loss and was unable to pay his rent.[30] One of the problems at Leicester was his disapproval of the audiences enjoying 'Blood and Thunder' pieces, for his ambition was to give entertainment of a higher and more worthy nature, but this didn't fill seats. In 1858, he suffered humiliation at the hands of the gallery in the role of '*Richard III*' at Margate Theatre Royal then under the management of Richard Thorne. His inability to pronounce the letter 'r' made it a lisping performance, which exasperated the house. "*When in the business of the scene he fell on his face a voice from the gallery shouted "Turn him over", a request that was chorused by many others.*"[31] His time on the boards was limited and he soon retired from thespian activities; maybe there was a surfeit of good tragedians.

Fewer companies came to the town outside the season as few of the 60,000 souls had the wherewithal to exist, let alone find money for entertainment. An 1861 season was not expected, but Powell decided to take the risk. It was deemed a gamble for reasons other than poor financial returns, "... *and not to wonder at if the few who are there are in a position to pay for amusement of this kind find empty spaces about them more potent to prevent a second visit than the performance to attract.*"[32] As one who can recall being in an audience of sixteen people for a variety show at the 800-seat Chesterfield Theatre, this statement reflects much truth. The local recession would have affected the wealthier classes less so. In addition to any dramatic disenchantment, there was a strong nonconformist element which promulgated the theatre as the anti-chamber to hell. This sentiment later transferred itself to the music halls. As late as 1905, when the Boscombe Grand became the Hippodrome variety theatre, the owner of the property opposite erected on his roof a marble figure of the devil, which was fixed facing the 'den of evil', as a timely warning to members of the public to keep away. This was not very effective as variety remained in full sway until the early 1950s.

In the face of worsening financial returns, all silver tickets were sold in July 1861 and the directors were barred from free or half price entrance. They had to pay full fare like everyone else.

Powell could not make money either at Coventry or Leicester and so gave up the former in 1861, to be replaced by John Mosley, who was described as being from the borough of Bradford.

Newspaper advertisements for the Royal were almost non-existent at this time, information being available only from the weekly criticisms printed in the local newspaper. There is little doubt that performance details were available on printed circulars, or 'fliers' pasted to walls and hoardings, and seen by the passing public. It is unlikely that the main supporters of the theatre, those who frequented the pit and gallery, bought newspapers. Theatre business seemed bad everywhere and the situation in Coventry was not helped by an eight week strike of ribbon workers in the summer months. Mr Johnson, a Wesleyan preacher from Derby, delivered a sermon in the theatre to a crowded house, resulting in a collection for the Weavers' Fund of £5 10s. Sermons were given there on succeeding Sundays for a while.

Mr and Mrs Charles Kean returned to play '*The Wife's Secret*' and '*John Bull in France*' in June, but there was no critical write up.

John Mosley [1806–1869]

John Mosley took over the lease at the beginning of the 1861–2 season for a fee of £150. Born in Nottingham, he spent many years touring the provinces, but branched into management by opening a theatre in Melton Mowbray around 1837 and the original Bradford Theatre Royal in 1846. Yorkshire became his home where he became responsible for theatres in Halifax, Huddersfield and Wakefield for many years until around the mid 1860s. The year 1857 saw him opening a new theatre in Douglas, Isle of Man, so he was a seasoned and experienced manager by the time he took on Coventry – perhaps one of the more challenging experiences of his life. The new Coventry season began with three weeks of Shakespeare and the classics, the company being swelled by Kate Saville and Tom Swinbourne, both from London, the latter being a member of Henry Irving's company at the Lyceum in later years. Kate Saville's father, John Faucit Saville junior, was connected with the theatres in Derby and Nottingham, the last being rebuilt in 1854, until his death at the end of 1855. Kate [d 1922] and her mother took over the old Nottingham Theatre Royal in St Mary's Gate from John until the opening in 1865 of the present theatre, which they leased between 1867 and 1869. Tom Swinbourne [1823–1895] had a deep toned 'quietness' and a manner of acting which was regarded as scholarly and expert. Although the Coventry silk trade began to improve, the great mass of unemployed, by their sheer numbers, perpetuated the cycle of low wages so that those who found employment were little better off financially.

Howe's work in 1858 had not permanently solved the drainage problem beneath the stage and in December 1861 the directors proposed that a mason be employed to repair them properly. Instructions were also given to have the dressing rooms repaired although the nature of the problem was not recorded in the Minute Book.

A taste of things to come was seen in September 1862 with the booking of Templeton's Renowned African Troupe, which offered a type of music hall entertainment. The result did not impress the *Herald*.

> "*. . . the musical part was a burlesque mirroring the Christy Minstrels. Voices made up in energy what they lacked in sweetness. The Music Hall is a sort of scientific cross between the theatre and pot house; but the want of order in the theatre on Monday night would have disgraced Music Hall or even gin palace, there was not the least effort made, that we could see, to suppress either the noisy blackguardism of the gallery or the smoking in the pit. The proprietary must irretrievably damage their property by allowing (it) to be used in such a way.*"[33]

John Coleman Chute [1819–1913]

The directors of the theatre recorded in the Minute Book that John Chute was to have the theatre for three months starting from 26th December, there being a stipulation that the theatre was to be open for not less than thirty nights.

According to the *Coventry Herald*, Chute had come from the Birmingham Theatre Royal. This was not the prestigious building in New Street, the successor of which survived until 1956, but the New Theatre Royal, later the Adelphi, in Moor Street which, during its short turbulent seven year existence, was adept in swallowing large fortunes of its many managers and Chute's short period of management did not improve matters there. Brother to James Henry Chute of the Bristol and Bath theatres in the 1850s, he had spread his theatrical talents far and wide, having controlled the Temple Street Theatre, Swansea, in the 1850s and 1860s. Later he was to try his luck managing the Liverpool Theatre Royal for three months from January 1880, and the Bury St Edmunds Theatre Royal between

October 2nd 1877 and 1882. This last was fully restored by him at the start of a ten year lease.

The *Coventry Herald* was silent regarding any theatrical activities at the beginning of the year possibly for the reason that Chute was proving elusive. The Minute Book contains copies of two letters sent on the instruction of the directors to the new manager. The first was dated 7th January, 1863.

> "*Dear Sir, At a meeting of the Directors of the Coventry Theatre Company held this evening their attention was called to the fact of the theatre having been closed the whole of this week and they have directed me as chairman to write to you for an explanation, an answer by return will oblige. Yours respectfully, W. Read*".

Chute's response was not recorded but it warranted an immediate reply which was dated 19th January, 1863.

> "*Sir, In reply to your letter the Directors wish me to say they cannot engage to assist you in increasing the attendance at the theatre. At the same time they will expect you to fulfil your engagement, or at once offer a compromise. Yours respectfully, W. Read.*"

The first productions advertised in the *Herald* did not take place until 27th March, which was but a week from the Easter holidays and the end of Chute's tenure, although it is likely the theatre was open before that. Chute was experiencing the same problems that befell Chart and other managers throughout the country.

Sensational pieces were tried at Coventry but only attracted small houses. Sam Cowell, once a common performer at the Royal, defected to the larger Corn Exchange. The continuing difficulty in trade only encouraged the management to stage the lightest of theatrical fare in the hope of attracting custom. Chute's tenure landed him into bankruptcy in July 1863, with debts of over £5000.[34]

J.H.Doyne and F. Maitland

Chute's failure led to another management team, J.H.Doyne and F. Maitland, later associated with the London Globe in the Aldwych, to try their luck from April with a season which heavily relied on box office favourites as opposed to the classics. G.V.Brooke, the '*idol of the provinces*', gave '*Othello*' at the end of the season on May 17, to "*a tolerable house.*"

Dolman

Doyne and Maitland chose not to carry on and the reins were assumed by Dolman, as the new lessee and manager, from the end of November 1863. Admission prices were lowered but thin houses continued. A rival in the form of Penny Readings made additional inroads into the theatre's profitability. These local amateur entertainments, arranged at the Corn Exchange, were given on a weekly basis and consisted of a dozen or more items including songs, instrumental music, speeches, scenes from Shakespeare, and extracts read from great works of literature – and all for a penny, although a few extra coppers would secure more comfortable accommodation nearer the front. The *Herald* blamed this weekly entertainment for reducing the attendance at the theatre to a new low. The boxes were already empty but now gaps were obvious in both pit and gallery.[35]

In December 1863 John Goode, a printer by trade, entered into a lease with Edward Shepheard, to rent 18, Smithford Street, for the sum of £43/8/- per annum. Part of the building had been occupied by Thomas Dewes, the solicitor who acted for *"The Coventry Lessee Company"* when the Theatre Royal was rebuilt in 1857. Number 18 had its own roadway access to the street. Was this Smithford Street property originally part of Rew's empire inherited by Henrietta Shepheard (nee Turland), and could it have been one of the buildings William Bennett failed to purchase in 1880 and which might have allowed him to rebuild the theatre nearer the main road?[36]

Godiva Music Hall

At the beginning of 1864, the first of the city's recorded regular public house music halls emerged to swell the opposition. A notice in the February 12 edition of the *Herald*, announced that the Godiva 'Concert' Room, at 21 Bond Street, had been considerably enlarged, *"and not withstanding that other places of amusement are comparatively a failure, this room is not infrequently crammed."* Run by Thomas Skeen Ratcliffe, the assembly room had been converted into a small music hall where, for a few coppers, many emerging entertainers in this form of working class entertainment could be seen whilst patrons upturned a glass of ale or ate a pork pie. A Godiva Inn has not been identified, in fact John Ashby (*"The Character of Coventry"*, John Ashby, 2001) lists the Castle Tavern at 21, Bond Street, so it is more likely the Godiva Music Hall was the name given to the assembly room there. A large scale map shows the building to have a frontage of approximately 27 feet and a depth of around 37 feet which cannot be described as large. Almost certainly the assembly room was placed on the first floor, and the conditions are likely to have given any Health and Safety organisation at the time a degree of apoplexy.

A typical evening's entertainment consisted of five or six acts. The names of those who appeared mean little to us in the twenty-first century, but in April there appeared Messrs Nunn and Montgomery, who had transferred from Holder's Music Hall, Birmingham. Outlets for performers were few, yet Holder's had a degree of prestige being one of two the principal music halls in Birmingham at that time, the other being Day's. Holder's later became the Gaiety Music Hall.

Richard Thorne [1813–1875]

Richard Samuel Thorne, actor, manager and dramatist and associated with theatres in Bolton, Blackburn, Preston, Dundee and the Pavilion in the East End of London, was also lessee of the Margate Royal at the time of assuming control of the

Coventry Royal in March, 1864, when much publicity was made of Shakespeare's ter-centenary. He was also father of the legendary Sarah and sired nine other children, all but one taking to the stage.[37] Attendance worsened and two performances were cancelled, money being refunded at the door owing to poor houses. The advice of the *Herald* was for the management to lower the admission prices still further – *"as elsewhere."*

The Royal English Opera, normally a guarantor for good houses, only managed meagre support during its week's stay in May. Meanwhile the Godiva Music Hall, often booking as many as five different performers a night, was open every evening for business.

Violet Campbell

Violet Campbell became the newest lessee on October 3, 1864. The *Herald* incautiously predicted the new company would enjoy a greater degree of success than previous managements.[38] Dion Boucicault's *'Streets of London'*, with its spectacular house inferno and horse drawn fire appliance, drew greater numbers into the pit and gallery for the three nights than hitherto. The play originated as the *'Poor of New York'* in 1857, and was adapted as the *'Poor of Liverpool'*, when presented at the Amphitheatre there in 1864. So successful was it that when the piece toured, the title was changed, localising the scenes wherever it went – the *'Poor of Leeds'*, *'The Poor of Manchester'*, and so on. The title finally changed to *'The Streets of London'* when it arrived at the Princess's in London's Oxford Street. Boucicault's melodrama contained vivid spectacle which probably appealed more than the plot to the pit and gallery audiences.[39] The attraction of similar visual exhibitions occurs in our own times; *'The Phantom of the Opera'* and *'Les Miserables'* being obvious examples.

The theatre literally went to the dogs with the exhibition of a troupe of performing canines in November, although it did not find favour with the *Herald*.

> *"If the playgoing public of Coventry will not support respectable tragedy, and will have nothing to do with genteel comedy, what can the poor players do but try something that may be considered a little more "spicy" by those whose intellectual palates it is their business to cater for."*[40]

The remainder of the season, despite expensive visiting performers of acclaim (Mr & Mrs Drayton and Madame Celeste), was a disaster. Comments in the *Herald* such as, *"attendances pretty fair"* and *"we feel constrained to make another appeal to the public in behalf of this much neglected institution"* and *". . . attractive programme which has not received the support deserved"*, indicated that matters could not last indefinitely. A week's opera in January 1865 did well, however the last dramatic performance was held on March 29, as a benefit for J. Barnwell, the performance being interspersed with Nigger melodists of the Christy Minstrel variety. Dramatic fare at the Theatre Royal was, to intents and purposes, over for the time being.

The Godiva, on the other hand, went from strength to strength. It could be favourably compared to similar establishments in other towns, and in order to accommodate the increasing patronage, a gallery was erected in December 1864, this being considered of great benefit for those not wishing to attend the body of the hall. From this one assumes the balcony was designed to be more attractive towards female companions of male habitués as they would not have to mix with the melee normally associated with an ale house bar. A proscenium was added, thereby making the hall more like a theatre in appearance. With an array of artificial flowers, neatly executed mottoes, flags and banners, the interior was considered very good. During the Christmas week, over 4,000 people sampled its wares.

Ratcliffe had summed up the mood of the populace by creating a market to fill a vacuum in local entertainment.

> "*His (Ratcliffe) establishment contrasts most favourably with very many similar places of entertainment in other towns and there is an air of propriety and order pervading the concert room...Music Halls are everywhere becoming a favourite resort of the people.*"[41]

The silk trade remained in a poor state, although business picked up later in the year in time for Latimer's Mammoth Travelling Theatre, which played a short season on the Pool Meadow ground (the site of the first corrugated iron Hippodrome in 1903), and a Marionette show was temporarily housed in the Chapel Yard, Well Street.[42]

Since 1862, the Theatre Royal Board of Directors had put forward resolutions to dispose of their unremunerative property and after years of prevaricating, they finally decided to dissolve the company and sell the lease in pursuant of the Companies Act of 1862. Henry Suffolk, accountant, was appointed liquidator and instructed to wind up the affairs and distribute the property. Detailed information for the years 1857 to 1865 is found in the Company's Minute Book (Coventry Record Office), and as nothing of the kind exists outside these dates, details of the owners, as opposed to lessees, are not always clear from that time onwards until William Bennett bought the property in 1880, one assumes, from the Shepheard family. In the meantime it is interesting to note that one of the directors, John Dell, acquired the lease of the building from the former company and renamed it the New Royal Theatre of Varieties. Drama did not work, perhaps music hall would.

1 Coventry Herald, 17 July, 1857.
2 Coventry Herald, 31 July, 1857.
3 Gorel Garlick, "To Serve the Purpose of the Drama", The Theatre Designs and Plays of Samuel Beazley 1786–1851, Society for Theatre Research 2003.
4 Theatre Notebook, Volume XXXIX 1984. "Thirty Years Struggle: Entertainment in Provincial Towns between 1840 and 1870" – Kathleen Barker.
5 Minutes of the Coventry Theatre, Coventry Record office.
6 Minutes of the Coventry Theatre, Coventry Record Office.
7 Coventry Herald, 13 and 20 November, 1857.
8 Coventry Herald, 20 November, 1857.
9 Coventry Herald, 13 November, 1857.
10 Coventry Herald, 27 November, 1857.
11 Coventry Standard, 25 December, 1857.
12 Antony Dale, "Brighton Theatre Royal", Oriel Press 1980.
13 Coventry Herald, 8 January, 1858.
14 Poole, "History and Antiquities of Coventry" 1870.
15 Theatre Royal Minute Book, Coventry Record Office.
16 Coventry herald, 26 March, 1858.
17 Leamington Spa Courier, 10 April, 1858.
18 Era Magazine, 2 May, 1858.
19 Coventry Herald, 7 May, 1858.
20 Coventry Herald, 30 July, 1858.
21 Coventry Standard, 10 December, 1858.
22 Chance Newton, "Idols of the Halls", EP Publishing 1975.
23 W. Macqueen Pope, "The Melody Lingers On", W.H.Allen.
24 Coventry Herald, 25 February, 1859.
25 Coventry Herald, 1 April, 1859.
26 Theatre Notebook, Volume XXXIX No 1 1985, "Thirty Years of Struggle: Entertainment in Provincial Towns between 1840 and 1870", Kathleen Barker.
27 Theatrical Journal, 25 May, 1859.
28 Coventry Herald, 27 January, 1859.
29 Coventry Herald, 24 February, 1860.
30 Richard and Helen Leacroft, "Theatres in Leicestershire", Leicestershire Libraries 1986.
31 Malcolm Morley, "Margate and its Theatres", London Museum Press 1966.
32 Coventry Herald, 11 January, 1861.
33 Coventry Herald, 3 October, 1862.
34 Cambrian, 10 July, 1863.
35 Coventry Herald, 4 December, 1863.
36 Theatre Royal Minute Book, Coventry Record Office.
37 Malcolm Morley, "Margate and its Theatres", London Museum Press, 1966.
38 Coventry Herald, 7 October, 1864.
39 Richard Fawkes, "Dion Boucicault", Quartet Books 1979.
40 Coventry Herald, 4 November, 1864.
41 Coventry Herald, 25 November, 1864.
42 Coventry Herald, 16 and 30 June, 1865.

Chapter 8

Music Hall

Mr John Dell

The new lessee was Mr John Dell, with Mr Tighe as his resident musical conductor and with an attractive bill the doors of the Theatre Royal Music Hall opened on November 13th, 1865, to a crowded house, many being turned away.

The opening programme sounds uninspiring by today's standards as it comprised: a prima donna, a ballad singer, a tenor, comic singer, gymnast, a baritone together with choruses and glees.[1] The entertainment went down well, and for a time the proceedings were overseen by George Allen, who was engaged from the Islington Philharmonic Music hall, afterwards known as the Grand and later the Empire theatre, a prestigious London suburban house which ended up as a cinema. The new prices at Coventry ranged from 3d to 1s. Booking a bill of individual acts was less expensive than arranging a touring dramatic company with larger overheads, and the new lower admission prices were more within the means of the local clientele.

For several months, workmen had been engaged on a number of internal alterations. Amongst these were the removal of the partitions which formed the back of the dress circle boxes and making a bar from the former ladies' cloak room. Other bars were added to the pit and gallery levels too (probably in what had been the manager's house) and in the latter, a portion of the floor was lowered but it is not stated by how much or exactly where this was. It is possible that the pit benches were replaced by a series of tables and chairs to create sufficient space for waiters to reach customers for their orders of food and drink, an amenity which, one assumes, was not available to patrons in the circle and gallery.

Drury of Warwick undertook a complete re-decoration of the interior which included touching up existing scenery and adding new sets. The music hall venture kept the building open and viable until a time when the return to drama was deemed sufficiently economic. A similar pattern was seen in the 1950s when Bingo companies opened for trade in former theatres, some of which have since returned to their original function.

The engagement of artists was not on a weekly basis, but seemed to last as long as their individual popularity remained buoyant. Marie Tressillian, prima donna, was on the opening bill along with Amelia Sestin, Mr Blewitt, Master Poole, Signor

Ellistra and she stayed until the following May. Others lasted a week or two, before being replaced by newer acts. The once nightly entertainment commenced at 7.00 p.m. and the theatre, once again, became popular and crowded houses were frequently reported.

Mr Tighe did not remain long, being replaced by Mr Rees after which "*a considerable improvement in the band*" was recorded.[2] Some artists of note for the period were booked. J.George Forde (1831–1873) was popular enough to warrant staging an earlier performance on March 27, to enable inhabitants of Bedworth, Nuneaton, Leamington and Warwick the opportunity of seeing him before catching their last trains home. He was acknowledged by the critic, H. Chance Newton, as

> "*one of the greatest comic patterers ever seen on the music hall boards. He never changed his dress for the stage and wore a long frock coat, a heavy black moustache, a little dab of red on his nose and a mop of black hair (his own) which was agitated violently whenever he reached a certain point in a remark.*"[3]

Reminiscent of Stan Laurel perhaps!

Advertising for the Godiva Music Hall completely disappeared from the *Herald* after the re-opening of the Royal. In the absence of other evidence, it is difficult to know whether it succumbed with the advent of weightier competition, or that hand bills were sufficient to attract a profitable business in which the two ran in tandem; however, the inauguration of the Royal Music Hall was probably an ominous event for the smaller house. The Castle Inn, where it is assumed the Godiva Music Hall operated, had become a butcher's shop by 1874, so any opposition to the Royal would have ceased by that date.[4]

The 1866 season opened on October 1st to crowded houses. The tide of fortune had seemingly turned for the better.

Fred Allford

A long summer break took place between June 9th and October 1st 1866, when a new manager, Fred Allford, took charge. George Allen later took up the post of manager at the Nottingham Alhambra Music Hall, previously known as the Theatre Royal before the building of the present theatre in 1865. During the recess, further decoration had taken place and a new drop scene painted. Allford engineered a different formula at Coventry which kept the populace returning time and time again. Sam Newsome, of the third Coventry Hippodrome, did exactly the same a hundred years later, when he put before the public the unique round of pantomimes, Spring Shows, tours, and Birthday Shows. Derek Salberg at the Birmingham Alexandra Theatre evolved his own successful formula, which was not commonly found elsewhere.

Allford introduced dramatic spectacle in addition to music hall turns, although newspaper reports indicated that these acts were incorporated into the plot. The productions, all written by Allford himself, had little dramatic quality about them but were light and frothy pieces of amusement, probably somewhat pantomimic in approach, and relied heavily on stage spectacle and music. The first was entitled "*The Colleen Oig*" or "*Donnybrook Fair*". Fifty local children took part in the fair scene, where one or two variety turns were found to be taking place. Whilst additional music hall artists varied from time to time, the "*Colleen Oig*" ran for six weeks before the pantomime "*Mother Goose*" opened on Boxing Day, with scenery especially painted by Mr De Bosco Hughes. He was the resident scenic artist of Holder's Music Hall, Birmingham – later the Gaiety. This curious connection between two seemingly unrelated halls manifested itself at other times and Hughes frequently worked for rival Coventry venues and in Burton-upon-Trent as well. When the overture was played "*the usual amount of impatience was manifested*", a statement showing that little has changed.[5]

One of Allford's ordinary music hall turns was Dr Newland who delivered a lecture on anatomy. His act was favoured with "*shouts of laughter and genuine applause*", so much so that he was retained for a second week. What he talked about can only be conjectured in the strangest of ways.

Another spectacular, '*The Chieftan's Choice*' or '*The Gathering of the Clans*', followed the pantomime and it was a production that had been previously staged by Allford at theatres in Manchester, Glasgow, Paisley, Edinburgh and Dundee. It will be recalled this was the title of the turn before the interval on the evening of the telephonic 'broadcast' in 1893. A range of entertainment covering instrumental and vocal music, ballet, drama and spectacle was available after the pantomime. Later in February 1867 fifty children, acting as marines and sailors, manned the guns and wielded cutlasses in a five weeks run of '*Love's Triumph*' or the '*Battle of the Breeze*'. Matters were enlivened by William Schofield who used his expertise in pyrotechnics to mimic naval warfare. Houses were filled nightly until the end of the season in May when the auditorium was redecorated by Mr Drury of Brighton.

Another unusually long summer recess lasted until September 23, 1867, when Mr Raymond assumed the conductor's baton. The dramatic spectaculars continued, although several weeks of normal music hall were included.

'*Fortune's Favourites*' or '*Christmas Eve*' was the seasonal fare for 1867/8 there being a spectacular scene of the Serpentine by Moonlight which featured a skating festival in which one hundred people took part, although one imagines many of them must have been static on such a small stage.

The final example of this light hearted amusement opened in February and was entitled '*Flying Jib*' or '*The Derby Lost and the Ledger Won*'. The piece "*was received with tremendous éclat, and at the fall of the curtain the principal artists had to cross and recross before it.*" This is an interesting observation of the manner in which the curtain calls were taken at that time and may give credence to the idea that the proscenium doors could have been retained from the rebuilding programme of 1857. D.B.Hughes was once again responsible for the scenery and the house was packed for weeks.

Return to Drama

This spectacle featured regularly until March when there was a return to straight drama. Why, when the formula appeared to be so successful, it is impossible to say at this distance of time. One possibility is that Allford moved to a more interesting challenge or a more lucrative engagement elsewhere. One of Allford's last music hall bills included 'Victoria [Queen of the lofty wire]' – a mode of publicity we would recognise today – together with the famed low comedian Alfred Walmisley, who became the next lessee.

January 1868 saw structural improvements undertaken at the Corn Exchange which, with a newly acquired theatrical licence, enabled touring plays to be presented. The stage was equipped with scenery and an act-drop, representing the Lake of Como, painted by D.B. Hughes.[6] The proscenium was of noble proportions, tastefully panelled, and the pilasters were painted in pale pink, green, white and gold.[7] The venture was probably an attempt to fill a vacuum created when the Theatre Royal became a music hall. However, the previous lack of dramatic success at the Royal did not deter the Exchange's management from leaping into the abyss. The silk business continued to pick up and the workers had successfully negotiated an increase in wages which, in turn, meant money for entertainment. Perhaps the time was ripe for more than two live entertainment outlets, assuming the Godiva remained in business.

From March 9, a fortnight's tour of Boucicault's 'The Colleen Bawn' was staged at the Royal, followed by Sarah Thorne (1837–1899) as the wronged heroine in 'Leah'. 'The Colleen Bawn', with a spectacular water cave scene, was one of Boucicault's most successful and significant plays being first produced in New York during March 1860, after taking only nine days to write.[8] It was also one of the first plays to use spectacular scenes in a domestic drama, a move which gradually lead to a greater degree of realism on the stage. 'The Colleen Bawn' was based on a true story, written as a novel entitled 'The Collegians' by the Limerick born writer Gerald Griffin, in which a young girl was murdered after being trapped into a bogus marriage. All harrowing stuff. 'Leah, the Forsaken' was another popular Victorian melodrama, by Augustus Daly, written on a Jewish theme.[9] Sarah Thorne, daughter of Richard, was a leading dramatic player of her time being responsible for running the Margate Theatre Royal, where she instituted a dramatic school for the training of promising actors and actresses. This was in the days before the formation of the Royal Academy of Dramatic Art by Herbert Beerbohm Tree in 1904. Earlier training grounds had been with the stock companies attached to every theatre in the land, but these had all but disappeared and the means of instructing young actors had been left in limbo. We have a similar situation now regarding performers in light entertainment. The disappearance of variety theatres has meant there are few outlets where such people can hone their art and afford to make mistakes.

The Sydenham Palace

From March 30th, 1868 the Sydenham Palace Inn, built by Mr Robert Higgitt in the previous year at the corner of Lower Ford Street and Cox Street, opened its assembly room with accommodation for an alleged 500 people. The assembly room,

Figure 33   The Sydenham Palace hostelry which included a music hall, one of the serious rivals to the Theatre Royal when it became the Empire

Coventry Local Studies, Central Library

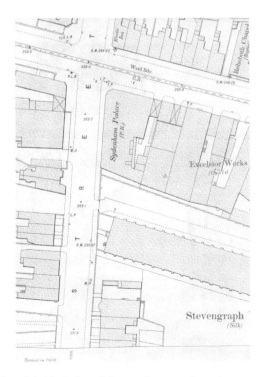

Figure 34   Position of the Sydenham Palace as shown on the ordnance survey map of 1888

Coventry Record Office

probably larger than the Godiva, was later to prove a serious rival to the Theatre Royal after it had become the Empire. Seats in the body of the Sydenham Palace were 3d and boxes, presumably around a single circle, were available at 6d, although box prices were reduced by a third from Tuesday to Friday inclusive.[10] The Sydenham Palace, situated opposite the Fair Ground, consisted of an Inn, an Assembly Room and a dancing saloon, each capable of accommodating about 500 people. The estimated capacity would seem exaggerated when looking at the ground plan of the ordnance survey map. The enterprise was run by Higgitt who had once been in charge of the 'Brewer and Baker' in East Street, and the 'Crystal Palace Wine and Spirit Vaults', Burges, only three years previously.[11] The name of Burges is a corruption of the word 'bridge' which spanned the divided section of the river Sherbourne. Vacillations of policy at the Theatre Royal now left Coventry without a music hall; another vacuum which the management of the Sydenham Palace was only too pleased to fill to its advantage.

Alfred Walmisley

The Theatre Royal reopened on September 21st, 1868, with a dramatic company under the management of Alfred W. Walmisley. The Music Hall part of the name was dropped until its conversion to the Empire Palace of Varieties in 1889, although variety made a brief re-appearance in 1871.

In the middle of October 1868 'After Dark' or 'The Scamps of London' was presented at the Theatre Royal. This was a spectacular drama, a forerunner of 'The Whip' produced at London's Drury Lane towards the end of the century, in that it contained an express train from which the heroine was saved in the nick of time before it thundered by. It was well carried out. "The express train is a wonder in itself and the thrilling situation of Louise, only just saved in time before it passes, is most capitally carried out."[12] This type of presentation disappeared with the rising of the cinema, which could do these effects so much better. The scene just described was often achieved using two dimensional effects. Constance Benson, wife of Sir Frank, spent her early days touring the provinces.

> "I remember a melodrama being put up, in which there was the most thrilling railway accident. The train was a cardboard one (in profile) and the whole strength of the company was enlisted to run this locomotive across the stage. The fact that our feet were visible did not seem to detract from the tragedy of the situation; and a piercing shriek from the wings, announcing the heroine's awful end, brought the curtain down with storms of applause."[13]

'Beauty and the Beast', regarded as the best ever seen in Coventry, began on Boxing Day 1868 and lasted until the middle of January 1869. The scenery was provided by D.B.Hughes, as usual, and new tricks were introduced part way through the run to encourage a second visit.

Figure 35 The sensation scene from 'After Dark' by Boucicault.
'After Dark' was used by the early film makers and the scene,
with Pearl White tied to the rails, was well known in the silent cinema

Reproduced by permission of Caroline and Christopher Calthrop

"Of course a great deal of rough work goes on, but nobody seems much the worse for it, although the wonder is that with so many assaults and hot skirmishes, the actors are not prostrated in reality before the scenes are half over."[14]

Performers in modern pantomimes confirm that this form of entertainment is an energetic pastime, and they often shed many pounds in weight during the season.

Local trades in silk, watches and woollen goods were in a depressed state again and from the end of February the theatre ceased weekly advertising in the press.

Figure 36 The Royal Britannia Vaults in which the Britannia Music Hall was situated. This was another rival to the Theatre Royal once it had become the Empire

Coventry Local Studies, Central Library

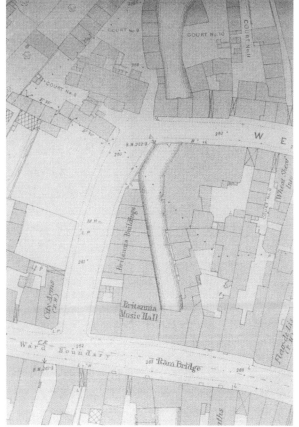

Figure 37 The position of the Britannia Music Hall as shown on the ordnance survey map of 1888. Ram Bridge was an extension of Smithford Street and therefore quite close to the Theatre Royal/Empire

Coventry Record Office

Britannia Music Hall

Our first introduction to the Britannia Music Hall occurred early in 1869, when it ran nightly turns of artists. The hostelry had probably opened in the previous year, but details of the music hall itself have yet to be unearthed other than it was situated at 38 Fleet Street, a continuation of Smithford Street.

The Sydenham Palace, having closed on January 15th, re-opened on March 29th, 1869 with the usual prices, although eventually all admission charges were dropped and it was to remain thus for a few years; the management recouped their expenses from sales of additional drink to the influx of patrons to the hall.

Pepper's Ghost

Professor Pepper, with his 'ghostly' optical illusions, was on the bill at the Guildhall for a number of weeks in April and May 1869. Pepper's Ghost was an enormously popular 3-D spectacle, whereby misty, transparent apparitions appeared nightly on stage and, in some instances, moved around. The effect was achieved using a large sheet of plate glass on stage placed at forty five degrees to the actor (ghost), who stood either in the orchestra pit or in the wings, depending on the position of the glass. The former location, apparently, gave a better result. Under the normal laws of reflection, light of a certain intensity from the actor was projected onto the glass and the image appeared some distance behind it on the stage. Designed by Henry Dircks, a retired engineer, the invention was sold to John Henry Pepper (1821–1900) of the London Polytechnic, who first used it in Dickens' 'The Haunted Man' in 1863. After that it was regularly performed and several companies constantly toured the novelty nation-wide. There were two disadvantages: the illusion was not seen to best effect from all parts of the house, especially in large theatres – the central positions in the auditorium were better – and the deception was dented when wags threw objects which bounced off the surface of the invisible glass. The former problem may have been linked to the size of glass which, in turn, would have been governed by the ability to get the apparatus into a hall or theatre, the weight that could be conveniently handled and the dimensions of railway wagons used to transport it from town to town. The smaller Guildhall would have been advantageous in these respects. Some 'Ghost' companies used multiple sheets of glass placed side by side in order to fill the stage opening, but this would have increased some of the difficulties already outlined.[15] Records of the illusion appearing at the Royal have yet to be found, although it appeared some time later at the larger Corn Exchange.

The new 1869 season at the Theatre Royal started on 14th August with Edward Askew Sothern [1826–1881] as Lord Dundreary, a part he created in the original version of 'Our American Cousin' by Tom Taylor when it opened in America in May 1858. Born in Liverpool, Sothern went over to America in 1851. The long side whiskers he adorned in the part eventually passed into the English language as 'dundrearies'. The play was first seen at the Laura Keene's Theatre, New York, but was a disaster and played to empty benches, the plot being described as nonsense and the dialogue not much better. In an attempt to improve matters, the cast extemporised upon Taylor's original script and the piece seemed to be enhanced. The role of Dundreary was conceived as a minor one, consisting of about forty lines or so, but bit by bit Sothern introduced extravagant business turning the character into a typical English Fop, which went down so well that the play became an instant success. He made his name by taking it all over the country and playing alongside members of resident stock companies who provided the other characters. At Coventry there was a better public response for the remainder of the season, although dramatically it was not particularly noteworthy.

The season had been successful with a report of good attendances, so it was surprising that Walmisley was replaced by G.B.Wright at the end of it.

G.B.Wright

Wright's first and only season began on 11th September 1869, with a programme consisting mainly of non-classical works. The musical conductor was Mr Costello and the band was described as very creditable. Boxing Night saw 'The Intruder' followed by the pantomime 'Prince Pippin the pretty, the Six Peerless Princesses, the Good Fairies of Coraldom and the petite army of Pettiness'. It only ran three weeks, almost as long as it took to say. Wright ran a stock company in which he took the leading roles, although for Easter week, by way of an additional attraction, he engaged extra actors to strengthen the corps. Violet Campbell, who had been lessee and manager from 1864 to 1865, joined the company in June 1870, mainly for leading parts. Her Juliet was well received ". . .with a little more energy, [she] would have made an excellent personation."[16]

The year 1870 began with two accidents. The first involved an unexplained explosion in a wines and spirits closet causing Miss Nolen, the barmaid, burns around the face, head and neck, although she survived.[17] The second happened on stage, or rather just off it. The production was 'The Broken Sword', with J. Hayden Sole in the leading role. The plot involved a bridge which crossed an imaginary river in which a boy was discovered in difficulties. A mattress had been placed behind the water scenery onto which the hero could leap when rescuing the boy, but the said mattress remained occupied by the lad when Sole leapt from the bridge. Although he avoided a personal collision, Sole badly dislocated his ankle which caused him great pain for the duration of the evening.[18] The remainder of the short season contained a higher percentage of classical works, including Shakespeare, than of late.

Frank George Venimore
A change in Policy

Wright's tenure was short and Frank G.Venimore became the new lessee from September 10th, 1870 after unspecified extensive alterations had taken place to the building. An improvement in local prosperity, coupled with a steady increase in the population, enabled the season to be lengthened to about nine months. It was still run on the repertoire system played by a stock company, although some touring groups were occasionally booked from Monday to Saturday. There were no one or two night stands any longer. Venimore, sometimes spelt with two 'Ns', was that interesting breed of professional who wore two theatrical hats; he was both manager and resident scenic artist, a previously known, but uncommon combination. There was a family of scene painting Vennimores, an Albert being recorded at the Llandudno Arcadia Theatre as late as 1960.

Whereas a majority of other managers took leading acting roles, Venimore did not. He was later recorded as being manager and scenic artist of the Royal Alhambra, Barrow-in-Furness, Royal County Theatre, Reading, Royal Court Theatre, Warrington and the Royal and Alexandra theatres in Sheffield. From there he went to be general manager at the opening of the Prince of Wales Theatre, Mexborough, in 1893 and for which he painted a set of stock scenes.

The Britannia Music Hall, re-opened on September 19th after undergoing alterations which transformed it into a spacious building of triangular proportions. It was reputed to hold 1,800 people, although the Era modified this to 1,300, with the stage placed at the apex, a situation similar to the Swansea Palace (the original Empire) and which remains one of the nation's 'Sleeping Beauties', awaiting a princely kiss to be brought back to life. One assumes that the holding capacity, like that described for the Sydenham Palace, was greatly exaggerated as the larger figure is equivalent to the current size of the Birmingham Hippodrome Theatre. Other references suggest this was nearer to 500. New 'drops' (backcloths) were painted by Charles Marshall and new scenery was provided by D.B. Hughes. Alan Sandford was the chairman who introduced the various turns and generally kept order in the house.[19] Readers only have to recall the television series "The Good Old Days", broadcast from the City Varieties Theatre, Leeds by the B.B.C., to get a flavour of the role. Unlike later music hall and variety theatres, artists at the Britannia were not necessarily booked on a weekly basis for many were frequently retained for a fortnight, or more, if their popularity warranted it and assuming they were not already booked elsewhere.

The Theatre Royal season opened on September 3rd, 1870 with the previous manager, G.B.Wright, as a member of the company. Everything was pronounced a great success with well filled houses frequently reported. Venimore, in a speech from the stage, promised to give the best productions to the highest standard and to include works by modern authors. More music hall acts were booked in place of the after pieces. *"There has been a falling off in the farces (after pieces) which hitherto have not been the least entertaining part of the performance."*[20]

The latest Revolution, which was occupying the minds in Paris at the time, closed all places of amusement in that city putting innumerable entertainers out of work. Venimore booked three acrobats, Faust, Hector and Petite Ted, from the Paris Cirque Napoleon for a fortnight. They appeared around 9.00 p.m. after the 'main course' and their performances took the place of the second play and farce.[21] Further artists were promised but never materialised.

December saw a new act-drop painted by Mr Smithers. The pantomime *'Harlequin Robinson Crusoe, His Man Friday, and Hoop-de-dooden-do, The King of the Caribbee Islands'* opened on Boxing Night 1870, and ran four weeks, the performance lasting over two hours not including the farce. The scenery was designed and painted by the lessee and an assistant, Mr Grainger, and Mr G.B.Wright was cast as the Clown.

Venimore changed the formula slightly during the early months of 1871, in that he booked a regular number of variety artists to occupy part of the evening's bill; in fact, for a period, the theatre was renamed Theatre Royal and Varieties. The main play or melodrama came first, then the variety artists, and a farce concluded the evening. This arrangement lasted until April, when the former dramatic fare made a re-appearance with a surge of plays based on the novels of Charles Dickens: *'The Old Curiosity Shop'* and *'Our Emily'* (*David Copperfield*), *'The Life and Death of Jo'* (*Bleak House*). The season ended on 29th July.

"In consequence of the near approach of the fair, business had not been very brisk."[22] Neither had it been so at the Britannia but the manager booked reinforcements to his bill to combat any defection. Any additional competition during the summer months invariably brings bad news.

Alan Sandford left the post of manager at the Britannia Music Hall in May 1871 and in July Mr E. Jukes was appointed pianist there. Considerable renovation and re-decoration took place before it re-opened *"and it now forms a very agreeable lounge."*[23] 'Lounge' is a curious word to use as the presence of scenery and drops would suggest a theatrical setting within a proscenium, as opposed to artists performing on an open platform as happened in the earlier music halls.

The Sydenham Palace, which operated a similar style of entertainment to the Britannia, re-opened on May 25th, 1871 for Fair Week and then re-opened again on June 27th, presumably for the remainder of the year. In October 1869, the owner, Robert Higgitt, was also lessee and manager of the Alhambra Music Hall on the corner of Gold Street and Horseshoe Street at nearby Northampton. Situated opposite the town's Marefair Theatre, the Alhambra was originally the Crow and Horseshoe Music Hall, and was to emerge into the twentieth century as the Palace twice nightly variety theatre. Higgitt ran it until March 1874, when he returned to Coventry and the Sydenham.[24]

Frank Venimore was sufficiently encouraged to open a new season on 25th September, 1871. In November, he provided the house with a sumptuous new act-drop depicting an Italian landscape on a ground of white satin drapery embroidered with gold tissue trellis work.[25]

'Jack the Giant Killer' opened on Boxing Day 1871 with the following advertisement; *"New and beautiful scenery the great feature of all pantomimes, and*

only possible to produce in a theatre – other establishments not having facility or machinery for the same".[26] This was an odd declaration, as no pantomimes were offered at any other venue in the town. The *'Giant Killer'* remained active until the end of January, although the Harlequinade section had been withdrawn slightly earlier. Good audiences followed in the spring and this was attributed to an upturn in local trade.

Just as books frequently appear a matter of weeks after an event, the Theatre Royal presented *'The Lost Heir'* in March 1872, a play based on the recently collapsed Tichborne case. Kenneth More, in his book *'More or Less'*, described how the management of the Newcastle Byker Grand Theatre would espy forthcoming films at the local cinema and immediately announce a similar sounding play destined to open beforehand. It would be home grown in a matter of days with dialogue mainly left to those on the stage during each performance.

In April it was announced that J.O.Halliwell had bought the Theatre Royal, Stratford-upon-Avon, with the intention of demolishing it and throwing the site into the Shakespeare property at New Place. The Royal was regarded as an ugly and unsuccessful theatre.[27]

In May 1872, there was a visit from *'Across the Continent'* touring company, or at least the principal members of it, they being ably supported by members of the resident stock company. The first night, May 22nd, was marred by the fact that the percussion cap of Mr Prescott's gun burst upon firing, part of the cartridge embedding itself in the side of his head and narrowly missing the eye.[28]

'Firefly', an equestrian drama, was about a horse (Etna) being led through flame and fire and it opened on June 24th, 1872 with Edith Sandford in the leading role. The advertisements announced this as her first appearance since a serious accident in Dublin, and that she was imminently to retire from the stage.[29] Whether it was the management's intention that audiences should flock to the Royal just in case of another accident, or to take their last chance to see this particular performer, was not made clear. In addition to *'Firefly'*, both she and Etna appeared in a version of *'Joan of Arc'*, *'The Ride for Life'* and *'The Child of Fire'*. She remained in Coventry for a second week.

Venimore made the Theatre Royal available for a benefit performance and included *'The Republic of France'*, together with the death scene of Willie Carlyle from *'East Lynne'*, in aid of Mrs Milward, widow, whose only bread winning son was murdered by Arthur F. Brown in Gosport Street. The support of public institutions and worthy causes always went down well and provided good publicity.

The Britannia re-opened for a new season on August 5th, 1872 with J.V.Green as the new musical director. Although the hall advertised a band, it is possible the musical director operated from a piano or violin. Green was reported as playing concerted pieces.[30] The hall had acquired a gallery, reputed to hold 500 people. This in addition to the 1800 previously reported would make a remarkable capacity taking it beyond that of the Corn Exchange. Perhaps mathematics was not a strong point in those days either. *"The interest in the fairy fountain is in no way diminished."*[31]

Redecoration and alterations

Venimore opted for another season which opened on 21st September, 1872 but not until after several alterations had been carried out to the auditorium during the recess. He, personally, redecorated the interior in the Greco-Italian style, which involved a background of pink and white panelling with gold relief and gold floral devices placed at intervals. The dress circle balcony front was adorned with tastefully shaped standards which relieved the floral decorations. Massive gold mouldings decorated the proscenium arch and the walls of the auditorium were painted to represent marble, possibly what we would now recognise as scagliola. The side galleries were closed to the public and the front seats of the gallery, which had lately formed part of the upper boxes, were restored to their original condition meaning that the central portion of upper tier of boxes was removed. No reason was given, neither was there any explanation for abandoning the side galleries – presumably on both levels. The sight lines and degree of comfort would not have changed, but it appears from an entry in 1878 that they had become unsafe. Such a move would have reduced the capacity of the house by over one hundred seats. That the side galleries were not immediately repaired may relate to their infrequent use and/or the lack of money, yet the impression given is that attendances were good. Charles Prague was installed as the new musical director, and the orchestra pit was arranged to take nine players, which was not large considering operas were served up from time to time.[32] This statement does not say whether the orchestra pit was reduced or increased in size, merely arranged.

The inaugural play was 'Married Life', and of the company the Coventry Herald critic reserved his judgement, but thought they were better than last year.[33]

Extensive machinery was installed in the upper and lower regions of the stage in preparation for Mr Levey's pantomime, 'Aladdin', or 'Harlequin the super-celestial sultan, the Vicious Vizier, the Pretty Princess or the Geni of the Lamp and Ring'. The structural changes can only be imagined, but it is safe to speculate that additional traps would have featured in both the scenery and stage. "For prices and times see the day bills", an indication of the importance these small pieces of paper were when displayed over the town. The pantomime closed on January 29th. Advertisements for the early spring programme were not put into the press, only the special visits made by visiting stars were publicised. However, the Birmingham Prince of Wales Theatre advertised on the front page of the Herald for it's 'Twinkle, Twinkle Little Star' or 'Harlequin Jack Frost and Little Tom Tucker' pantomime. One wonders whether Venimore tried to lure Birmingham citizens to his small Coventry Theatre Royal in like manner, possibly not. The seasonal show was better received than most and managed to attain an additional week's run.

J.G.Taylor replaced J. Eaves as the next proprietor of the Britannia in February 1873 where Leotard Bosco, the illusionist, appeared later in June. Farther into the century Bosco leased music halls in Hanley [Gaiety], Hull [Springthorpes, later Empire], Warrington [Gaiety], Stockton [Star], Bradford [Jollity], Birmingham [Aston Royal] and was a highly successful entrepreneur. Advertisements appeared that the 'police were in attendance'. One must assume that such an announcement was designed to encourage both confidence and re-affirm custom. What reaction would a similar statement have today?

March 9th saw the termination of Mr Powell's engagement with '*Mazeppa*' and '*Dick Turpin*', two equestrian pieces in which the rider quitted himself with honour. The title role in the first piece was normally played by a woman, but was apparently initially conceived as a male role.

Barry Sullivan, (1822–1891) the well known tragedian, and no relation to Sir Arthur Sullivan the composer, played in four classical productions at the end of April to packed houses at the Theatre Royal. These included, '*The Lady of Lyons*', '*Richard III*', '*Richlieu*' and '*Hamlet*'. Born in Birmingham, he made his first stage appearance in Cork in 1840, and was said to combine pains and care into the interpretation of his roles. A very thin person to start with, his voice was regarded as rather limited. There is an anecdote of Sullivan's '*Hamlet*' which bears repeating. It happened at the Theatre Royal, Portsmouth (date unknown) and at the beginning of the speech "*To be or not to be*", one of the tars in the gallery shouted, "*Hi, Barry, give us a hornpipe*", and then as an after thought added, "*mind as it's the sailor's one*". The demand was taken up by others in the gods and Sullivan moved down to the footlights and delivered a stern reproach whereupon the speech was resumed. "*Ere, Barry!...are you going to give me and my friends that hornpipe or am I to come down and make yer?*" By this time Sullivan was inwardly convulsed with laughter, but he eventually acquiesced and did it to satisfaction, for he was well versed in this dance having played Black-Ey'd Susan's William so often. Only then did the play resume without further interruption.[34]

John Laurence Toole [1830–1906], one of the 'stars' of the London stage and a frequent visitor around the country, might have been expected to perform at the Theatre Royal, but at the beginning of May he went into the Corn Exchange instead, thus highlighting the increasing frequency of professional productions at that place. Toole, a close friend of Irving, played the winter months in London for many years and toured the provinces in the summer. He took over the London Charing Cross Theatre in 1882, giving it his own name. This theatre lasted until 1895 when the land on which it stood was incorporated into extensions of the adjacent Charing Cross Hospital.

Limelight

Edward Dean Davies, proprietor of the Royal Lyceum, Sunderland, late lessee of Drury Lane, and theatres in Liverpool and Newcastle-upon-Tyne, came to Coventry with a list of popular plays together with new scenery and limelight effects, but performed to almost empty houses. Limelight is a word associated with the theatre that has passed into the English language; the phrase, '*being in the limelight*' being the most common example. Developed by Thomas Drummond (1797–1840) for surveying purposes, it made its way to the stage in the mid to late 1820s. A block of compressed quicklime (calcium oxide) was heated with a flame of combined oxygen and hydrogen gas, or sometimes a mixture of oxygen and coal gas, which is mainly hydrogen anyway. The result was a brilliant light which could be tinted to give various effects. Almost all theatres used it. However, anyone versed with chemical knowledge will inwardly blanch at the thought of mixing the two gases and then igniting them, as a combination of both can be highly explosive and, indeed, a number of devastating accidents, caused from this source, have been recorded in the annals of theatre history.[35]

The little known drama '*Naomie*' played for a week at the Theatre Royal and in the cast was the actor Colin Harford Hazlewood. His father ran the West Bromwich Theatre Royal and Wolverhampton Star Theatre (later the Prince of Wales and the second Theatre Royal). Colin fought in the Boer War as a member of the Staffordshire Imperial Yeomanry and was later invalided home with enteric fever. He died in 1900 after undergoing operations for cancer of the tongue.

Isidore de Solla's Opera company, the first lyric corps to visit Coventry since the alterations to the Corn Exchange, spent a week at the Theatre Royal in June 1873, where smoking and drinking were strictly prohibited, except in those places reserved for the purpose and an official made his rounds to ensure this rule was obeyed. The company, which rendered, '*Il Travatore*', '*La Sonnambula*', '*Bride of Lammermoor*' and '*Maritana*', was not of the best but was well received.[36]

The Sydenham Palace re-opened on June 13, 1873 "*with a first class band*" and R. Higgitt in full control.[37]

At the Britannia the police were in attendance making sure there was law and order.

A company belonging to Miss Foote, a grandniece of Marie Foote, Samuel's daughter, who became The Countess of Harrington in 1831[38], visited the Theatre Royal in July and played to awful business before the theatre closed for the summer recess.

Pantomime, '*Babes in the Wood*', was reduced to a burlesque during the winter of 1873/4 and played as an after piece to the main programme.

John Garner Taylor and a rudderless theatre

The theatre re-opened on September 20th, 1873 with John Garner Taylor as the new lessee. Taylor was the proprietor of the very successful Coventry Britannia Theatre of Varieties, although quite what he wanted with a legitimate theatre is difficult to fathom and it would seem he had second thoughts before the season was out.

A new company was booked at the Theatre Royal and they played familiar works in repertoire, that is a different play most nights. They began with the perennial '*The Lady of Lyons*' on 20th September, and the interludes between the various plays presented each evening were filled with operatic pieces rendered by Viotti Glover and Edith Percy, both of whom remained at the Royal for several weeks. This arrangement lasted until November 8th, when the company was disbanded. Henry Bradford's Company played for two weeks, as did that of W.R. Waldron, and then the theatre went dark until Christmas. No pantomime was in the offing, merely more plays with a seasonal flavour; '*The Mistletoe Bough*', '*Christmas Eve*' and so forth, but the Britannia reopened under the guise of the Victoria Theatre, although the policy remained that of purveying music hall entertainment. The German Reeds spent Christmas at the Corn Exchange performing music of an 18th century flavour. '*Babes in the Wood*', in burlesque form, was served up at the Theatre Royal in January along with other dramas, then came another period of closure during which Sefton's Comedy Company occupied the Corn Exchange. In mid February the Royal was open but only on Mondays and Saturdays, when members of Taylor's variety bills at the Britannia, performed their same acts at the theatre immediately after their initial appearance in Fleet Street. The correspondent for the *Era* complained that the two venues were offering exactly the same fare.[39] A three weeks closure at the theatre followed, which was ended by the Excelsior Burlesque and Dramatic Company playing '*Four Knaves in the Pack*', billed as being full of startling incidents although these were not enumerated in the press. A series of companies presented plays and variety in the Royal, which opened and closed with regularity, until Barry Sullivan re-visited the theatre at the end of April. The theatre, shut more than it was open, had no firm policy and it must have been difficult for members of the public to know what to expect there. The season finished at the end of June with Glover and Stubb's English Opera Company presenting the by now familiar works, '*Lucia di Lammermoor*', '*Il Travatore*', '*Faust*' et al, over a two week period. Taylor decided his best interests were to concentrate on the Britannia and he handed over the lease of the Theatre Royal to Fred Cooke, who reopened the house to huge acclaim on September 26th.

Fred Cooke

Fred Cooke took hold of the reins on September 26th, 1874 his inaugural play being the American drama '*The Green Hills of the Far West*', presented by a brand new stock company. A string of melodramas followed: '*Octoroon*', '*East Lynne*', '*The Iron Mask*', which attracted excellent business during the autumn although Don Edgardo Colonna, from Mexico, attracted fair houses only. He came as a star to play various Shakespearean roles relying on the resident stock company to fill the supporting parts. He was acknowledged as having an intelligent study of the parts, if somewhat unorthodox, although "*his ideas of Richard III, though not strictly in accordance with our own, was (sic) good...*"[40] W.C.Middleton came in early December also to play leading roles with the stock company, all of which were mirror images of theatrical affairs in the 1820s and 30s when Kean and Macready travelled the provinces.

J.G.Taylor's Victoria Theatre reopened on October 12, 1874 with J. Lowe in the chair.

Cooke was also a dramatic author and presented his '*Maureen na Lareen*' in November shortly before '*Sleigh Bells*', for which William Mallalieu, who was later to assume the role of lessee in 1878, acted as stage manager. The play attracted good audiences, partially through the euphoria of a visit by the Prince and Princess of

Wales to Coventry, although they did not sample the wares at the theatre. The pattern of melodrama was interrupted with the presentation of the *'Forty Thieves'* pantomime at Christmas, along with *'The Idiot Witness'*, a curtain raiser. The leader of the cut throat band of thieves was a woman, Nellie Smith, offering shades of our familiar female principal boy, and the settings, including the four seasons transformation scene, was from the brush of Tannet. The orchestra was led by Mr Wilson who later defected to the rival Britannia Theatre of Varieties. The pantomime, plus Harlequinade, offered a full evening's entertainment and continued until the end of January 1875.

The transformation scene in modern pantomime reflects but a small relic of its Victorian counterpart. There, the main character would be 'transported' through scene after scene into the realms of fairyland via the mechanical movement of scenery with the use of flying (or rolled) cloths, and the appearance of stage sets, or groups of characters, or both, rising out of the cellar on stage bridges. One reason for the curtailment of this stage spectacle in the twenty first century is the complete absence of the necessary stage machinery, except in a handful of British theatres.

Benefit nights were a test of an artist's popularity, so long as something didn't prevent the locals from supporting it.

> *"We have often seen this place full, but we never remember to have seen it more crowded than it was at the benefit of William Mallalieu."*[41]

In April both the Britannia and Sydenham Palace music halls were running in opposition to the Theatre Royal and, reading between the lines, the *Era Magazine* correspondent felt this made an impact. Partially to combat the opposition Fred Allford, who had run the Royal in its music hall days from 1865, returned in April to perform and organise other burlesque productions. However, the Sydenham Palace appeared to bow out of the scene after Easter, leaving the Britannia as the leader of the opposition.

The remainder of the spring and early summer saw the Theatre Royal closed on and off, before the redecoration of the building took place during the summer break. J.G.Taylor, previously of the Britannia and Royal, took a benefit performance at the Corn Exchange, there being *"a fair attendance present."* The Theatre Royal re-opened on August 2nd with Fred Allford in charge and a series of light entertainments including, *'The Gathering of the Clans'*, a seemingly popular title which re-appeared from time to time, and *'Donnybrook Fair'*, which had also been seen in the 1860s. This was the prelude to a season of legitimate drama starting on Saturday August 28th with a resident stock company.

The Victoria Theatre reverted to the name Britannia at the end of March 1875, as Robert Leggett took over control from Taylor. Leggett, who later ran the London Sun Music Hall in Knightsbridge in the early 1880s, was an active member of the Coventry Local Volunteer Fire Brigade.

The autumn programme included a further visit from Don Edgardo Colonna with *"a fair amount of success"*. On November 9th, a benefit performance was given in aid of the widow and orphans of Charles Harcourt, formerly of the Royal, although in what capacity he worked we do not know. There was a crowded house.

The pantomime in December 1875, '*Ye Lady Godiva, Harlequin Leofric, Peeping Tom, Ye Good Days of Queen Bess and the pretty Fairies of Kenilworth Castle*', had a run inversely proportional to it's titular length and only survived three weeks. It abounded in satire and local humour but didn't attract to any extent. Nellie Smith, a member of the stock company, was Leofric and Queen Bess played by William Mallalieu, shades of our modern principal boy and dame. Burlesques were introduced at the Britannia and marked an initial departure from pure variety, a move which may have affected business at the theatre. That chosen for Christmas was also of a local flavour and entitled '*Beneath the Spires*', the scenic artist being Mr Stoner. The title referred to the three spires which rose from the cathedral, later blitzed in November 1940.

Vesta Tilley [1864–1952]

Only in March 1876, did the Royal open with any degree of regularity. The London Drawing Room Opera Company came down on March 6th with, '*The Barber of Seville*' and '*The Bohemian Girl*', together with other works not familiar today. They had good houses the first week but outstayed their welcome during the second, being rewarded with a poor response. Meanwhile at the Britannia, one of the new artists was "*a wonderful girl called the Great Little Tilley*", who was such a draw with "*her sweet singing*", that she was retained for three weeks and made two return dates during the year. This was Vesta Tilley (Matilda Powles), aged twelve, who made music hall fame in later years and eventually married Lord de Frece, finally retiring from the stage in 1925. Also on the programme was Harry Ball (Harry Powles), billed as a comic and instrumentalist. Harry was Vesta's father, and chaperone, born in Worcester and a former employee at one of the Worcester China works. In the Lowesmoor district of that city is the shell of the Prince of Wales Music Hall, now re-named the '*Vesta Tilley Centre*'. The connection between the star and the hall is tenuous. Certainly she never performed there although her father may have been the chairman before moving to the Theatre Royal, Gloucester, to act in that capacity in 1867. Vesta made her stage debut in 1868 at the age of four, on the stage of the Nottingham St George's Music Hall, where her father had been made manager. At the time she performed a gamut of female characters from baby songs to old maid's ditties; most being written by her father who, from 1872, resigned his position to become her personal manager. At that time she experimented with her male impersonation act, first seen at Birmingham Day's Concert Hall in 1872. The *Coventry Herald* does not itemise her performance, or refer to her male roles, so it is possible, for whatever reason, she temporally reverted to her former act.[42]

Yet another area of competition appeared, this time in Alma Street with Coventry's first skating rink which offered morning, afternoon and evening sessions to the accompaniment of a resident band.

The Theatre Royal had intermittent periods of closure, the reasons for which are not known. '*The Life and Death of Jo*', an adaptation of Dickens' '*Bleak House*', re-opened the theatre on May 15, but *"the attendance has not been commensurate with the merits of the piece."*[43] Perhaps some were losing the habit of regularly attending the theatre which, curiously, had no attraction for the Whitsuntide holiday. This pattern of mediocre attendance continued up to the summer break.

Boucicault's *'The Shaughraun'* (The Vagabond), came to the Theatre Royal during the week beginning September 4th, 1876, after a brief closure. First produced at Wallack's theatre, New York in 1874, the manager there complained of the title, believing no one would be able to pronounce let alone understand it. *'The Shaughraun'* was another of Boucicault's original and great melodramas, the story having roots in Irish history during the times of the Fenian insurrection of 1866. It made the author a lot of money. Coventry's reaction was not recorded.

Edward Bell

Edward Bell, advertised as coming from the Royal Adelphi, London, took the lease of the Theatre Royal and opened the house on October 9th, 1876 with *'All for Her'*, played by a formidable stock company recruited from many of the major provincial houses.

> *"The band under the able leadership of Mr Morris Edmundsen performs some excellent music and is certainly not the least item on the evening's amusement."*[44]

Little is known of the new manager. Advertisements always capitalised on new managers having London connections as it appeared to give them high status, but a majority had their roots in the 'sticks' and spent most of their time there. There was an E. Bell at the Prince of Wales Theatre, Rochdale, in 1874, and an Edward Bell at the Macclesfield Theatre Royal in 1875, the year it closed, and an E. Bell at Ryde Theatre Royal between 1878 and 1880. It is possible they are one of the same as the dates fit.

As in previous years, the advertisements ceased until the run of *'Cinderella'*, which opened on Boxing night and ran until January 26. *"The introduction of Cinderella's carriage drawn by two beautiful ponies, is quite a feature"*, suggesting that this now common practice was then a novelty.[45] For the first time there were two pantomimes in the city. *'Jack the Giant Killer'*, complete with transformation scene designed by the resident artist, Mr Stoner, was the rival attraction at the Britannia Theatre of Varieties. It is interesting to contemplate how this, together with a number of music hall artists, who performed separately during the evening, and a Harlequinade could be squeezed onto a stage much smaller than that at the Royal; and where did they all change? Dressing room accommodation was a luxury rarely given much attention by proprietors in those days, not that present day conditions are always regarded as perfect by those who have to use them. When the Britannia pantomime was withdrawn in mid January, the transformation scene was kept on as an added attraction. Vesta Tilley and Harry Ball were back there straight after the pantomime. She did the rounds of small provincial halls making another London appearance at London's Wilton's Music Hall two years later in 1878.

John Coleman was again in financial trouble and appeared at the bankruptcy court in October 1876. He ran the Great Northern Circuit which included theatres in: York, Leeds, Doncaster, Liverpool, Lincoln, Isle of Man, Glasgow and Hull. His venture in leasing the London Queens Theatre (Long Acre) was a disaster and the burning of the Leeds Theatre Royal in 1875, which was only 50% insured, made matters infinitely worse. It was Coleman's custom to play the more spectacular productions at the larger Leeds and York theatres where expenses could be recouped. After much to-ing and fro-ing with the authorities, Coleman's bankruptcy eventually prevented him from exercising his claim on the lease of the York Theatre Royal, and his place was taken by W.A. Waddington, who had attempted to wrest the theatre from Coleman on a previous occasion.[46] On gaining control, the Waddingtons immediately abandoned the stock system and went over to full time touring for many years.

William Duck [1820–1892] arrived in the early spring with his 'Our Boys' and played to good business. He, and his production, were frequent visitors to the Royal over the following years. Written by Henry J. Byron, the comedy 'Our Boys' ran for four years at the London Vaudeville Theatre, and held the record for the longest consecutive run until the appearance of 'Charley's Aunt' in 1892. The policy at the Theatre Royal was one of presenting tours for the time being. Although the stock company regime made a couple of 'come-backs', it was in it's death throes.

Auguste Creamer and his 'Eileen Oge' and 'Clancarthy' company, visited for a week in August 1877. The plays had been written by Creamer himself, a provincial touring manager who eventually fell on hard times, as did many of his contemporaries. Early in 1906 he was 'resting' – a theatrical euphemism for being out of work – in Manchester before being contracted to play at the Oldbury Palace in the Black Country. The figure offered was less than his usual fee and he insisted on a month's booking to cover the rail fare. However, the Palace was not a theatre in the recognised sense of the word, being a hall, which only had a music and singing licencce, attached to a public house. Creamer, and his wife, performed sketches for the first two weeks, but it was discovered that Thomas Pritchard, owner of the premises, was offering such entertainment illegally and to keep within the law Creamer would have to perform solo, which he refused to do, reminding Pritchard he had been billed as an actor in a sketch. This neatly illustrates the knock on effect from the days when the Drury Lane and Covent Garden managements monopolised dramatic presentations; now it was the turn of the music halls to be attacked by those managers who had been freed from this constriction. Judge Smith, at the West Bromwich County Court, found in favour of Creamer, with costs.[47] He had seen better days, being once manager at the Great Yarmouth Theatre Royal in the early 1880s and the Leith Princess Theatre in the early 1890s, but touring was his life and forte. This Irish playwright had been criticised at Wakefield in February 1886 for touring three political plays into the town; Boucicault's 'The Shaughraun', 'Colleen Bawn' and his own 'Irish Life'.[48] It seemed he had an axe to grind.

Figure 38   The Oldbury Palace Music Hall where Auguste Creamer appeared in 1906. The building opened as the Museum Varieties in 1870 and was attached to a public house, like so many other music halls of the period

Author's collection

The early photograph of the Oldbury Palace is interesting on several counts. It opened in 1870 as the Museum Palace of Varieties and was an assembly hall attached to a public house in Church Street. Known as the Bird Show owing to the decorations of stuffed birds that adorned the interior, it functioned as a music hall and became the Palace in 1906, not long before Auguste Creamer made his debut there. An initial glance gives the appearance that the hall was larger than it really was. Oblong in construction, like the Leeds City Varieties Theatre, there was a shallow balcony on three sides. The three rows of side benches, together with leg room, are unlikely to have taken up more than approximately six feet of space. The rear bench is continuous whereas the front two have spaces for movement. Working by proportion the proscenium width can have been little more than fifteen feet with a height to the crown of just over sixteen feet. The act-drop, painted to resemble fabric (as can be seen at the Chatsworth House Theatre, Alexandra Palace and Normansfield Hospital Theatres), was operated by being rolled up from the bottom as there was no fly tower. The photographer stood at the front of the end balcony which may have been as deep or a little deeper than those at the two sides. There is an absence of boxes. Seating on the ground floor is not shown but is likely to have been benches only. The orchestra pit appears to have five or six stands. The date of the photograph is not known but gives the appearance of being around the 1880s or 1890s. There seems to be an absence of footlights and the central chandalier most probably used gas for illumination. In the absence of any evidence to the contrary, it is likely that this style of building resembled the interiors of the Britannia and Sydenham Palace music halls, both of which were attached to public houses. There were, no doubt, a great number of similar pub music halls throughout the country, some of which were converted into modern theatres of variety but the majority must have simply faded away under the weight of mightier opposition.

The beginning of 1877 saw more weekly touring companies at the Coventry Theatre Royal. There were odd periods of closure caused, possibly, by the lack of available companies. The London Haymarket and Lyceum theatre companies were the first to tour the country with any degree of regularity; John Coleman's players were a close third.[49] The opportunity of seeing, on a weekly basis, fresh actors and actresses, often of a high standard, put the final nail in the coffin of the national resident stock system. Dickens was a popular author and 'Nicholas Nickleby' did the rounds in February. "*The departure of the coach, the thrashing of 'Squeers' by Nicholas, the escape of 'Smike' and the death of the poor outcast, all tend to realise the author's great work*", which suggested the kind of melodrama and realism so popular with the pittites and gods.[50]

If the Royal was taking more touring companies, the Britannia Theatre of Varieties ventured onto new ground at the beginning of August by installing a stock repertory company which performed a different work each night. Many of them were 'pot boilers', although plays such as 'Frederick the Great', 'Hamlet', and the 'Corsican Brothers' were attempted, possibly as truncated versions of the originals. No details of the last named were given but it is highly unlikely the Corsican stage trap was installed for the performance. This resident company included Mr Temple Collings, actor and scenic artist, who would transfer to the Royal later in the decade. The Britannia did not revert to variety until December 1877.

Touring may have been gaining in popularity but it could have its problems. John Coleman was due to open at the Coventry Theatre Royal with 'Henry V' on October 7th. The audience assembled but a few minutes after the advertised start, Bell came before the curtain and explained there had been a hitch and there would be no performance. He quickly introduced John Coleman to furnish the explanation and, presumably, take any flack. The play had ended a week's run at the Brighton Theatre Royal the previous Saturday, and Coleman's stage crew had packed the scenery and properties until three or four o'clock on the Sunday morning. Sunday rail services were a problem even then, and the five or six tons of luggage could not be taken out of the town until the Monday morning which, in consequence, arrived too late at Willesden Junction to catch the early Coventry express. The effects were wheeled into the theatre in the early to mid afternoon which gave insufficient time to get everything ready for the 7.30 p.m. performance. Money was refunded and everyone was urged to return the following night with a friend in tow to make up for the lost revenue. The play was adapted by Coleman himself to include a series of historical tableaux, which were well received.

> "... the grandest production that has ever been seen or will ever be seen on the Coventry stage."[51]

The Brighton correspondent for the *Era* wrote,

"Never within the memory of the oldest playgoer has Brighton seen such a combination of grand and effective historical tableaux as have been presented through the medium of the revival of Henry V."[52]

The Coventry audiences liked it too.

It is interesting to record the vast quantity of scenery and properties travelled by Coleman for this production. Not all the scenery for a play was toured at this time, companies frequently relied on the host theatre to provide something suitable out of stock. If there was nothing available, the resident scenic artist was kept busy painting cloths, borders and wings to order, after company managers had forwarded their requests a few weeks in advance.

On the assumption that Robert Higgitt had died, we find the Sydenham Palace was now in the charge of Mrs Eliza Higgitt who, four years later, left the taproom and sawdust floor in order to run a confectionery establishment in Cross Cheaping. There is nothing to suggest that the music hall side of The Sydenham was operating at this time.

Bell supervised the annual pantomime *'Little Red Riding Hood'*, which opened at the Theatre Royal on Boxing night 1877, and ran until 19th January 1878, the transformation scene being painted by Mr H. Becker, also mentioned as manager of the theatre.

Mr Western, a well and respected member of the Britannia Music Hall received, from his admirers, a token of their esteem in the form of a silver medal, not at the Music Hall but on stage of the Theatre Royal after a performance of *'Our Boys'* on 21st January, which might suggest the capacity of the latter was greater despite the reputation for the music hall holding over 2000 people.

May 9th began a three nightly engagement at the Theatre Royal by Jolly John Nash, whose real name was Jimmie Taylor, in a show entitled *'Be Merry and Wise'*. Nash was one of the first music hall performers specialising in comedy songs, and who later became chairman of the Strand Musick Hall, the site of which later sprouted the first London Gaiety Theatre. He was also one of the first light entertainers to be commanded to appear privately before the Prince of Wales whom he greatly offended, on one occasion, by slapping the royal personage heartily on the back after some buffoonery or other.[53] The prefix Jolly came from his merry infectious laughing songs.

The spring and early summer months proved a difficult time for the Theatre Royal as it was closed more than it was open, rather like the previous year. No apparent reason is forthcoming unless Edward Bell was in deep financial water.

There were no signs of a similar malaise at the Britannia, whose music hall season closed on July 6th after which another drama company, including William Mallalieu, remained for several weeks. The usual dramatic favourites, *'Catherine Howard'*, *'Hamlet'* and *'East Lynne'* were served up. This was the Britannia's second venture into drama and may have been more successful owing to fluctuations at the Theatre Royal.

James Walton

The Theatre Royal reopened on September 7th, 1878 with J. Walton, lessee, and William Mallalieu as manager after his transfer from the Britannia. Towards the end of the century, Mallalieu would be in charge at the Leicester Theatre Royal. Workmen had been busy altering the upper boxes which were then deemed 'safe' by the City Surveyor, although the original problem was not recorded. It will be recalled that the upper side galleries were closed in 1872. The interior lighting was renewed and the staircase entrance widened. It is not known whether this refers to the box access, gallery or both. Mander, of Coventry, supervised the decorating.[54] Other work included relining the seats with crimson cloth, a new carpet, a new stage, improved lighting, a complete set of new stock scenery and an act-drop painted by Edwin Day of Birmingham. Day was a member of the family who owned and ran Day's Concert Hall, later Frank Matcham's Empire, in Hurst Street. The Empire, situated almost next door to the present Hippodrome, was bombed in 1941.

The season opened with a stock company, as opposed to a weekly touring one, but this lasted no longer than a few months. The Britannia continued with its summer season of dramatic presentations until mid October, when music hall artists took to the stage once more. The dramas '*Joan*' and '*Catherine Howard*', recently seen at the Britannia, were served up relatively warm at the Theatre Royal. The '*Corsican Brothers*', a regular over the years, re-appeared for the week beginning 30th October.

Appropriately the Royal staged '*Guy Fawkes*' at the beginning of November, a play which may have been written by George Macfarren (father of the composer) and first produced at the London Coburg (now the Old Vic), in 1822. The following month, Fred Smith's '*Spectral Opera Company*', including Professor Pepper's Ghost effects, took Coventry by storm but at the Corn Exchange and not the theatre. One wonders how this illusion fared in so large a building.

'*Sinbad the Sailor*', opened at the Theatre Royal in December 1878 and drew excellent crowds. The mechanical arrangements by George Cawdery and the transformation scene '*Aeriel's Dream*' being described in superlatives, with Jennie Hardcastle carrying on the tradition of the female principal boy.

In March manager Mallalieu was replaced by Temple Collings, another refugee from the Britannia Theatre of Varieties. Collings's versatility exhibited itself as manager, actor and scenic artist.

Tom G. Warry

Kate Santley (1837–1923), whose operetta company normally performed at the London Royalty Theatre and where Gilbert and Sullivan's '*Trial by Jury*' received its first performance, brought opera to Coventry in February 1879. She had led a varied theatrical existence making a big success at the London Oxford Music Hall as an early 'serio'. This booking was followed by Charles Dillon and Bella Mortimer in a series of classics and Boucicault's melodramas. Dillon (1819–1881) began as a young teenage player in Simpson's Penny Theatres in the Vine Yard on the other side of Tooley Street, London. From there he acted as a fourteen year old in a dog play at London Bridge Theatre.[55] He had an eccentric personality, although his power of acting was regarded highly and his power of pathos was described in superlatives. He was a rough, unintellectual character whose visual characteristics lacked charm and beauty. A 'well built' man, he never doffed his heavy moustache and beard for any part whether it be Hamlet or that of a young romantic. Once he also gruffly feigned not to know Henry Irving, whilst the two were standing side by side outside the Lyceum in the days of the latter's fame. Irving, as a young man, was considerably helped and encouraged in the learning of his profession whilst a member of Dillon's Stage Company.[56]

The Britannia had been closed for a short while but re-opened in July 1879 with a return of J. Eaves as proprietor. He immediately instigated a new short dramatic season, a feature to be repeated with both comedy and burlesque in January 1880.

Touring was becoming increasingly more popular and many big names in the business were taking advantage of it. The shows made available often followed successful London productions and several companies would be launched to take the play on tour. The most important, or number ones, would visit the better equipped theatres in towns and cities whilst smaller number twos, with less experienced casts and simpler sets, would serve smaller but properly equipped theatres. The number threes would take in the smallest theatres and the number fours would frequent village halls and assembly rooms in the more remote areas. The Coventry Theatre would have opened in 1819 as a main provincial house, but by 1879 it probably functioned as a number two date, gradually slipping down the hierarchical ladder as the century progressed and as newer better equipped buildings became available. In October 1879, the Theatre Royal received a John Hollingshead tour and later in the same week another from Charles Wyndham. Neither august personages appeared with their companies but their names would have created sufficient clout to command an audience.

There was no pantomime on Boxing Day 1879, the bill of fare being 'Simon' and 'Christine the Dutch Girl' both provided by John Taylor's touring company. At the Britannia, however, a series of comedies, given by the Standard Comedy and Burlesque company, gave 'Ali Baba' as an after piece. Pantomime did not completely desert the Royal; 'The House that Jack Built' or 'Mother Hubbard, Dame Trot, Mother Goose, and their comical cat, dog and goose', ran for three weeks from 1st March. Afterwards came another season of 'in-house' stock plays with Mallalieu and Collings, who became the new manager in that month. The remainder of the year was occupied mainly by weekly touring companies, some coming back to fulfil return dates.

'The Streets of London' returned to the Theatre Royal on May 24th for the week, the *Herald* correspondent praising the scenery, especially that of the Thames Embankment at night with electric lamps giving a mysterious atmosphere over the setting. Electricity at the Royal is only mentioned on one other occasion, when lights adorned the proscenium arch in 1892. It must be assumed that gas remained the main illuminant and that electrical power was provided by other means, possibly a small steam generator nearby. It is interesting to find that Temple Collings was the scenic artist for this play and that it was an in-house production.

> *"This theatre is, we regret to say, in the market, and our reason for regret is the probable loss of its present lessee, who has done his utmost to give the public pleasure combined with comfort."*[57]

In August 1880, the Theatre Royal went up for auction at the White Lion Hotel in Smithford Street. It was listed simply as the theatre with residence for a manager. Beneath in the cellars was a wholesale wine and spirit warehouse occupying 580 square yards, originally let to Whittems and later used by Andrew Summer. The lot was sold to William Bennett for £1,150, although he did not purchase the other adjacent properties in the Theatre Yard which were up for sale at the same time. These were the Times printing works and other printing offices.[58] As Sir Skears Rew had owned much property there and as it was now all on offer, it is reasonable to suppose that most of these buildings had been in the same ownership over the years, probably that of the Shepheard family. This was a period when many provincial theatres which were too small to be adapted into main receiving houses, were rebuilt, closed or replaced. The limitations of the Royal must have been increasingly obvious to managers and public alike, so the opportunity not to replace the theatre with a larger one, by demolishing adjacent property, is somewhat surprising.

[1] Coventry Herald, 10 November, 1865.
[2] Coventry Herald, 2 March, 1866.
[3] Peter Honri, "John Wilton's Music Hall", Ian Henry Publications 1985.
[4] John Ashby, "The Character of Coventry", John Ashby 2001
[5] Era Magazine, 30 December, 1866.
[6] Coventry Herald, 3 January, 1868.
[7] Era Magazine, 16 February, 1868.
[8] Richard Fawkes, "Dion Boucicault" Quartet Books 1979.
[9] M.W.Disher, "Blood and Thunder", Frederick Muller 1949.
[10] Coventry Herald, 3 April, 1868.
[11] Morris Directory 1866, Coventry City Library.
[12] Era Magazine, 25 October, 1868.
[13] Russell Jackson, "Victorian Theatre", A & C Black 1989.
[14] Coventry Herald, 8 January, 1869.
[15] Theatre Notebook, Volume XLIII No 1. 1989, "Professor Pepper's Ghost", George Speaight.
[16] Era Magazine, 10 July, 1870.
[17] Coventry Herald, 7 January, 1870.
[18] Coventry Herald, 28 January, 1870.
[19] Era Magazine, 25 September, 1870.
[20] Coventry Herald, 28 October, 1870.
[21] Coventry Herald, 11 November, 1870.
[22] Era Magazine, 11 June, 1871.
[23] Era Magazine, 27 August, 1871.
[24] Lou Warwick, "Theatre Un-Royal", Lou Warwick 1974.
[25] Coventry Herald, 1 December, 1871.
[26] Coventry Herald, 22 December, 1871.
[27] Coventry Herald, 12 April, 1872.
[28] Era Magazine, 26 May, 1872.
[29] Coventry Herald, 21 June, 1872.
[30] Era Magazine, 11 August, 1872.
[31] Era Magazine, 15 September, 1872.
[32] Coventry Herald, 20 September, 1872.
[33] Coventry Herald, 27 September, 1872.
[34] H. Chance Newton, "Cues and Curtain Calls", John Lane The Bodley Head Limited 1927.
[35] Frederick Penzel, "Theatre Lighting Before Electricity", Wesleyan University Press 1978.
[36] Coventry Herald, 27 June, 1873.
[37] Coventry Herald, 13 June, 1873.
[38] Lou Warwick, "Theatre Un-Royal", Lou Warwick 1974.
[39] The Era Magazine, 22 February, 1874.
[40] The Era Magazine, 6 December, 1874.
[41] The Era Magazine, 21 March, 1875.
[42] Sara Maitland, "Vesta Tilley", Virago Pioneers 1986.
[43] The Era Magazine, 21 May, 1876.
[44] Coventry Herald, 13 October, 1876.
[45] Era Magazine, 7 January, 1877.
[46] Sybil Rosenfeld, "The York Theatre", Society for Theatre Research 2001.
[47] The Stage, 12 April, 1906.
[48] C.M.P.Taylor, "Right Royal", Wakefield Historical Publications No 35. 1995.
[49] John Coleman, "Fifty Years of an Actor's Life", James Pott & Co, 1904.
[50] Coventry Herald, 23 February, 1877.
[51] Coventry Herald, 12 October, 1877.
[52] Era Magazine, 7 October, 1877.
[53] W. Macqueen Pope, "The Melody Lingers On", W.H. Allen.
[54] Coventry Herald, 20 September, 1878.
[55] Theatre Notebook, Volume 14. 1959, Drama at London Bridge", Malcolm Morley.
[56] H. Chance Newton, "Cues and Curtain Calls", John Lane The Bodley Head Ltd 1927.
[57] Era Magazine, 22 August, 1880.
[58] Coventry Herald, 27 August, 1880.

Chapter 9

William Bennett [c 1838–1911]

The Royal changed hands after the start of the new season and Bennett took control on September 27th, 1880 with Temple Collings as his acting manager. Performances in the opening week were given by Charles Morton's Danites

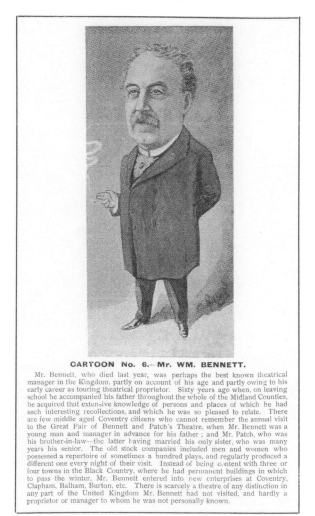

CARTOON No. 6.—Mr. WM. BENNETT.

Mr. Bennett, who died last year, was perhaps the best known theatrical manager in the Kingdom, partly on account of his age and partly owing to his early career as touring theatrical proprietor. Sixty years ago when, on leaving school he accompanied his father throughout the whole of the Midland Counties, he acquired that extensive knowledge of persons and places of which he had such interesting recollections, and which he was so pleased to relate. There are few middle aged Coventry citizens who cannot remember the annual visit to the Great Fair of Bennett and Patch's Theatre, when Mr. Bennett was a young man and manager in advance for his father ; and Mr. Patch, who was his brother-in-law—the latter having married his only sister, who was many years his senior. The old stock companies included men and women who possessed a repertoire of sometimes a hundred plays, and regularly produced a different one every night of their visit. Instead of being content with three or four towns in the Black Country, where he had permanent buildings in which to pass the winter, Mr. Bennett entered into new enterprises at Coventry, Clapham, Balham, Burton, etc. There is scarcely a theatre of any distinction in any part of the United Kingdom Mr. Bennett had not visited, and hardly a proprietor or manager to whom he was not personally known.

Figure 39   A cartoon of William Bennett which appeared in the 'Coventry Celebrities in Cartoon' in 1912

Coventry Record Office

Company. Bennett was well versed in theatrical matters, for his family ran the Theatres Royal in Kidderminster and Leamington, together with other theatres at Burton-upon-Trent and the Shakespeare in Clapham, London. He was also brother-in-law to Wally Patch who was associated with the Stourbridge Alhambra Theatre and who also ran the Burton-on-Trent Alhambra Music Hall in tandem with Bennett during the early 1880s.

Bennett did not regularly use the *Herald* for advertising purposes; one can only assume he felt other forms of propaganda were more effective and cheaper.

He secured a two day booking of Ellen Terry starting on November 10th. Both she, and her stage partner Henry Irving, had played the Birmingham Theatre Royal during the previous week but he did not follow to the city of her birth (1847), where her father, Ben, had been a member of Henry Bennett's stock company. Making her debut at the age of nine at the London Princess's theatre under Charles Kean, she quickly climbed the ladder of fame which pinnacled in her association with Henry Irving at the London Lyceum Theatre; her most well remembered role being '*Portia*' in '*The Merchant of Venice*'. At Coventry, Irving's place was taken by Charles Kelly, known in private life as Charles Wardell. He, and Ellen, were husband and wife although the three year union of this, her second marriage, was to end in 1881 after he had become jealous of her talents and taken to drink. He died in 1885.[1] The *Herald* was to remark, "*It is rarely that a 'star' of Miss Terry's magnitude takes a provincial tour and not always that Coventry is visited when such a course is adopted.*"[2] He might have added that some who ventured forth were sometimes rewarded with 'beggarly houses', although on this occasion, full and fashionable audiences were noted. Prices of admission were not advertised in the paper but there is little doubt they were raised for the occasion. Pit stalls were created on the ground floor and the boxes were converted into a dress circle. Since the centre boxes were already designated 'dress circle' in the 1857 rebuild, it must be assumed this reference concerned the side box seats. The plays performed were '*The Merchant of Venice*' and '*New Men and Old Acres*'. This was Ellen Terry's last professional venture to Coventry until 30th June, 1906 when she laid the Foundation Stone of the second Empire Theatre, which was modelled out of the Corn Exchange in Hertford Street into a fashionable music hall. By that time the Theatre Royal was no more.

A stock company reappeared on November 29th, 1880 but "*business has not been as good as might be expected. . .and the company have acquitted themselves tolerably well.*"[3]

The Christmas pantomime was '*Jack and the Enchanted Beans*'. "*The whole of the machinery has now been got into perfect working order*" suggesting there had been problems from the opening night, but then the inaugural performance of any pantomime is frequently plagued by theatrical gremlins.[4] Temple Collings was the scenic artist and also took an acting role. It was heralded as "*the best pantomime that had ever been put upon the Coventry stage*" but then almost all reviewers used similar sentiments every year.

"New Babylon", performed by George Lash Gordon and Percy Bell's Company, was seen in February 1881. In the company was Gladys ffolliott, an Irish actress of great character, wit and a personal friend of Marie Lloyd. Once, when suing her landlord, she appeared in court. The young barrister, Harris, rose.

> *"Miss Gladys ffolliott with two small 'ff's', I notice."*

> *"'It has been spelt in that manner since the days of Edward the Second', she returned."*

> *"Ah, a name redolent of romance."*

> *"Exactly as yours, Mr Harris, is redolent of sausages"*. (The firm Harris, like Walls, purveyed this delicacy at that time).

The judge laughed and she won her case.[5] Little wonder she and Marie got on well.

'Little Bo-Peep' made a three day appearance at the end of February. Pantomimes are usually complicated affairs from almost every standpoint, and it stretches the mind to imagine scenery and costumes being turned around in such a short space of time.

The Britannia Music Hall, at the corner of Fleet Street and Smithford Street, was bought by William Bennett in 1881. It is difficult to assess the force of the opposition offered by the Britannia to either the Theatre Royal or the Corn Exchange as neither operated a Music Hall policy at this time. The Britannia remained in Bennett's ownership until the Co-operative Society bought the freehold for a drapery and footwear shop in 1892.

Barry Sullivan made one of his regular appearances at the Theatre Royal in May, followed by a two day visit from the Edward Compton Comedy Company in, *'She Stoops to Conquer'* and *'The Lottery Ticket'*. Edward Compton, born Edward Mackenzie in 1854, quickly established himself as a first rate light comedian. The change of identity occurred when his father, Charles Mackenzie, a member of a family with strict Puritan connections, chose to go on the stage. Rather than disgrace the family name, he chose an alias, Henry Compton, which remained until the cognomen was reinstated by Edward's son, Compton Mackenzie who became the well known novelist. In 1881 the Compton Comedy Company was inaugurated at the Southport Winter Gardens on February 7th, financed by a legacy from Edward's fiancee, Lillian Adelaide Neilson, who died suddenly in Paris.[6] In the Company was an actress, Virginia Bateman, who later became Mrs Edward Compton. The Batemans were of American stock, choosing to settle in England at the time of their Revolution. Her father, Hezekiah Linthicum Bateman, ran the Lyceum Theatre and introduced Henry Irving to the London stage, with one of his (Bateman's) four daughters, Isabel, as his leading lady, a position later taken by Ellen Terry.

The Compton Comedy Company is probably an organisation little known beyond the knowledge of theatre historians, and yet for forty three years it attracted hundreds of thousands of people into the provincial playhouses and kept the flags of good drama and first rate acting flying high.[7] From 1920 to 1923 its headquarters was based in the Nottingham Grand Theatre, which the company re-named the

Nottingham Repertory Theatre. The Grand, which was situated in the Hyson Green area of the city, became a cinema from 1925 and was demolished around 1964.

The *Stage* newspaper reported the Coventry Royal being closed for almost ten weeks during the summer of 1881 while alterations were effected. Reopening took place on August 15th, 1881 with a complete new set of stock scenery painted by T. Hall, a scenic artist imported from the Prince of Wales Theatre, Birmingham and the Holte Theatre, Aston.[8] The proscenium arch was striking in that it was painted in light colours and the panels ornamented with *"chaste and well executed designs."* The lower tier of boxes was painted the traditional green and the upper tier a shade of pink. An elaborately designed Coventry Coat of Arms was worked into the central panel of the lower tier. A cloakroom for ladies was also installed on this level[9] Perhaps the gentlemen had to fend for themselves at the Theatre Vaults, for it is not known the degree of toilet accommodation, if any, provided for the genders in many theatres at this time.

Although many of our theatres are decorated in red hues, playhouses originally were green in colour even though this is regarded as unlucky by many thespians. Nottingham Theatre Royal and the Plymouth Palace reverted to green during their refurbishments, and the Douglas Gaiety has kept faith with turquoise, the colour with which it opened in 1900. The opening production at Coventry was the farcical comedy 'The Major and Husbands and Wives'.

The traditional pantomime was usurped by a fortnight's appearance of the Compton Comedy Company over the Christmas period.

> *"So anxious are people to witness the doings of this clever company that they are willingly paying increased prices to secure seats."*[10]

The year 1882 continued with the usual round of touring productions, some of which gave the same performance every night in the week, others offered a different play each night. In August 1882, bills were circulated announcing the postponement of the 'For Gold' company which was advertised to appear on the 21st. The theatre was undergoing further renovations which took longer than estimated to complete. The pit floor was lowered about eighteen inches and new refreshment bars and smoking saloons were added. Orchestra stalls were now a permanent feature in the front part of the ground floor. Reasons for further structural alterations can only be surmised. It is likely that the lowering of the pit, and the installation of orchestral stall seats were connected. One imagines that only the front part of the pit was sunk so as to enable the armchairs, with backs to them, not to interfere with the sight lines of those sitting on the pit benches behind. Even though the stalls armchairs might have been slightly higher than the former benches, one wonders whether the sightlines from the new seating were impaired especially as the stage remained in its former position. Bearing in mind the rebuilding undertaken in 1857, the front of the pit was now just around five feet below the original 'plimsoll' line of 1819. For the first time, the pit holders were pushed back as the front rows of their territory were given over to orchestra stalls patrons who paid a higher price for admission.[11] Most London theatres were doing the same, as a means of recouping greater box office returns to meet increased costs of production. At Coventry it is almost certain a

Figure 40   The Theatre Royal, Bristol (1941) showing the distribution of chairs in the more expensive parts of the house and benches elsewhere. Coventry Theatre Royal is likely to have had a similar appearance in 1882 apart from not having the extra gallery and the fact that the pit extended beneath the first tier of boxes. It was unusual for pit benches to have survived so late into the twentieth century

Reproduced by permission of English Heritage. NMR

wooden barrier dividing the pit and orchestra stalls was installed and was probably similar to that re-introduced into the Douglas Gaiety theatre in 2000. (see page 68) The Royal reopened with the play '*Craft*', written by Arthur Sketchley.

The Britannia, which used to feature in the weekly reviews in the *Era* theatrical paper, disappeared from these pages during most of 1882, but it reopened in November.

> "*This hall having undergone some important changes will undoubtedly again secure popularity.*"[12]

The pantomime '*Ali Baba and the Forty Thieves*', opened at the Theatre Royal on Boxing Day 1882. It was written and produced by H.C.Hazlewood, a member of the family which controlled the West Bromwich and Wolverhampton Theatres Royal at the time. The part of Abdallah was taken by J.B.Mulholland, who was later to run the Nottingham Grand Theatre from 1888, the London Camberwell Metropole (later the Empire) from 1894, the Hammersmith Kings Theatre from 1902 and the Wimbledon Theatre from 1910. The lieutenant of the unsavoury gang, Kalulu by name, was played by eight year old James Jones who, in addition to his prowess of the '*man-management*' of his tribe, had the confidence of an older actor and was able to clog dance with precision and dexterity. However, he was described as a precocious infant capable of making a fortune from his talent, assuming he was 'spared' before being out of his teens.[13] Rules of employment of children became more strict as the century wore on. Later, a Parliamentary Act of 1889 prohibited those under seven from appearing on stage, and licences were required for those between the ages of seven and ten, an action not popular with managements who were in the habit of exploiting children as they were cheap. Up until the latter part of the twentieth century, when excessive rules and mounting finances took over, children always played a prominent part in pantomimes and gave them a special character. It was reported that the Harlequinade in 'Ali-Baba' was shorter than usual, a sign that this part of the traditional fare was beginning to wane in popularity.

> "Owing to his success attendant on Mr John Coleman's visit here, this theatre has remained at his disposal for this week and results have justified the venture."

John Coleman was 'officially' booked for a week but stayed two. A common publicity stunt was to suggest that the huge popularity during the first six days warranted a prolonged visit, but it was just that – a stunt. Theatres, like visiting companies, had to book their dates well in advance. To say that Coleman was retained was to suppose he had no where to go during the second week and that no company had been booked into the Royal. The theatre was a commercial concern and businesses could not be run like that. An almost modern equivalent occurred with a pantomime, starring Arthur Askey, at the Coventry Hippodrome during the 1960s. The run was suddenly extended by a week due to 'public demand'. A spokesman for the theatre told me that there was no booking during the week in question, and it was cheaper to run the pantomime with meagre houses than to keep the house dark. Pantomime contracts, at that time, included a clause to extend the run if the decision was taken some weeks before the scheduled closure. That is exactly what happened at the Hippodrome; there was certainly no sudden 'public demand', but the phrase looked well in the local papers.

Miss Bateman's company was a frequent visitor to Coventry, and she returned for the week beginning May 20, 1883 with a round of plays including 'Mary Warner'. As frequently happened in Victorian times, the finesse of Miss Bateman's histrionics was such, that some members of the audience forgot they were watching a professional actress performing a rehearsed play written by an author. In the plot, she was falsely accused of some misdemeanour or other in front of an officer of the law, when one member of the audience could stand it no longer and informed the policeman that, "It was the other lodger, Sir."[14] It is not clear which of Hezekiah's four daughters visited Coventry, the fact that initials, or forenames, were often omitted in Victorian literature doesn't help solve such matters.

Bennett continued to make serious attempts to remedy the shortcomings of the building, and to make it function as a profitable touring theatre. The Theatre Royal closed on June 8th, 1883 for yet another series of alterations to the stage and dressing rooms. It was reported that the former was lengthened by thirteen feet and widened by eight.[15] Just how this was accomplished is not detailed in any paper, for no alterations to the outer walls were recorded on the Ordnance Survey map of 1888. It is possible that the rear of the old stage had been used for storage purposes, and that this was cleared to enable more elaborate sets to be accommodated. Where the extra width came from is not so easily explained. The additional room can only have been found by re-arranging the existing space. No amount of juggling could have added one 'jot or tittle' to the stage left wing, and any changes affecting the size of the proscenium opening can be ruled out. The theatre reopened on August 6th with the 'Crutch and Toothpick' company. The new season carried on much as before, a high note being Frank R. Benson's Shakespearean company coming for a week on October 16.

Frank Benson [1858–1939]

Frank Robert Benson was a professional stalwart who not only provided one of the few nurseries for aspiring actors and actresses, but did sterling service as an actor-manager in taking Shakespeare, and other classical plays, into the provinces for so many years. Donald Wolfit was to assume a similar mantle in the twentieth century. As a student at New College Oxford Benson produced 'Agamemnon', the first play to be done there in the original Greek. He first appeared professionally in Henry Irving's company at the London Lyceum, and was responsible for organising twenty six Shakespearean Festivals at Stratford-upon-Avon from 1888, as well as being a governor there. He entered into management two months before his first Coventry appearance, when he took control of Walter Bentley's company (of which he was a member) in 1883. Bentley abandoned the troupe and shipped himself off to Australia. The repertory of Benson's first season included, 'Romeo and Juliet', 'Hamlet', 'Lady of Lyons', 'The Corsican Brothers', 'Money', 'Rob Roy' and 'The Merchant of Venice', most of these being presented to the patrons at the Coventry Theatre Royal. He was a keen sportsman and eagerly recruited young actors who could demonstrate their prowess on the playing field, as it was common for the company to challenge local teams wherever they played. Stories of advertisements for a 'Mercutio who was a good left hand bat' are, no doubt, apocryphal for the actor's ability always came first. During an interview Frank Benson was greatly impressed with Basil Rathbone's football colours, his trial as a fast bowler and success on the track.[16] Benson believed physically fit men made better actors, however he met his match on one occasion when he, and his Shakespearean Company, entered a local swimming competition. There was a pile (wooden stake) in the river; Benson never saw it but it gave him a black eye just the same and no amount of make up could hide the fact during the evening's performance.[17] King George V knighted him at the conclusion of 'Julius Caesar' at Drury Lane on May 2, 1916, using a stage property sword.

On Tuesday November 26th, an accident occurred on the stage during a performance of 'Youth' given by Wilmot's Company. A rifle, loaded with blank charges, was fired in front of the Joseph Swift, who was playing the character Frank Darling, and much of the discharge entered into his left eye. There is no account of how bad the injury was but such occurrences were by no means rare. Swords and firearms have frequently caused serious, and sometimes fatal, injuries in the theatre.

Harold Norman, playing the part of Macbeth, was fatally stabbed in a duel with Macduff at the Oldham Coliseum Theatre in 1947.[18]

The weeks before Christmas have always been difficult on account of seasonal pressure on everybody's time. 'Grelley's Money', which opened on December 9th was no exception. *"The pantomime being in view was no doubt the cause of meagre attendance's."*[19]

The 1883/4 pantomime was *'Little Bo Peep and the Old Woman who lived in a Shoe'*, together with Boucicault's *'Octoroon'*, which alternated with *'The Dumb Man of Manchester'*. Audiences certainly got their money's worth.

Public Transport

It is known that theatre attendance in general improved upon the introduction of public transport into our towns and cities. Whereas theatres had a localised clientele, public transport would have brought the outlying districts that bit nearer to the front door, even though the art of walking was more practised then than now. Coventry's first public carrier opened in the form of a steam tramway between the railway station and the coal mining town of Bedworth, some six or seven miles to the north, in 1884. The route ran along the end of Smithford Street and it seems reasonable to assume it made some difference at the box office, although there are no official records to show one way or the other. The remainder of the tramway system did not open until after the theatre had finally closed.

Tom C.King, actor and manager (1825–1893), headed a classical week at the end of January 1884 which gave, *'Othello'*, *'Ingomar'*, *'The Merchant of Venice'* and *'Hamlet'*. It was King who played Othello when Henry Irving ventured onto the boards, for the very first time, to portray Cassio at the Dublin Queens Theatre in March 1860.[20] A man of ample proportions, King was well known for his portrayal of Hamlet and he had an unusually thunderous voice, of barnstorming qualities, quite capable of filling the cavernous Drury Lane.[21] He was another who never shaved off his moustache for any role. Born in Cheltenham, he made his first appearance at Birmingham Theatre Royal, then went onto the York circuit to learn his trade before performing at the London Princess's Theatre under Charles Kean in 1857.

The Coventry Theatre Royal closed for more alterations on March 1st, but was open the following Monday. What changes took place are unknown, but they could not have been very substantial.

On March 22nd a comic concert party, headed by Witty Watty Walton, opened with those who had taken part in the Birmingham Prince of Wales' pantomime. Two local turns were included, one being the Wood's children, who appeared as white minstrels, and the other was Professor Newman, the ventriloquist.

Further alterations to the stage were effected during a closed period from May 25. They were in preparation for the production of *'Mazeppa'*, with Maude Forrester in the title role riding her steed *'Lightning'*. The production ran for a fortnight, and the Godiva Procession Committee presented Maude Forrester with a handsome illuminated address at her benefit during the second week. She reappeared at the Royal in later years in the title role of 'Lady Godiva'.

The Strand Comedy Company opened the autumn season on July 17th, with Ada Swanborough [1845–1893] in 'May' and the burlesque 'Out of the Ranks'. Business was moderate.

September 20th saw 'Called Back', by Hugh Conway, and a pantomimic burlesque of 'Aladdin' or 'The Lamp and the Scamp'. One wonders whether it deviated from the original in a similar manner to Jim Davidson's "Sinderella", an adult skit on the well known pantomime and offered towards the end of the twentieth century, although Conway's production was, no doubt, not quite as daring.

Wilton B. Payne's 'Way of the World' company attracted depressingly small audiences in October, although members of the cast played with considerable spirit. Better attendance figures greeted Wilson Barratt when he toured his play 'The Silver King', also in October. The play, written by Jones and Herman, saw the light of day at the London Princess's Theatre in November 1882, and was based on Ibsen's 'Nora', or 'A Doll's House'. Although it was invariably on tour, it was not quite the grand success of Wilson Barratt's other 'smash hit', 'The Sign of the Cross', which netted him enough money with which to build the Leeds Grand and London Lyric Theatres. There is no record of this last play ever visiting the Coventry Royal, but it did play at the Opera House in March 1897.

The Britannia Music Hall re-opened as the New Gaiety Theatre on Monday 3rd November, 1884, to a crowded audience. *"It is some years since this city has enjoyed the peculiar privileges and benefit of a really good music hall"*, which suggests that both the Britannia and Sydenham Palace had been closed for some considerable time. Alterations were carried out to the designs of W. Langley. The stage was fourteen feet deep with a proscenium width of eighteen feet, dimensions similar to those found at the present Leeds City Varieties Theatre. T. Hall provided the scenery and painted the proscenium and act drop. Around 800 people were accommodated in pit, stalls and a *"prettily shaped"* balcony, a number which must surely have rivalled the capacity of the Theatre Royal. The figure of 800 is more realistic than that of 1800 made earlier. Mr Arthur Dashwood kept order as chairman, and the entertainment consisted of up to eight performing acts including, an American comic, a male impersonator, a bone soloist, Irish vocalist, wire walker, duettists and character vocalist.[22] Dashwood remained until November 29th, although he turned up later at the Theatre Royal, and was replaced by Sidney Ogle. Dashwood eventually became lessee and manager of Swansea's Fletcher's Music Hall in 1885, and at the Kirkcaldy Gaiety Varieties in the 1890s.

Sidney Cooper (lessee of the Reading Theatre Royal) brought the 'Little Jack Horner' pantomime to the Corn Exchange for eight nights starting from Boxing Day, whilst the Theatre Royal made do with the spectacular drama 'Michael Strogoff'. T. Hall's special scenery for the battle scenes, the 'Tartar's Camp' and 'The Burning City' were much commended. Pantomime made a delayed appearance at the Royal when '*Dick Whittington and His Cat*' played for two weeks at the end of January 1885.

On March 22nd, 1885 the Gaiety reverted to the name of Britannia, R.E. Mackintosh taking charge of the house.

John Lawson and Lester Collingwood appeared there in '*After Dark*' on 8th August, 1885. Lester Collingwood became a well known figure in Birmingham, taking over the Lyceum Theatre in John Bright Street in 1902 and renaming it the Alexandra, a place he ran until his death in 1910. A fortnight later John Lawson was at the Britannia in the sketch '*Redemption*' in which he played the part of a Jew. He was part Jewish himself.

September 27th and 28th saw Vesta Tilley, with a complete supporting variety cast, at the Corn Exchange. This was a far cry from her appearance at the humble Britannia in 1876.

At the Theatre Royal, ordinary touring dramas occupied the boards for the rest of the year, there being little of note save another visit by Benson's Company. Although closed for three weeks in July, there were no reports of alterations being undertaken to patch up a building which was becoming progressively unsuitable for modern productions.

Emily Charlotte Kennion's '*Nina*' stayed a week at the end of October 1885. She was "*complimented upon attention to detail that distinguishes the performance.*"[23] She was the lessee of the Leicester Theatre Royal (1885–1887) at the time, and had entered into negotiations to acquire the control of the larger Nottingham Grand Theatre which was to open in 1886. Emily and her husband, Captain Kennion, ran both theatres for a while; he as business manager and she directing her company. Although she had a family of seven to support, the couple lived apart. Her financial situation, which reflected heavy losses of around £1,700 on a Leicester Royal pantomime, was not helped by the fact that she kept no books of accounts. The situation did not improve and in July 1888 she and her estranged husband appeared at the Nottingham Bankruptcy Court.[24] She mainly engaged touring companies and it was stated in the proceedings that she worked on a system by which they were paid 55% of the gross receipts, leaving 45% for the host theatre to make ends meet. It appears that this was a common practice at the time. One understands that in this part of the twenty first century the percentage gained by some touring companies can be higher than 55%.

'*Young Mrs Winthrop*' appeared for only three nights from November 5th to the 7th 1885, with Miss Nellie Bouverie in the lead. Business was bad for the first two nights but picked up on the Saturday, but only at the expense of an extremely rowdy gallery, members of which were tongue lashed for their effrontery from the front of the stage by Miss Bouverie herself. The theatre occasionally booked productions for three nights only, the remainder of the week being dark. This is not easy to understand as there were over a hundred companies touring the country week by week at the time. It is possible only a few of these were suitable for the conditions offered by the Theatre Royal.

Later in the month, a benefit performance was held at the Britannia for Mr J. Wagland, retired manager at the City's King's Head. Whether this was the King's

Head Hotel in Smithford Street, or the King's Head Tavern, Little Park Street is not made clear, neither is the reason for this unusual performance.

'*The Streets of London*' reappeared at the beginning of December 1885, this was a company sent out by Andrew Melville [1853–1896], a seasoned actor responsible for giving the citizens of Derby their Grand Theatre in 1886 and those of Birmingham their Grand in 1883, although he did not personally appear at Coventry.

Star Trap

'*Cinderella*', ran for a three week season from Boxing Day, 1885. It was considered well written, by James Horner, being witty with an abundance of puns and free from vulgarity. The story was told in nine scenes; that in the kitchen contained much good star trap business. A star trap was an adaptation of a corner trap and consisted of a circular opening filled with triangular segments, rather like slices of a round cake. Each segment was hinged to a square frame but was only capable of opening in an upwards direction. With suitable lighting, the segments were invisible to members of the audience and that part of the stage looked solid. An actor stood on the trap platform at the bottom of the shaft below the stage, with his head just touching the underside of the star. Upon a given signal, the stage hands heaved on the ropes and the actor rose, apparently through the solid stage, so quickly that he would leap some feet into the air. The quicker he was propelled, the higher he went. By the time he landed on the stage again, the solid platform, upon

Figure 41 A rare example of a star trap as seen at the Grand Theatre, Llandudno (1984). Its origins are unknown for the frame could not be made to fit into either of the square corner trap openings. A better model would not have had a hole in the centre

Photo – Author

141

which he had been standing, was beneath the star and presented a solid floor. Using this piece of machinery was a specialised business and not without a certain amount of danger. Some performers managed to achieve between one and three pirouettes before landing back on the stage. It was not uncommon for some pantomime producers to employ a large number of these traps in their productions. The author has only ever seen one version of this once common trap and it was in a pantomime at Coventry Hippodrome in the late 1960s. Like most other forms of stage machinery, the star trap is all but confined to history.

Four Shetland ponies did duty in taking Cinderella to the ball and it is obvious, from the report, that many of the artists came out of character from time to time to perform speciality acts. This was in line with 'Gus' Harris' regime at London's Drury Lane and, to some extent, remains with many of the present large scale pantomimes still, although other 'in-house rep' productions prefer to tell an elaborated story with no extraneous interruptions. At Coventry the Zulu Queen (we don't see such a character in present day Cinderella productions), danced with boots twenty inches in length; perhaps a forerunner of Little Tich. The last scene, a chamber in the Baron's Castle, was followed by the transformation and then the Harlequinade. Transformation scenes now come immediately before the interval, the end being reserved for the 'walk down'. The Harlequinade had all but disappeared at the turn of the century, although the author can remember a revival of it at a Birmingham Aston Hippodrome pantomime in the late 1940s, when a cut down version was presented during the interval.

Touring drama, with many companies returning for a second date, was now the mainstay at the Theatre Royal, there being no further ventures into stock companies – with the exception of one week in 1895. Coventry did not have a number one theatre until the Opera House opened. The Royal was becoming increasingly unable to accommodate productions with the large and elaborate sets so much enjoyed by the late Victorian audiences. The lack of a fly tower, which speeds up scene changes, would have been a serious drawback at the Royal. Some theatres, especially those with a viable future, constructed their own, an example of which took place at the Leicester Theatre Royal in 1888. At Coventry cloths had to be rolled when taken out of sight. Bennett's new Opera House (1889) in Hales Street, had a tower which was described as *"a most modern arrangement."*[25]

Variety made a come back in June 1885 with a display of Mdlle. Eugenie Garrette's *'Pigeon Show'*. Onda, the female Apollo on the trapeze, fell nightly into a safety net, Dr Harley conjured and Nellie Goodwin was the serio comic.

The Corn Exchange saw the arrival of Edward O'Connor Terry and his comedy company for three evenings from 3rd to the 5th May, 1886 presenting, *'In Chancery'*, *'Weak Woman'* and *'The Rocket'*. Edward Terry was the leading comedian at the London Strand Theatre from 1868 to 1875, and in 1887 went into management in his own Terry's Theatre in London.

John Lawson [1865–1920], who was seen at the Coventry Britannia the previous August with his *'Redemption'* company, now returned to the Theatre Royal for the week beginning May 24th 1886, with *'Humanity'*, *or 'A Passage in the Life of Grace Darling'* – in four acts. The last act of the play, based on a terrible fight to the death of two crooks – Murray and Roberts – in 1861 London, was about a Jew (played by Lawson) whose wife was unfaithful with a Christian. The immediate connection between this and Grace Darling is not obvious, but in the final part the two men chased each other around the stage throwing furniture and crockery, of which there was an abundance, at each other. According to Naomi Jacob's *'Me'*, or *'A Chronicle about other people'* (Hutchinson and undated), Lawson used to advertise that £20 of pots were smashed at each performance. Certainly the beer bottles were doctored out of rubber and the furniture designed so that no lasting injury would occur. Later, when sketches were finding their way into the music halls, Lawson lifted the last act of *'Humanity'*, cut it to eighteen minutes, toured the variety theatres and made a fortune out of it.[26]

Completion of Upper Circle boxes

The Theatre Royal re-opened on July 26th, 1886 with Mrs Weldon's *'Not Alone'* company. During the summer recess, the front of house had been redecorated in extremely bright colours and there were improvements in the region of the upper boxes where *"a complete run from one side of the house to the other"* was formed.[27] The changes were seen as *"greatly enhancing the paying property of the building"* even though the front of the gallery had to be sacrificed thereby reducing the seating capacity in that region. This suggests that the auditorium was reversed to its appearance in 1857, or thereabouts. It is not easy to explain why the front tier of boxes was removed in the first place. It is possible that with a rise in greater prosperity, there were more patrons willing to pay for upper circle box seats which commanded a price higher than those in the gallery alone. It will be remembered that these central boxes in the second tier were removed in 1872. It is unlikely the box structure was very substantial.

T. Morton Powell, as Sir Clement Huntingford, visited the Royal in the drama *'World'* on October 24th 1886. Powell leased a number of theatres including Birmingham Bordesley Palace, Cannock Hippodrome, Liverpool Grand Theatre and the Farnworth Queens in the first part of the twentieth century.

Prior to the annual Christmas pantomime, Balfe's Opera Company brought round *'The Bohemian Girl'*, but *"the unsatisfactory performance gained such disapproval that the lessee decided to close the theatre for the remainder of the week."*[28] A similar situation occurred at the Leicester Opera House just twelve months later in January 1888, when Percy Wyndham's *'Fred'* or *'A Lancashire Lad'* opened on the Monday night only to have the lessee, Elliott Galer, stop the performance at 9.0. o'clock, return the money taken at the box office and close the theatre for the rest of the week. The audience applauded his decision. The company originally booked was unable to appear and a replacement was engaged, unseen, which turned out to be below the standard normally expected at the Opera House. Another story, with humorous overtones, occurred at Plymouth Royal some time before 1886, when the stock company put on *'Octoroon'* by Dion Boucicault.

"At the end of the first act. . .he (the manager) got up and addressed the audience: 'Ladies and gentlemen, my cast have acted so badly that they will now, with your permission, do it all over again', and they did."[29]

M'Culloch and Green's *'Blue Beard'* pantomime (an obsolete title for present day audiences) opened on Boxing Day 1886, with the transformation scene appearing after the twelfth or final scene. The scenery was painted by Phil Lovett, who coupled his artistic talents with that of appearing as an elephant. The run was cut short due to a spell of bad weather which affected audiences, reminiscent of a Frank Maddox's pantomime at the Bath Theatre Royal around 1963, which was curtailed owing to unseasonable snow drifts preventing his traditional rural clientele travelling in from the surrounding countryside.

Barry Sullivan played one of his many returns to Coventry early in February. For one who revelled in gloomy roles, he was a great humorist at heart and would occasionally get other actors to insert comic business into otherwise serious plays, although he drew a line at despoiling Shakespeare. The tale is told of his appearing in Birmingham before a thin and very unenthusiastic house, when he had to mark the end of the act by presenting the heroine to the leading Juvenile. He took liberties with the tag line and uttered, *"Take her and with her take the blasted Birmingham audience into the bargain."*[30] It is not recorded whether the Coventry patrons were held with the same degree of esteem. The 'tag' is the last line of a play and by tradition is not spoken until the first night.

Frank Roden retired from the managership of the Britannia in February 1887, and activities at the music hall were not reported in the columns of the *Era* for some time.

'Little 18 Carat' opened at the Theatre Royal on 13th March, 1887 with J.P.Moore as Colonel Billy. Moore was another entrepreneur who had connections with theatres in the Midlands and especially the West Bromwich Regent, which operated from 1895 to 1896 as a temporary replacement whilst the Royal in that town was being rebuilt after a fire. He took charge of the Kidderminster Theatre Royal from 1898.

The D'Oyly Carte Opera Company brought the *'Mikado'* to Coventry in June 1887 for two nights, but to the Corn Exchange and not the Theatre Royal. Since there were several D'Oyly Carte Companies on the road at any one time, each new opera was seen in most towns of importance shortly after the Savoy first night. No evidence has come to light of the D'Oyly Carte ever appearing at the Smithford Street house.

Edmund Tearle's *'Julius Caesar'* was on display during the week beginning April 10, 1887. Tending to be rather 'heavy', Tearle was considered an inferior interpreter of roles compared to his cousin Osmond and Osmond's son, Godfrey. However, Edmund cut a popular figure in Coventry, *"Mr Tearle has been accorded such a reception here as will no doubt induce an early return visit."*[31] It did, on several occasions.

An accident, not an uncommon one, befell Mr Bray, a stage hand, on May 23rd, 1887 when he fell through an open trap and collided with the stage on his descent thereby sustaining several internal injuries.[32] The incident, no doubt, occurred during the daytime when a minimal amount of lighting would be provided so that the darkness of an open cut would be indistinguishable from the dimness surrounding it. In the absence of social security, one wonders whether victims of accidents, such as Bray, had outside financial support when no money came into the home from employment. There were benefit clubs, but they seemed to be local ad hoc arrangements rather than nationally organised affairs. Leppington in 1891 refers to chorus girls paying a few coppers into such a fund per week in case of illness or accident, and being able to withdraw sufficient money to enable them to exist during the interim period.[33] The incident is interesting, being the first information found at Coventry concerning the provision of stage cuts and traps. The theatre, in keeping with the others of the nineteenth century, is likely to have been favoured with the usual complement of corner, grave, several bridge traps and sloats.

'Dick Whittington and His Cat' pantomime appeared at the Theatre Royal in the back end of June 1887. Summer pantomimes were not altogether unknown but they never seriously caught on. Easter ones were staged towards the end of the century but like their summer counterparts, faded from popularity.

Further alterations to the Theatre Royal were undertaken during two weeks at the end of July, but details were not specified. It seems that Bennett was making strenuous efforts to improve a building which was becoming more and more obsolete.

In September 1887, alterations were proposed to improve the acoustic qualities of the Corn Exchange, which were described as far from ideal. One has to visualise a large interior with little other than the outer walls, windows, roof lights and stage. It would have been a cavernous building and difficult to fill with sound which didn't echo and there were no artificial aids such as microphones on hand. The corridors were part of the interior and it was suggested that these were shut off by constructing interior walls, probably in a similar fashion to that at the Newark Palace in 1988. The blocked off corridors were intended for additional dressing rooms. Five openings, or balconies, on each side of the hall had been closed in with wood and a proposed new shallow gallery, seating an additional 500 people, was to be erected on three sides of the auditorium. The net increase in seating would be 300 due to the loss of 200 from the corridors. The total new capacity would be increased from 1500 to 1800, probably over twice that of the Royal, and this must have been an added incentive for larger companies to visit the Exchange.[34]

It was hardly surprising, therefore, that larger companies by-passed the Royal which was inconvenient and too small to attract the larger touring companies. This must have been true about almost every surviving early nineteenth century theatre; certainly Wallace Revill, in a letter dated 6th May, 1897, to the proprietors of the Leicester Theatre Royal, complained about the unsatisfactory accommodation and poor holding capacity which prevented better class companies from being booked.[35] When reseated using second hand materials from Birmingham Day's Music Hall in October 1893, the Coventry Royal was still described as *"bijou"*.[36] Bennett had to do something. He did. In November 1887, *"Mr Bennett announces in a footnote to this week's bill that plans are being prepared for a new theatre and opera house to be erected*

145

in Hales Street, Coventry, of which he will be the proprietor. It is intended, when the new building is finished, to convert the present theatre into a music hall and palace of varieties."[37]

Exeter Fire

It is an interesting exercise to speculate why Bennett did not rebuild and extend the Theatre Royal. The Ordnance Survey map for 1888 shows that the theatre was hemmed in on three sides by other properties. Only the north, facing the Theatre Yard, was available for access, and this would have had serious implications for large numbers of people emerging into one small area from a burning building. This was a time when the water remained turbulent from the aftermath of the 1887 Exeter theatre fire.

Although matters of public safety had surfaced before, especially in London, many theatres which were regarded as fire risks remained in use and, with the average life of a theatre being short, eventual conflagration seemed an accepted way

Figure 42 (*Left*) This illustrates the constriction when the large door was swung across the gallery entrance in order to make patrons file past the pay box in single file. The example was photographed from the street side of the pay box at the Northampton Royal Theatre and Opera House (1983)

Figure 43 (*Right*) The same constriction as seen from the other side of the door by patrons leaving the gallery and descending to the street. The narrowing at the Exeter Theatre Royal was permanent and it is easy to appreciate the bottleneck caused by hundreds of people trying to hurry out in a panic. It was stated that a similar door at the Coventry Theatre Royal was fastened back once the performance had started and therefore there was nothing to impede the flow when patrons left. This gallery pay box at Northampton is no longer used and the door is normally fastened back. There is another entrance and exit to the gallery and this passageway is only used in emergencies

Photos – Author

of life. In general, the main material for theatre construction was wood, especially backstage, and theatre exits in the main were often described as being restricted thereby making a mass exodus during an emergency difficult. The heat backstage generated from gas lighting was considerable and it had the effect of completely drying out all the timbers which became all the more vulnerable to fire. The London Opera Comique and the old Globe in East Strand, were constructed back to back. Both were 'Jerry' built, probably as a speculation for gaining generous compensation with the Aldwych reconstruction in the early twentieth century, and were known as the 'Rickety Twins'. The Opera Comique had the added nickname 'Theatre Royal Tunnels' which left nothing to the imagination.[38]

On Monday 5th September, 1887 the most appalling loss of life resulted from a devastating fire during a touring performance of 'Romany Rye' at the Exeter Theatre Royal. Around 180 people perished, many trying to make their way from a single entrance to the gallery. Theatre fires were not new; it was estimated that the chances of a theatre surviving before being burnt was seven years, but alarm bells rang loudly this time since the Exeter Royal was less than two years old, having replacing a theatre also destroyed by fire. The most eminent theatre architect of the day, Charles Phipps, designed it and it was assumed that all modern safety precautions had been incorporated into the plans. Surprisingly there was no safety curtain and the gallery, where most of the casualties took place, had but one entrance which narrowed into single file at the pay kiosk half way down the staircase.

People questioned that if such a disaster could befall a new building, what would happen should a similar calamity overtake an older one. After the fire, licensing authorities all over the country sent inspection teams into all places of local entertainment for immediate surveys; some buildings were closed on the spot, others were given a limited period in which to carry out remedial work and the remainder received a clean bill of health. It was proposed that all theatres should have a brick proscenium arch which, with an iron safety curtain, would present an impenetrable barrier against the spread of fire from stage to the auditorium. Some authorities seemed to insist upon this more than others. It is almost certain that the proscenium at Coventry was made of wood and plaster and not brick or stone, indeed it is likely the whole of the interior, both sides of the footlights, was constructed of timber apart from the outer walls. To carry out such remedial building work on a theatre with no access on three sides, and of a relatively low seating capacity, would not be cost effective, and this must have had a bearing on Bennett's decision to build his Opera House elsewhere.

Local reports on places of amusement in Coventry were described as efficient regarding their ability to extinguish fires and provide a rapid and unobstructed exit. Many theatre managements were introducing electric light, a safety curtain and sprinklers to minimise conflagration, but the Theatre Royal had none of these, yet the authorities seemed satisfied and did not insist upon any remedial work. A sprinkler consists of a perforated pipe, or pipes, over the stage, the holes being stopped with a fusible substance which melts on the surrounding temperature being raised: once dissolved the water is free to flow. In current theatres the pipe is placed at the top of the safety curtain in order to prevent it from overheating and buckling.

The means of exit from the theatre were considered sufficient from all three licensed buildings, as work had been carried out under the orders of the City Surveyor a few years previously.

The Theatre Royal was described as never having been an ideal building (just what did this mean?), but it compared favourably to other theatres of a similar size and probably reflected the numerous alterations made by Bennett since he took control. All exits from the pit, and the two tiers of boxes, converged into a couple of passages which opened into the Theatre Yard. The gallery entrance had but a single four feet wide stairway which was regarded as being outside the theatre itself, as it passed through the extension which incorporated the manager's residence. All doors leading to the gallery folded outwards and were fastened open during performances. There were no obstructions in the form of pay kiosks and barriers. It has to be borne in mind that the capacity of the gallery had been reduced upon completion of the upper circle boxes. Even so, the only escape from the Yard was approximately 100 feet from Smithford Street through an archway approximately eight feet in width. The Yard was shared with the 'Coventry Times', Robertson and Gray's publishing and printing offices and the National Telephone Exchange, although it is

 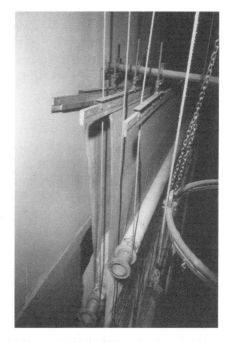

Figure 44 (*Left*) A view of two rolled backcloths hung in the flies and a third which as just been let down using the visible ropes. This example of changing cloths can still be found in amateur theatres but must have largely disappeared from the professional scene. Saxondale Hospital, Nottinghamshire, 1986

Figure 45 (*Right*) The same cloths viewed from the flies where there is no tower above into which scenery can be hoisted bodily. Note the frames from which the cloths are suspended. This would make the changing of cloths on, say, a weekly basis more cumbersome than the flying method. Rolled cloths did not pose the same fire risk as those already hanging and surrounded on two sides by a plentiful supply of air. This scene, and the previous picture, would have been replicated at the Coventry Theatre Royal. Saxondale Hospital, Nottinghamshire, 1986

Photos – Author

reasonable to assume that those employed in these buildings would make their way to and fro at times outside normal theatre hours. Rebuilding with access to the main thoroughfare would certainly have required the costly purchasing of occupied land between the theatre and Smithford Street, and it will be remembered that Bennett chose not to take this course of action when much of the surrounding property came up for sale in 1880.

As far as the stage was concerned, all wing gas lights and battens were covered with wire gauzes. Above the battens were catwalks to enable flymen to reach burning material and cut it down to the stage should the need arise which, it was reported, had happened on occasions. At each side of the stage was "*a considerable space*" available for the storage of properties and to where burning material could be taken out of the way. It is difficult to regard the stage left wing area as being 'considerable', as the proscenium opening would have permitted a width here of approximately eight feet, whilst that on stage right was greater after the rebuilding work undertaken in 1857. Fire extinguishers were available on the stage. It was stated that in the absence of a fly tower, all cloths were rolled and as such were almost non-flammable, as opposed to a hanging cloth with an abundant supply of air on both sides. Exits from the stage were approved, and the dressing rooms were not in the theatre but connected by a staircase.[39]

The *Herald* was not beyond making suggestions of its own. They thought a standpipe near the stage would be appropriate but according to the report, that area was well equipped with extinguishers. They thought a large emergency door at the rear of the building would improve egress, but had forgotten that the back of the auditorium shared a wall with other property and no access was possible. Stress was made on the no-smoking rule being adhered to, and they cited examples of where members of the audience frequently broke this edict.

The Corn Exchange also received official approval, even though it was described as an '*ill constructed and ill adapted*' building. It had three exits, to: Vicar Lane, King's Head Hotel Yard and Hertford Street, which enabled a large audience to be evacuated easily.

The only other building mentioned was the Co-operative Assembly Room, West Orchard, licensed for stage plays and having a capacity for 400 people. Being situated over the shop, it had three separate entrances and could be cleared in four or five minutes. Neither the Britannia, nor the Sydenham Palace were mentioned suggesting both were 'dark' at the time.

It will be remembered that this degree of safety scrutiny aimed at theatres in 1887 did not manifest itself in the football industry until a century later, after calamities at Sheffield and Bradford.

On Monday 3rd October, the Corn Exchange gave the proceeds from the performances of '*Family*' and '*The Loan of a Lover*' solely to those who had suffered in the Exeter Theatre fire. Many other theatres up and down the country made similar provisions.

There was the possibility that the local authority would eventually refuse a drama license for the Theatre Royal, or insist upon a further reduction in capacity. By some quirk of licensing logic, the regulations for opening and running a music hall were less stringent than for a legitimate house. In 1892, The Wakefield Theatre Royal was refused a dramatic licence as it did not comply with fire regulations, yet it reopened with a singing and dancing licence and functioned as a music hall for a short period afterwards, until the present Royal was built.[40] The old building was unsuitable for people to watch a play, yet when run as a music hall it was the same building and similar people sat in the same seats. Wakefield was not an isolated example. Music halls were viewed by some as the antechambers of hell, so perhaps it was thought that if a fire did break out the occupants would be part way to their destination anyway. Since the Coventry Theatre Royal was considered satisfactory, no further alterations were required when the venue became the Empire Theatre of Varieties two years later.

Last couple of years

Tearle presented a folio of Shakespearean plays over the Christmas period, and H.S.Dacre brought '*Little Red Riding Hood*' to the Theatre Royal boards for the week beginning January 15th, 1888.

The following week, the Britannia Music Hall reopened under the proprietorship of J. Randall whom, we must assume, leased it from William Bennett. Possibly small music hall sprats were of less interest to Bennett who was becoming increasingly more interested in catching larger fish for his empire. On April 1st, The Britannia became known as the Old City Music Hall, entering upon yet another phase of its existence. On the opening bill was a six year old clog dancer by the name of Andy Reynolds.

There were several periods when the Theatre Royal was closed for a week, or for three days when some companies were booked for half a week only. The flavour of products began to change. Plays such as '*A Mother's Sin*', '*The Wages of Sin*', '*Dr Jeckell and Mr Hyde*', brought the sensational element to Coventry. '*Fun on the Bristol*' was all about the shenanigans on board ship with Widow O'Brien (shades of Charley's Aunt to come) leading the frolics.

The Vokes family spent a three night engagement at the Theatre Royal at the beginning of June 1888. There were five of them: Barbara, Victoria, Fred, Fawdon and pretty, moonfaced, kittenish Rosina. Their father was a theatrical costumier whilst Fred initially spent time as an assistant to Professor Anderson, the 'Wizard of the North' and who frequented the Coventry Royal in 1854. The Vokes's were on the downward path of success having been a great influence as dancers in the Drury Lane pantomimes under Chatterton from 1869.

> "*But clever as they were, the Lane was to get a bit too much of the multitudinous Vokes'. In 1874, they were playing all the principal parts in "Aladdin". They even took a call as a family, and did a special dance whilst taking it.*"[41]

They monopolised the following three Christmas shows so that others did not get a chance, then the public tired of them, and finally Chatterton's regime failed and the theatre was closed. Their reign, except for one year under 'Gus' Harris, was over. Longevity was not built into the Vokes's genes as most died in their 40s or early 50s.[42]

Rarely did any artist of national note appear at the Britannia, Sydenham Palace or the Empire yet on 30th September 1888, Sam Torr [1849–1923] made an appearance at the Old City Music Hall (formerly the Britannia), in an ordinary variety bill. A native of Nottingham, he ventured into an unsuccessful managership of the Gladstone Vaults, Leicester in 1883, which he converted into the Gaiety Music Hall. From there he went around the London halls where his fortunes revived. Between 1911 and 1914, he was manager of the Malt Cross Music Hall, Nottingham, when it was refused a licence on moral grounds. He was regarded as one of the last red nosed comedians who stubbornly stuck to his battered hat, seedy frock coat and huge bow cravat, which was more typical of Sam Cowell thirty years before.

October 1888 Mr and Mrs Warwick Gray's Children's Opera Company played at the Theatre Royal with '*Billie Taylor*' and '*Les Cloches des Corneville*', which were played on alternate nights.

'*Siberia*' was the Christmas offering which opened in December 1888, although pantomime came on January 13th in the form of T.R.Nugent's '*Sinbad the Sailor*', which marked the last seasonal fare to be staged under Bennett's regime at the Theatre Royal.

Figure 46 Bennett's Opera House, Hales Street, which opened in 1889. It began as a touring house and ended as weekly repertory theatre also spending some time as a cinema. It was a casualty of the bombing raids during 1940 and was demolished in 1961

Coventry Local Studies, Central Library

Miller and Elliston's '*Harbour Lights*' Company closed the theatre on March 17th, when it ceased to be the town's main receiving drama house. This melodrama saw the light of day at the London Adelphi Theatre, the theatre associated with William Terriss, in 1885 complete with spectacular scenery by Bruce Smith, William Perkins and Walter Johnston and it ran for 500 performances. Reduced scenery was made for touring the national circuits and it is interesting to speculate what eventually turned up at the Coventry Royal.

So ended eighty years of almost continuous drama at the Theatre Royal. It was now destined to function as a music hall, with odd weeks of plays, until its final closure in 1895. From March 17th, the building remained in limbo except for occasional weeks of variety, which were masterminded by Bennett himself. Starting on Easter Monday April 21st, the place re-opened for light entertainment, and was followed by another week towards the middle of May, otherwise it remained dark until it entered into its next chapter as the Empire Palace of Varieties under the leadership of 'Gus' Levaine on 16th June 1889.

In the meantime, The Opera House in Hales Street, a mere stone's throw from the 1937 Hippodrome, was duly launched on March 28th, 1889 with Fred Benson's Company performing '*A Midsummer Night's Dream*'. An examination of the productions booked into the Opera House during its first year show a large proportion of spectacular dramas, and operas, which could never have been accommodated within the confines of the Theatre Royal.

1   Nina Auerbach, "Ellen Terry", Dent & Sons 1987.
2   Coventry Herald, 12 November, 1880.
3   Era Magazine, 5 December, 1880.
4   Era Magazine, 8 January, 1881.
5   Naomi Jacob, "Me, A Chronicle about other people". Hutchinson.
6   Lou Warwick, "The Mackenzies Called Compton", Lou Warwick 1977.
7   Lou Warwick, "The Mackenzies Called Compton", Lou Warwick 1977.
8   Coventry Times, 10 August, 1881.
9   Coventry Times, 10 August, 1881.
10 Era Magazine, 7 January, 1882.
11 Era Magazine, 10 September, 1882.
12 Era Magazine, 11 November, 1882.
13 Era Magazine, 13 January, 1883.
14 Era Magazine, 26 May, 1883.
15 Era Magazine, 16 June, 1883.
16 J.C.Trewin, "Benson and the Bensonians", Barrie and Rockliff 1960.
17 H. Chance Newton, "Cues and Curtain Calls", John Lane the Bodley Head, 1927.
18 James Carter, "Oldham Coliseum Theatre – The First Hundred Years", Oldham Leisure Services 1986.
19 Era Magazine, 15 December, 1883.
20 Madeleine Bingham, "Henry Irving", George Allen and Unwin 1978.
21 H. Chance Newton, "Cues and Curtain Calls", John Lane the Bodley Head Ltd 1927.
22 Era Magazine, 8 November, 1884.
23 Era Magazine, 31, October, 1885.
24 Leicester Journal, 13 July, 1888.
25 Coventry Herald, 23 September, 1887.
26 H. Chance Newton, "Cues and Curtain Calls John Lane The Bodley Head Ltd 1927.
27 Era Magazine, 31 July, 1886.
28 Era Magazine, 11 December, 1886.
29 John M East, "Neath the Mask", George Allen and Unwin 1967.
30 H. Chance Newton, "Cues and Curtain Calls" John Lane the Bodley Head Ltd 1927.
31 Era Magazine, 16 April, 1887.
32 The Stage, 26 May, 1887.
33 Russell Jackson, "Victorian Theatre", A & C Black 1989.
34 Coventry Herald, 23 September, 1887.
35 Minute Books of Leicester Theatre Royal, Leicester Record Office.
36 Midland Daily Telegraph, 17 October, 1893.
37 Era Magazine, 26 November, 1887.
38 Raymond Mander and Joe Mitchenson, "Lost Theatres of London", New English Library 1976.
39 Coventry Herald, 23 September, 1887.
40 The Stage, 17 November, 1892.
41 W, Macqueen Pope, "Theatre Royal, Drury Lane", W.H.Allen 1945.
42 H.G.Hibbert, "A Playgoer's Memories", Grant Richards 1920.

Chapter 10

The Empire Palace of Varieties

'Gus' Levaine [1854–1936]

The Empire opened on June 18th, 1889 under the command of 'Gus' Levaine, with a variety bill consisting of: Marie D'Este and Henry Coran [vocal comedians], Andy Reynolds Nix [the demon head] who had appeared at the Britannia not long back, Sisters Thomas [song and dance], Will Woodgate [character comedian] and Mons. Henri Sardon [conjurer]. Two days before, on June 16th, the Old City Music Hall was renamed the City Palace of Varieties, and both offered similar styles of entertainment which was demonstrated by Harry Wingate who, in July, completed a week's engagement at the City Palace only to venture across to the Empire to commence another. There were no barring clauses then. Barring clauses were later written into contracts to prevent an artist from appearing at rival halls within a specified period of time. This operated more especially when a town or city had more than one music hall so, for example, a performer appearing at Nottingham Empire would be prevented from appearing at the neighbouring Hippodrome for, say, six months before *and* after the engagement.

In the January of the same year, Levaine opened the Grand Variety Hall in Gold Street Northampton, which was the same building that Robert Higgitt had run as the Alhambra some years previously.[1] In addition, Levaine had another finger in the music hall pie, being proprietor of the Royal Albert, Gloucester, also known as the Empire.

At the end of November 1889 Fred Heath and Flora Gayton introduced their '*Living Pictures*' at the Coventry Empire to excellent effect.

The City Palace had a new musical conductor in November 1889, when Harry Lambourne took over from Herr Otto Dettmann. At the same time, a young boy comic took to the stage under the name of James Lambourne who is likely to have been the son, or a close relation, of the conductor. The lad went down so well that he was retained for a second week.

Not long after the inception of variety at the Empire, there came a tragedy on the stage towards the end of Christmas Eve 1889. Henry Mudge, who went under the stage name of Leyton, and his wife, took to the boards at 11.00 p.m. for a song routine which lasted five minutes. At 11.08 p.m. they returned with a second number. In-between each verse Mudge launched himself into a vigorous dance routine. At the end of the fourth verse he staggered and fell uttering *"Oh, I am going."*

He was pulled from the stage into the wings where restoratives were applied and Doctor Hicks sent for, but the 27 year old performer was dead. At the inquest his elder brother, a grocer from the New Cross suburb of London, said Henry had suffered from intussusception and had undergone an operation at St Thomas's Hospital but it did not cure the valvular disease which finally caught up with him. This is a curious statement as intussusception, which is a condition of the gut, and valvular (heart) disease, are not connected. It would seem the entertainer suffered some kind of heart failure at the time. Henry Cave, the resident stage manager, closed down the evening's entertainment, after which Mudge's body was transferred to the Workhouse mortuary at 12.20 am Christmas morning.[2]

At the beginning of January, audiences at the Empire were treated to Mons. Olvene and Young Nestal. They were not strangers to Coventry, having performed at the Old City Music Hall previously and they were to appear at the Empire again in 1892 and 1895. Olvene was a seasoned wire walker, juggler and gymnast and Nestal performed on the trapeze. Back in the 1880s, whilst appearing at the Metheringham Varieties, Nottingham, Olvene acquired a fourteen year old Frederick John Westcott as Nestal, his stage partner. Westcott later changed his name to Fred Karno who became an internationally known entrepreneur and introduced the world to Stan Laurel and Charlie Chaplin.[3]

Shows at the once nightly Coventry Empire commenced at 8.00 p.m. and attracted good custom with admission prices ranging from: boxes, circle and stalls 1s, pit and upper circle 6d, and gallery 3d. The bills, composed of 'run of the mill' artists, were given favourable reports in the local press. The Musical Director was James W. Appleton R.A.M. 'Gus' had an eye for business, for at the foot of his newspaper advertisements was the following, *"To the committees of Flower Shows, Galas and Sports, Mr Levaine is open to supply the best talent from the Empire at very moderate terms."* His successor carried on the tradition. John Varney, proprietor of the Nottingham Weekday Cross Music Hall, offered a similar service there in 1891.[4]

'Gus' Levaine took his annual benefit on 5th and 6th June, 1890 when artists and friends presented him with a massive gold Albert chain and a leather travelling trunk. H.J.Potter was the resident musical director.

The City Palace gave a performance for the Poor Children's Boot Fund in December 1890, which would have provided footwear for some youngsters who normally went about in bare feet.

"Special performances, promoted by a committee of local gentlemen, will be given on Tuesday and Wednesday next, the 23rd and 24th February 1891 with the object of recouping Mr Levaine for the very heavy loss he sustained by the burning of the Old Star Vaults" (in Market Place), of which he was tenant.

The Old Star was located at 72 Cox Street, near to the Sydenham Palace, and must have been refurbished as it carried on trading until c1920.[5] It would appear that 'Gus' had business interests outside the stage.

Artists from the other side of the Atlantic were no strangers to variety even then. At the Empire in May 1891, Messrs Clements and Foster were described as American stars rendering an exceedingly funny sketch.

The Sydenham Palace music hall, which appears to have been closed for around fifteen years, re-opened on September 7th, 1891 with twenty 'stars' on the bill which lasted until midnight. Why the management re-opened it is not known, but it seems likely that the popularity of this form of popular entertainment was an inducement. The building alterations were designed by Mr H. Quick and included lengthening the assembly hall by 45 feet to give accommodation for about 500 people. The stage and proscenium were removed from one end of the building to the other which meant that all the arrangements were turned around. It is likely there was one circle and that the music hall was situated on the first floor, with the normal public house rooms beneath.

The new act-drop, painted by Jesse Lee, represented the entry into the city from Grey Friars, and including the famous three spires. The area of the former stage now accommodated a bar and audience entrances were available from both Cox and Ford Streets.[6] Thomas Owen, a much respected figure and a member of the City Council, was the proprietor who provided serious competition to the Empire which, in the end, favoured neither establishment. It employed a resident chairman to introduce the turns (a relic of the 'pub music halls' and made famous in the television programme, "*The Good Old Days*"). The Empire appeared to rely on speedy continuity, more in keeping with the American style. There were now three

Figure 47 Thomas Owen, proprietor of the Sydenham Palace Hotel and music hall
Coventry Local Studies, Central Library

halls offering similar types of entertainment within the city and only one legitimate theatre and the Corn Exchange which offered a broad canvas of entertainments. It is difficult to ascertain whether the Sydenham Palace had provided music hall turns continuously from 1871, as the newspapers and the *Era Magazine* failed to mention anything about it over a number of years. Since there was no advertisement fee involved with the *Era*, failure for any notice is likely to reflect that the hall did not function. On the other hand, John Ashby, in his *"The Character of Coventry"*, brings to the attention an 1890 edition of a publicity booklet, which mentions that the Sydenham was presenting music hall entertainment every Saturday and Monday evenings for *"harmless amusement."* Possibly the 1891 alterations were meant to modernise it more into line with current music hall practice. In addition to the normal music and dancing licence, it was granted permission to stage plays.

The turns which appeared at the Empire, Sydenham Palace and Britannia music halls were many and varied. Over a period of time audiences could be expected to see any of the following: comedians, (there were many from Ireland and many Negro comics too), contortionists, mesmerists, cartoonists, slack wire dancers, serios, boot dancers, clog dancers, duettists and dancers, male impersonators, female impersonators, ventriloquists, trapeze and gymnast performers, jugglers, magicians, instrumentalists, knockabout comedians, ballad vocalists, quick change artists, a number of one legged performers, dioramas, marionettes, impressionists, shadowists and sketches. The list is not definitive. All three halls invariably changed their programmes weekly, although it was not unknown for the Britannia to retain a strong bill for a second week with, presumably, artists changing their material for the second showing.

Levaine chose '*Aladdin*' as the subject of his 1891 Christmas pantomime, which ran until Saturday 11th January 1892, and in which he took a leading acting role although we are not told what. There was no hint that this was to be his last production, and he left Coventry to take over the Pavilion Music Hall at Bath later that month.[7] This hall, directly opposite the present Theatre Royal, eventually became the Lyric and finally the Palace, managing to survive until 1956 as a twice nightly variety theatre. By 1896, Levaine was managing the Raikes Hall, Blackpool, then in 1902 he moved to the Midlands to lease the Birmingham Ladywood Palace in Morville Street, and which formerly had been Inshaw's evocatively named Steam Clock Music Hall. He was lessee and manager of the Empire Palace, Riddings in Derbyshire during the 1920s, and remained in the area until his death in 1936.

Henry William Thomas

The closure of the Empire was short and on Monday 22nd February, 1892, Henry William Thomas, aged 29, became the new lessee with Arthur Vining as his house manager. Thomas, a native of Worcester, had been 'mine host' of the Theatre Vaults, a popular tavern at the corner of Smithford Street and Theatre Yard since the mid 1880s. There is no connection between this gentleman and an earlier

William Thomas, who ran the Northampton Crow and Horseshoe Inn, also known as Thomas's Music Hall.

Bennett still owned the theatre and he leased it to Thomas. The leases appeared to have been issued on an annual basis as Bennett, probably, kept his options open on getting a better deal if one came along. Details of the 1892 lease exist[8] and state that Thomas was to have the theatre but not the stable or wardrobe rooms. These are areas which have not surfaced before. The rent was £4 per week or 20% of the first £50. Beyond that Bennett took 15% of the residue of the gross takings. Payment was not to exceed £300 a week and was to be paid promptly every Saturday. Bennett made certain stipulations: the scenery was not to be altered or painted in any way, no stage play was to be presented neither was boxing or sparing permitted. He had to provide good artists, not permit any obscene or suggestive material, make sure there was an efficient band (not less than four in number), provide trustworthy checktakers, see that the performances terminated by 11.00 p.m. each evening and make sure the building was securely locked. Thomas was responsible for all rates, taxes, repairs to the property and the gas bill. The agreement between them could be dissolved by either side with three months notice given. By 1894 some alterations to the agreement had been made. Twelve pounds was due on the first week and if the box office returns did not exceed £30 a week only £4 was due to Bennett. If the takings were between £30 and £50 the rent was increased to 20% and this fell to 15% if the citizens of Coventry dropped more than £50 into the till during the week. If the theatre was closed then only £1 was demanded.

During the short closure between tenants, Thomas undertook a number of alterations. The stage was re-laid, a new act-drop and scenery installed, the proscenium surrounded with brightly coloured lights and the plaster mouldings and emblems of music picked out in bright colours. It has to be assumed these mouldings were the same as those added in 1872. The positioning of lights around the proscenium indicates a use of electricity. No evidence has been found to suggest this form of energy superseded gas for the auditorium and stage lighting, so it may have been powered by a small unit locally. It is interesting to note that the Opera House went over to full electric lighting from gas in the summer of 1896.[9] Circle, stalls and box seats were reupholstered and the sanitary arrangements were overhauled. The house reopened two weeks earlier than had been expected, and the indulgence of the audience was craved for the unfinished state around them. Prices remained unaltered although it was possible to get in for reduced charges at 8.45 p.m.[10]

The opening bill on Monday February 21st 1892, consisted of: Mons. Henri Sardon (conjurer), Olvene and Nestal (gymnasts), J.P.Macnally (Irish comedian), Nellie Darrel (electric spark), Brothers Venola (gymnasts), Norah M'Evoy (Irish Colleen), Harry Cambridge (vocal comedian) and Master Charl (wire walker).

On Tuesday March 14th, J. Randall, of the Britannia, took a farewell benefit although he and the hall staggered on for two or three months, but it was the end of the road for this minor music hall. The Empire was up for sale too. At an auction in March 1892, it attracted £2,000, but this was short of the reserved price and the sale was withdrawn.[11] A condition existed that any prospective purchaser should not apply for a theatrical licence although, oddly, Bennett himself renewed the annual stage play licence for the Theatre Royal, according to the City Council minutes,[12] until 1898, some two to three years after its final closure.

In April 1892, J.H.Stewart took a short lease of the Sydenham Palace where he booked at least two touring drama companies in place of the usual weekly variety bills. The first was Miss Maino Donnell's company in 'The Warning Light' in which Arthur Carlton [1866–1931] was a member. By the end of the decade, Carlton was very much into the theatre bricks and mortar business investing heavily in provincial theatres, mainly in the Midlands but not exclusively so. His interests were bound up in a registered company, Tours Limited. One of his last properties was the Theatre Royal, Worcester, which he ran from 1903 until his death.[13]

A fortnight later, John Lawson presented 'Siberia' and 'Humanity' at the Sydenham Palace; the last is likely to have been the cut down version seen at the Theatre Royal in May 1886. Other artists made up the remainder of the programme. Lawson stayed on to direct the burlesque 'Aladdin up to Date', also at the Sydenham.

On 9th May, 1892 at the Britannia an entertainment, made up of songs, glees, an instrumental solo, a whistling solo and a ventriloquist's act, brought the venue to a final close before a crowded audience.[14] The building had been purchased by the Co-operative Society for the sum of £1,200 at auction and was to be converted into one of their retail outlets. The Coventry Standard suggested that had the brewers known it was going for such a low figure, they might have taken a more positive interest in the place.[15] So ended one of the Empire's rivals. In its comments, the press made reference to the familiar site of the coloured placards of 'The Brit', thus emphasising the importance of what we know as 'fliers', often in place of newspaper advertisements, and which were posted all over the area.

Dwindling Audiences

During the first six months, the Empire attracted reasonable business although a report in the Herald during March 1892 reported "so far attendance has fluctuated." Despite endeavours to make the place comfortable, comments like, "on the whole the Empire is well worth visiting" did not sound wildly encouraging.[16] Henry Thomas was 'accused' of attempting to elevate the tastes of his patrons which suggested a laudable aim on the one hand, but resistance on the other. Whether this was due to a lack of 'top liners', rather like the No 2 and No 3 variety halls in post Second World War years, is a debatable point.

Stewart's lease was up in June, and Owen resumed charge of the Sydenham Palace with the usual fare of music hall artists.

'Robinson Crusoe' and the Harlequinade enjoyed a good season over the 1892 Christmas period at the Empire. The character 'Dumps', created as a foil to Tommy Atkins, was played by Albert Edmands who was destined to be the last lessee of the Empire over the 1895 Christmas period.[17] A chorus of fifty local girls over the age of ten was required. They were *"drilled to perfection"*, and no doubt their parents paid at the box office to verify this.[18]

After the initial weeks, it was customary to bring out a new edition of a pantomime in order to encourage patrons to visit a second or a third time. Fresh songs, dances and comedy routines were brought out on January 9th, but the production only lasted the week, finally closing on January 14th.

The year 1893 seemed to progress quite well. In August of that year, when the telephonic broadcast was made, the house was personalised under the title, "Thomas's Empire", and audiences were described as *'large'*. During October, the hall was re-seated with fittings taken out of Day's Concert Hall, Birmingham, then being rebuilt as the Empire by the legendary Frank Matcham. The redundant furniture consisted of upholstered seats with brass fitted glass rests, which were superior to the plain wooden benches they replaced.[19] These glass plates enabled patrons to rest their ale during the performance. Waiters going round plying for trade required sufficient space between rows to gain access to customers. This format had disappeared from a majority of music halls by the turn of the century, when the licensing authorities had a fit of moral conscience and thought that the abolition of liquor consumption within the auditorium would help to reduce drunkenness. Bars were confined to spaces away from the audience which killed the atmosphere of the halls. The seating arrangements then resembled those of the legitimate theatres which had people sitting in neat rows. This was also the period when the promenade, a space for perambulation at the rear of each level, was similarly abolished in an attempt to redress the presence of prostitutes. Both measures simply drove the problems elsewhere.

On August 6th, after a few months closure, the Sydenham Palace of Varieties reopened as the Pavilion under the proprietorship of A. Brandon, but the venture did not last long and Owen was back in charge by September, under the old name.

Whilst the 'smalls' from the world of music hall were booked for the Empire and Sydenham, Chirgwin, the *'White Eyed Kafir'*, one of the giants on the variety circuits, played two nights at the Corn Exchange and was followed two weeks later by the legendary Charles Coborn who later went to the Empire. With a capacity of at least twice that of the Empire, the proprietors of the Corn Exchange could afford to book the more expensive artists, although it has to be said this was not a regular feature. Albert Chevalier made an appearance the following August in 1894.

There was no recognisable pantomime at the Empire but a spectacular *'The Bad Baron of Kenilworth Castle'* opened Boxing Day 1893, and lasted a fortnight. At the end of 1893 and the beginning of 1894, however, trade went 'off' at the Empire. During the interval of the programme on Monday January 22nd, Henry Thomas went before the curtain to announce that he would be compelled to close the house on Saturday February 10th on account of the lack of support.[20] The reasons for public apathy are not immediately obvious, although the competition from the Sydenham Palace, which offered a similar class of programme, did not help. Having said this, the Sydenham advertised the last week of the 'present season' on January 6th 1894, which one might have assumed would be a buoyant time for the hall did not have to compete with conducive summer weather. It has to be assumed that trade was bad at both halls. The Sydenham reopened for a week on January 15th when 'Gus' Levaine brought his own variety company back to Coventry, but it soldiered on intermittently until it, too, closed on October 27th 1894, *"until further notice"*, as the newspapers put it.[21] It never reopened, except for Julia Hepburn's Company in *"Aladdin"* at the beginning of January 4th, 1896. According to the *Era*, the show appeared to last only one week. Gil Robottom ('*Over Ninety Years of Cinemas and Theatres in Coventry' – 1992*), suggests that the Sydenham Palace was an early venue for cinema in the 1890s but information is sparse. Silent films made their first appearance in music halls as an ordinary turn from 1896, and it is reasonable to assume that the Sydenham experimented with this new form of entertainment, but any venture there is likely to have been short lived.

Business failed to pick up at the Empire and Thomas closed the hall on the 10th February.

A Reopening for the Empire

With the opposition from the Sydenham Palace having disappeared and the winter season approaching, Thomas must have hoped that this was a propitious time to re-open the Empire, which he did on Saturday December 22, 1894, with what was described as a *'first class London Company'*. Excluding local artists who were also invited to appear, the bill consisted of the following acts: Jessie Albini (burlesque actress), Minnie Jacobson (serio), Fred Newby (ventriloquist), Sibb and Sibb (trapeze artists), "She" (illusion and wonder), Princess Lula (trapeze artist), Cantrell (ventriloquist). Archie Howells, who later went to the Bristol Empire, the London Canterbury and the Crouch End Hippodrome, was taken on as the new musical conductor.

One supposes that in a time of desperation Henry Thomas might rally a few of the bigger names in the business in an attempt to restore his fortunes. His coup was the 43 year old Charles Coborn, (1852–1945), whose real name was Colin Whitton McCallum, a Scot, famous for, *"The Man Who Broke the Bank at Monte Carlo"* and *"Two Lovely Black Eyes"*, booked, at 'enormous expense', during the week beginning February 4th, 1895. His adopted name came from Coborn Road, a thoroughfare in the London district of Bow. He was now back in Midland territory having once appeared at The Talbot Palace, Market Street, Nottingham (later the Gaiety & Kings Theatre and within sight of the present Theatre Royal) at a salary of £3 10s in 1876.[22] In 1885, he founded the Music Hall Artists' Association, later the Music Hall Benevolent Fund, the first performers' trade union formed to counter the power of the managers and as a result he was occasionally refused work for challenging the power of the bosses.[23] His wife and Lottie Albert were friends of Belle Elmore, better known as Mrs Crippen, and alerted their suspicions of her disappearance to the police. Their initiative led to the arrest of Crippen and his subsequent execution.

Coborn was contracted to appear in one of the ordinary two hour programmes Thomas booked week after week and he appeared with a trapeze artist, a Negro comedian, a pack of performing dogs, duettists and dancers, a pantomimist and a serio. He sang eight songs in all but the audience grew restless until he rendered *"The Man who broke the Bank"*, the house joining in until the rafters shook. Monday and Tuesday audiences were reported as being packed and one assumes the remaining performances would have been equally well attended.

Coborn aimed to lead an improvement in the general tone of music hall performances but without recourse to Puritanism or cant. He gave them nonsense but ruled out material that was offensive, unlike some performances in the legitimate theatre. In a newspaper interview, Coborn blamed local clergy and political representatives in Coventry for not regularly attending music halls to give them respectability.[24] He thought the city quite capable of supporting a thriving music hall which could be profitable, and he confirmed his engagement was the most expensive Thomas had entered into in the ordinary way.[25] There can only be three answers to the question why Thomas did not book more artists of his calibre: one, they were not interested in small theatres like the Empire, being able to make more money at the larger halls in other cities; two, the theatre was not large enough to

FATHER OF THE PROFESSION

COBORN singing
"The Man Who Broke The Bank
At Monte Carlo."

Figure 48   Charles Coborn (1852-1945). One of the few famous
music hall artists to visit the Empire

Author's collection

make money – perhaps Thomas lost on the week after all – and; three, the citizens of Coventry were not very supportive even of star material. The first argument is unlikely to hold much water since the massive halls like the London Coliseum, The Palladium and others of their kind, had yet to be built. Many music halls in other cities had greater seating capacities but buildings as large as the Birmingham Empire, one of the first in the Moss Empire chain and which opened in 1894, were only just coming on stream. One assumed Thomas did not embark upon booking a star like Coborn if there was not the possibility of the balance sheet being in the black at the end of the week, so one has to come to the conclusion the fault lay in Coventry and its people who, for some reason, did not support variety artists, either good or ordinary, in sufficient numbers or were willing to pay a high enough ticket price to guarantee a profit. This theory is somewhat confirmed by what occurred during the weeks following the Coborn booking and the fact that few stars of note ever appeared at the larger Corn Exchange. However, this analysis is unlikely to be the only factor as will be discussed later.

Good, but not capacity, business was done the following week when another top ranking comic singer, Arthur Lloyd (1840–1904), topped the bill. Born in Edinburgh, he was a comic vocalist, sketch artist, and songwriter making his debut at the Glasgow Whitebait Tavern. Dabbling in legitimate theatre, he once appeared with the Negro actor Ira Aldridge. His first London appearance in 1862, was at the Knightsbridge Sun Music Hall where he sang '*swell songs*' in the style of Vance and Leybourne. He was regarded as the last of the 'Lion Comiques'.[26] Nevertheless, attendances were not as large as those for Charles Coborn.

Thomas took his third annual benefit on February 19th when additional turns, including Charles Coborn, who was working in Birmingham at the time, came to give support.

Joe Darby, the champion jumper of the world, interrupted his French tour to appear in the week beginning March 4th, and for whom the stage was strengthened for his leap of eighteen feet over six chairs. One has to wonder from which direction this gymnastic feat took place bearing in mind the narrowness of the proscenium arch. The city's response was rather chilly, thereby making the engagement questionable regarding profitability. It is possible that Thomas made money on the Coborn week but lost on the other 'stars' which discouraged further experimentation along those lines. Coventry audiences seemed not to be interested. Even the printed exhortation in the newspaper advertisements "*Once you have been you are sure to come again*" did not sound totally reassuring.

Struggling along and Final Closure

On March 11th, 1895, the house was renamed the Old Theatre Royal and Empire, as variety gave way to drama given by a stock company booked by Thomas. It was not unusual for theatres to change their name depending on the fare being offered. The King's Lynn Theatre was known as the Theatre Royal from Monday to Wednesday when drama was staged, and the Hippodrome for the rest of the week for variety. The theatre in Burton-upon-Trent alternated its title between the Opera House and Hippodrome, depending on the type of show being staged. The old pot boilers were dusted and put on the boards, *'Flowers of the Forest', 'Green Bushes', 'Simon Lee' and 'Ben the Boatswain'* but people were seeing better at the Opera House, so why should they patronise the Royal?

The Easter offering (for the week beginning April 15th), was a spectacular production under the title *'On Parade'* employing 80 local children. The programme included a number of variety acts but no 'top-liner' and attendance was, again, poor. The writing was on the wall, very much as in the 1950s when managements tried anything to keep their theatres open despite the competition from television. Thomas threw in the towel and closed the Empire on Saturday April 27, 1895, with an ordinary bill headed by Azella, another trapeze artist. It came as no surprise. The local critic praised Thomas for his tenacity in providing varied and acceptable entertainment,

> *"A Music Hall, even on a small scale cannot be carried on without a considerable amount of risk and expense. No one will deny that Mr Thomas has done his utmost to provide an entertainment (that is) varied and acceptable to the general public. But if the latter will not patronise his enterprise, it is not to be expected he will continue an undertaking that is un-remunerative."*

and,

> *"It is to be hoped that in the last few days that Mr Thomas keeps the "Empire" open he will have far larger audiences than that of last night."*[27]

To students of music hall and the variety theatre, it may seem strange that the Empire never offered twice nightly performances, a system which developed with Tom Barrassford and his syndicate in the 1890s, although it had been tried in Liverpool and Sunderland in the 1860s and 1870s respectively.[28] Disliked by the artists, it had the advantage of offering the public cheaper admission since each performance was short and twice the payload could be admitted every evening. On the other hand if Thomas was finding difficulty filling his theatre for one performance in the evening, he was unlikely to fill it for two.

Henry Thomas, together with manager Charles Kingsley, with a degree of foresight, had constructed a prefabricated wooden theatre which was assembled in New Bridge Road, Nuneaton and opened as the Theatre Royal on July 15th, 1895. This convenient 'end on' of dates is unlikely to have been mere coincidence but suggests careful planning when the business at Coventry showed signs of collapsing. This prefabricated Temple of Thespis lasted until 1900, when it was dismantled and re-assembled at Rugby upon the reopening of the permanent Nuneaton Prince of Wales Theatre. Thomas remained connected with the Coventry Theatre Vaults until the end of the century.

As a temporary measure, Bennett reopened the Empire theatre on June 3rd, 1895 (again as the Theatre Royal), with the melodrama *'Man's Ambition'*, a play with comic interludes by a couple of quaint comedians, Messrs Spry and Monti who sang, danced, told funny stories and otherwise exerted themselves with the result of creating incessant merriment. But this appeared to be a 'one off' occasion.[29] It was reported that there were *"fairly large houses."*[30] The theatre remained closed, yet for two nights in August, Charles Coborn returned to Coventry, but to the larger Corn Exchange. It was reported that the popular parts of the auditorium were well filled but *"there was room in the higher prices seats"*,[31] so it would appear there was insufficient support from across the broad spectrum of society for this form of light entertainment. Perhaps this, together with the unsatisfactory appearance of the buildings, says it all.

Undaunted by previous failures, Albert Edmands, who appeared in the 1892/3 pantomime and was later manager of the Coventry Jubilee Circus in October 1897, leased the Empire and reopened it for the Christmas season on December 23rd 1895, with *"first class variety."*[32] Prices remained unaltered and the opening night was attended by an appreciative, but small, audience watching a good bill. The press advertisements appeared for two days only and the theatre was probably open for no more than the week. This was the last show in the theatre. For the record, the bill consisted of: Marie Stewart [burlesque actress], Dick Geldard [comic], Rose Wynne [serio], The Three Angelos [acrobats], Violet Grenville [ballad singer], Our Jack [wire walker], Flo Wilson [song and dance artist], Fred Kelmar [ventriloquist] and Will Dawson [comic].

Why, at this time, was variety a failure at both the Coventry Empire and Sydenham Palace? They were both small venues, one adapted from a public house assembly room and the other built for theatrical presentations of a previous age. Neither was sufficiently adaptable for the 'modern' style of variety, unlike newer theatres in Birmingham to which, undoubtedly, many of the citizens of Coventry visited by train. Indeed the Birmingham Prince of Wales theatre regularly advertised in the columns of the Coventry papers. There was a modern Opera House in the town and two second rate music halls displaying second rate artists. However, it must be assumed that these performers appeared successfully elsewhere and made a living in their profession and, indeed, other towns of similar size were not without their lower order of music halls. Birmingham had its Metropole (colloquially known as the 'Blood Tub') in Snow Hill, as rough an area as any in Coventry. Nottingham and Derby had their Palaces, Northampton had the Empire so why should Coventry be different? The theatre was not reported for the rowdiness of its patrons so it is unlikely people were deterred on that account. The most plausible explanation is that the theatre had become old fashioned, looking much as it must have done in 1819, and with a stage too small for some of the newer variety acts to be decently presented. Today neither objection would be a deterrent to its preservation on account of the antiquity it represented. The Sydenham Palace probably seemed even more out of date and not even the upsurge in popularity of music hall entertainment could save either. Variety was metamorphosing out of the public house music hall image where drinking was available in the auditorium. The newer buildings of Moss, and others, reflected the change in style – an example of Cinderella going to the ball. Many other 'pub' music halls had closed, or were about to do so, and were replaced by modern theatres of variety which appealed not only to the working classes but to other strata of society.

[1] Lou Warwick, "Death of a Theatre", Lou Warwick 1978.
[2] Coventry Herald, 27 December, 1889.
[3] Richard Illiffe and Wilfred Baguley, Victorian Nottingham Vol 12, Nottingham Historical Film Unit 1974.
[4] Nottingham Evening Post, 12 August, 1891.
[5] John Ashby, "The Character of Coventry", John Ashby 2001.
[6] Coventry Times, 9 September, 1891.
[7] Midland Daily Telegraph, 12 January, 1892.
[8] Coventry Record Office.
[9] Coventry Herald, 8 August, 1896.
[10] Midland Daily Telegraph, 23 February, 1892.
[11] Coventry Standard, 1 April, 1892.
[12] Coventry Record Office.
[13] Suz Winspear, "Worcester's Lost Theatre", Parkbarn 1996.
[14] Coventry Herald, 13 May, 1892.
[15] Coventry Standard, 1 April, 1892.
[16] Midland Daily Telegraph, 8 March, 1892.
[17] Midland Daily Telegraph, 27 December, 1892.
[18] Midland Daily Telegraph, 10 January, 1893.
[19] Midland Daily Telegraph, 17 October, 1893.
[20] Midland Daily Telegraph, 23 January, 1894.
[21] Midland Daily Telegraph, 27 October, 1894.
[22] Geoff Mellor, "Northern Music Hall", Frank Graham 1970.
[23] Peter Honri, "John Wilton's Music Hall", Ian Henry Publications 1985 and W. Macqueen Pope, "The Melody Lingers On", W.H.Allen.
[24] Midland Daily Telegraph, 6 February, 1895.
[25] Midland Daily Telegraph, 7 February, 1895.
[26] Peter Honri, "John Wilton's Music Hall", Ian Henry Publications 1985.
[27] Midland Daily Telegraph, 23, April, 1895.
[28] Geoff Mellor, "Northern Music Hall", Frank Graham 1970.
[29] Coventry Reporter, 8 June, 1895.
[30] Era Magazine, 8 June, 1895.
[31] Coventry Evening Telegraph, 13 August, 1895.
[32] Midland Daily Telegraph, 23 December, 1895.

Chapter 11

Plans which Failed to Materialise

There followed a period of rumour, counter rumour and indecision regarding theatrical provision in Coventry. In April 1897, a curious and tantalising announcement appeared in the press[1] to the effect that William Bennett and Charles Machin (proprietor of more than one theatre in Sunderland, and joint owner of the Shakespeare Theatre, Clapham, with Bennett) had employed one of the foremost leading theatre architects, W.G.R.Sprague, to prepare a suitable building to be called the Grand Theatre, to be designed in the Italian Classic style and destined to replace the Theatre Royal. Sprague, who once worked in Frank Matcham's office, was one of the foremost theatre designers of his day. His surviving buildings include the Sheffield Lyceum, and a number of smaller London houses including: Wyndham's, Albery, Strand and Globe (now the Gielgud).

After the successful launching of the Opera House, it is possible Bennett sensed that the time was ripe for a second first class modern theatre in Coventry, but interestingly this was intended for drama and not variety. The Grand was designed to hold 2,500 people on three levels using the cantilever principle which obviated the need for pillars. According to the *Midland Daily Telegraph* (April 3, 1897), the frontage was designed to be on Smithford Street which would have meant Bennett purchasing the intervening property, an option he chose not to take in 1880 and 1889. Each level would have first class retiring rooms and the artists would be provided with up to date dressing accommodation with special attention paid to sanitation and ventilation. Just what the theatre would have looked like is open to speculation since the plans, if any were drawn, have disappeared as nothing can be traced at the Royal Institute of British Architects. It was announced that the new theatre would be open for the 1897 Christmas pantomime, but it was not to be. Perhaps the site, and the expense, were too impossible after all.

Shortly afterwards, in 1898, Bennett paid £15,500 for the purchase of the Corn Exchange from John Brown Izon, Edward Lynes and Thomas Burbidge, and he published his intentions to turn this into a permanent drama house. Early in 1898, Bennett announced that W.G.R. Sprague was to convert the Corn Exchange into a theatre along the lines of Bennett's two London theatres, the Shakespeare, Battersea, and the Royal Duchess, Balham, both designed by Sprague. There was no mention of the Theatre Royal at this time, or Sprague's intentions for it. The interior of the Corn Exchange was to be gutted and the auditorium extended downwards in what were the King's Head stables, which would give sufficient vertical room for a dress circle, amphitheatre and gallery along with ten boxes. A new proscenium, stage and dressing rooms were included. Such a grand place of entertainment would become the main theatre in Coventry and the Opera House would go over to varieties. Such intelligence opened the proverbial can of worms, mainly from the farming and agricultural communities, for where would they go to trade? They threatened to take their businesses away from the city and patronise the Exchanges in Birmingham, Warwick or Rugby which, in turn, upset the local retailers who had visions of vanishing business.

Bennett promised a new Corn Exchange and where better than to place it than on the site of the Theatre Royal. In 1898, Bennett contacted the firm of Owen and Ward, well known Birmingham theatre architects responsible for many theatres in what is now known as the West Midlands (including the West Bromwich Theatre Royal, Smethwick Theatre Royal, Bordesley Palace, Walsall Her Majesty's and the first Birmingham Alexandra), to draw plans for an Assembly Rooms on the ground floor (which would double as a Corn Exchange during the day), and a modern ballroom on the first floor with up to date catering facilities.[2] He planned to offer the new building to local corn merchants and farmers for day-time use, on a five year lease, as happened at the current Corn Exchange. Negotiations were made with other owners in the 'Yard', possibly for extending the entrances and exits, but once again, nothing materialised.

Why did Bennett's plans never materialise? One excuse given was that he was too busy organising his London properties, but he was in business to make money and someone of Bennett's financial acumen was unlikely to turn down such an opportunity unless insurmountable obstacles were put in his way. This was the man who sacked his entire Opera House orchestra rather than pay them an additional eight shillings per week to bring them in line with the remuneration other theatre musicians received. Bennett remained the owner of the Corn Exchange until 1906 when it was converted into the second Empire Theatre of Varieties. Coventry's only opportunity to have a theatre designed by a well known national architect, unfortunately, never materialised.

Despite the fact that many theatrical plans were forming a whirlwind within the city, Bennett continued to apply for, and be granted, a stage play licence for the Theatre Royal right up to December 1898.[3] Perhaps this was habit, as it was clear he had little intention of re-opening it as a live venue. Did he make his annual application so that the licence could be transferred elsewhere when the time was right?

At the City Council meeting held on 16th June, 1903 it was passed that a planning application for an extension to Illiffe's Cycle Workshop should be extended into Smithford Street thereby including the site of the Theatre Royal. Oddly the same meeting passed a planning application to construct the first Hippodrome on Pool Meadow, a case of 'music hall is dead, long live music hall'. This was the first of the twentieth century variety theatres in the city and took place in a corrugated iron structure holding around 1200 people. It is interesting to note that the artists who appeared on the twice nightly bills seemed of a similar calibre to those who performed at the Empire and Sydenham Palace ten years previously. Later the *Coventry Herald*[4] signified that the Empire was no more, and its passing appeared to generate no public comment or sadness unlike the closures of theatres after the Second World War. Before 1906, the site had been swallowed up by Illiffe's Printing Works, which had spread from the Vicar Lane base and is shown on the O.S. map of that year. Suggestions by Marguerite Steen in her biography of Ellen Terry[5] that the theatre, was not demolished until 1913, would seem to have relied upon the faulty memory of Ellen who played in '*The Merchant of Venice*' at the Royal in November 1880.

The situation to the year 2004

So ended seventy six years of entertainment in Smithford Street, which began when George III was on the throne. Bennett's Opera House, the home of weekly repertory in later years, was bombed during the Second World War. The second Empire, in Hertford Street, fashioned out of the former Corn Exchange, purveyed variety from October 1906. Films made their appearance in mixed cine variety bills

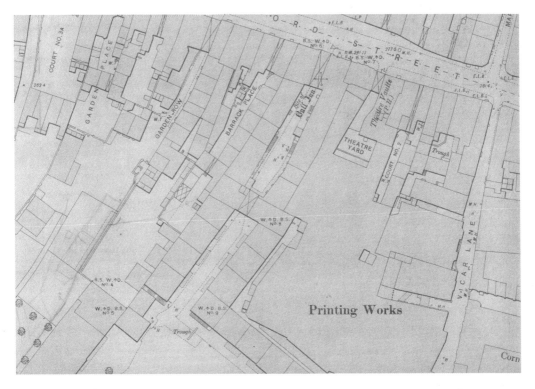

Figure 49 The ordnance survey map of 1906 shows how the site of the Theatre Royal and Empire had been covered by Illiffe's Printing Works. The former access for scenery to the dock doors from Vicar Lane remained as did Court No. 2 which led to the dressing rooms. The Theatre Yard was not altered presumably because it gave access to other buildings. Thomas's Theatre Vaults continued to trade under that name and survived until the whole area was destroyed in the bombing of 1940 during the Second World War

Coventry Local Studies, Central Library

from around 1909, and remained an important part of the entertainment. This hall, too, had a very short life as a variety theatre, being converted into a permanent picture house which was gutted by fire in 1929. This left the Hippodrome, Hales Street, which opened in 1906, (not to be confused with the Pool Meadow Hippodrome of 1903), to carry the flag. Replaced during 1937 by a new theatre, designed by W.Stanley Hattrell and Partners, in the style of a modern cinema, it was a nationally well known variety hall until the end of the 1960s, when various major tours of opera, ballet and drama brought a different style of culture to the city in place of weekly music hall. The Hippodrome closed in 1985, became a bingo hall and was demolished, despite much public objection, by the City Council in 2002, who required the site for part of their plans to mark the Millennium. This leaves the sole representative of live entertainment to the Belgrade, a relatively modern but small theatre, which opened in 1962. Some theatrical events also take place on the Warwick University campus which lies within the Coventry city boundary.

CURTAIN

[1] Midland Daily Telegraph, 3 April, 1897.
[2] Coventry Herald, 8 July, 1898.
[3] Coventry Record Office.
[4] Coventry Herald, 19 June, 1903.
[5] Marguerite Steen, "A Pride of Terrys", Longmans 1962.

Bibliography

Newspapers, Magazines and Record Offices:

Aris Birmingham Gazette.
Cambrian.
Coventry Herald.
Coventry Mercury.
Coventry Record Office.
Coventry Standard.
Coventry Times.
Era Magazine.
Leamington Spa Courier.
Leicester Journal.
Leicester Record Office.
Midland Daily Telegraph, Coventry.
Minute Books off the Leicester Theatre Royal.
Minutes of the Coventry Theatre.
Morris Directory.
National Telephone Journal.
Nottingham Evening Post.
The Stage, London.
Theatre Notebook, Society for Theatre Research, (STR).
Theatrephile.
Theatrical Journal.
Victorian Nottingham.
Warwickshire and General Advertiser.

Books:

John Ashby.	The Character of Coventry.	John Ashby 2001.
Nina Auerbach.	Ellen Terry.	Dent 1987.
Leslie Baily.	The Gilbert and Sullivan Book.	Cassell 1953.
Henry Barton Baker.	Our Old Actors.	Bentley & Son 1878.
Martin Banham (ed).	Cambridge Guide to the Theatre	CUP 1992.
Walter Baynham.	The Glasgow Stage.	Forrester 1892.
Madelaine Bingham.	Henry Irving.	Unwin 1978.

Michael Booth.	Victorian Spectacular Theatre 1850–1910.	Routledge 1981.
John Booth.	A Century of Theatre History.	Steads 1917.
Asa Briggs.	The Birth of Broadcasting.	OUP 1961.
R.J.Broadbent.	Annals of the Liverpool Stage.	Blom 1908.
T.L.G.Burley	Playhouses and Players of East Anglia.	Jarrold 1928.
James Carter.	Oldham Coliseum Theatre.	Oldham 1986.
John Coleman.	Fifty Years of an Actor's Life.	Pott 1904.
John Coleman.	Players and Playwrights.	Gebbie 1890.
Gilbert B. Cross.	Next Week – East Lynne.	London 1977.
J.E.Cunningham.	Theatre Royal, Birmingham.	Ronald 1950.
Antony Dale.	Brighton Theatre Royal.	Oriel 1980.
M.W. Disher.	Blood and Thunder.	Muller 1949.
John M. East.	Neath the Mask.	Unwin 1967.
Richard Fawkes.	Dion Boucicault.	Quartet 1979.
Moira Field.	The Fisher Theatre Circuit 1792–1844.	Norwich 1985.
Percy Fitzgerald.	A New History of the English Stage Vol 11.	Tinsley Bros. 1882.
Derek Forbes.	Illustrated Playbills.	STR 2002.
Richard Foulkes (ed).	Scenes from Provincial Stages.	STR 1994.
Gorel Garlick.	To Serve the Purpose of Drama.	STR 2003.
Elizabeth Grice.	Rogues and Vagabonds.	Dalton 1977.
Terry Hallett.	Bristol's Forgotten Empire.	Badger 2000.
Theodore Hannam-Clark.	Drama in Gloucestershire.	Marshall 1928.
Phyllis Hartnoll (ed).	Oxford Companion to the Theatre.	OUP 1965.
H.G.Hibbert.	A Playgoer's Memories.	Richards 1920.
Peter Honri.	John Wilton's Music Hall.	Ian Henry 1985.
Russell Jackson.	Victorian Theatre.	A & C Black 1989.
Naomi Jacob.	Me, A Chronicle about other People.	Hutchinson.
William G. Knight.	A Major London Minor (Surrey Theatre).	STR 1997.
Richard Leacroft.	Development of the English Playhouse.	Methuen 1973.
Richard Leacroft.	Theatre and Playhouse.	Methuen 1984.
Richard & Helen Leacroft.	Theatres in Leicestershire.	Leicestershire 1986.
Angus MacNaghten.	Windsor and Eton in Georgian Times.	MacNaghten 1976.
Sara Maitland.	Vesta Tilley.	Virago 1986.
Raymond Mander & Joe Mitchenson.	Lost Theatres of London.	New English Library 1976.

Herbert Marshall & Mildred Stock.	Ira Aldridge – The Negro Tragedian.	Macmillan 1958.
Geoff Mellor.	Northern Music Hall.	Graham 1970.
Kenneth More.	More or Less.	Hodder & Stoughton 1978.
Malcolm Morley.	Margate and its Theatres.	London 1966.
Christopher Murray.	Robert William Elliston.	STR 1975.
H. Chance Newton.	Cues and Curtain Calls.	John Lane 1927.
H. Chance Newton.	Idols of the Halls.	EP Publishing 1975.
Harold Oswald.	The Theatres Royal in Newcastle-on-Tyne	Northumberland 1936
Frederick Penzel.	Theatre Lighting Before Electricity.	Wesleyan U.P 1978.
Giles Playfair.	The Prodigy (Master Betty)	London 1967.
Poole.	History and Antiquities of Coventry.	Coventry 1870.
W. Macqueen Pope.	The Melody Lingers On.	Allan.
W. Macqueen Pope.	Theatre Royal, Drury Lane.	Allan 1945.
Michael Newman.	The Golden Years – Hippodrome Coventry.	Baron 1995.
Cecil Price.	The English Theatre in Wales.	U.Wales Press 1948.
Paul Ranger.	Under Two Managers	STR 2001.
George Rowell.	The Victorian Theatre.	OUP 1956.
W. Clark Russell.	Representative Actors.	Warne
Dr Terence Rees & Dr David Wilmore (ed).	British Theatrical Patents 1800–1900.	STR 1996.
Sybil Rosenfeld.	The York Theatre.	STR 2001.
Gil Robottom.	Over Ninety Years of Cinemas and Theatres in Coventry.	1992.
Philip B. Ryan.	The Lost Theatres of Dublin.	Badger 1998
Paddy Scannell & David Cardiff.	A Social History of Broadcasting, Vol 1.	Blackwell 1991.
Marguerite Steen.	A Pride of Terrys.	Longmans 1962.
Herbert Sullivan & Newman Flower.	Sir Arthur Sullivan.	Cassel 1927.
C.M.P.Taylor.	Right Royal – Wakefield Theatre 1776–1994	Wakefield 1996.
J.C.Trewin.	Benson and the Bensonians.	Barrie 1960.
Lou Warwick.	Death of a Theatre.	Lou Warwick 1978.
Lou Warwick.	Drama That Smelled.	Lou Warwick 1975.
Lou Warwick.	The Mackenzies Called Compton.	Lou Warwick 1977.
Lou Warwick	Theatre Un-Royal.	Lou Warwick 1974.
Sue Winspear.	Worcester's Lost Theatre.	Parkbarn 1996.

Also published by The Badger Press

"No Sails on Huttoft Mill" by J. O. Blake (out of print)
"A Glossary of Terms used in Variety, Vaudeville and Pantomime" by Valantyne
  Napier
"Laughter in the Roar" by Brian O'Gorman (available from the author)
"The Lost Theatres of Dublin" by Philip B. Ryan
"Bristol's Forgotten Empire" by Terry Hallett

In preparation:
"Variety at Night is Good for You" by J. O. Blake
  One hundred London Variety Theatres remembered by a compulsive theatre-goer;
  profusely illustrated in line by Nicholas Charlesworth, together with bills and
  programmes from each theatre

Publishers of Theatrical Postcards, Books, Greeting Cards and Notelets

Lists sent on request

THE BADGER PRESS
Westbury, Wiltshire BA13 4DU
www.vaudeville-postcards.com
email: nc@vaudeville-postcards.com

INDEX

Productions shown in italics

179